Human Relations

Principles and Practices

Human Relations

Principles and Practices

Barry L. Reece
Virginia Polytechnic Institute
and State University

Rhonda Brandt
Human Resource Development
Specialist

Houghton Mifflin Company   Boston
Dallas   Geneva, Illinois   Palo Alto   Princeton, New Jersey

Library of Congress Catalog Card Number: 89–82118
ISBN: 0-395-52994-8
    BCDEFGHIJ-D-99876543210

Total Person Insights

p. 9: Marsha Sinetar, "Do What You Love...The Money Will Follow," *Network News*, March/April 1987, p. 12.

p. 13: William Raspberry, "Topmost Priority: Jobs," *Washington Post*, 1977.

P. 18: Alice Sargent, *The Androgynous Manager*, p. 1; Reprinted by permission of the publisher. (New York: AMACOM, a division of American Management Associations, 1981).

p. 32: Denis Waitley, *The Winning Generation: The Self-Esteem Training Program for Youth* (Cedar Falls, Iowa: Advanced Learning, Inc., 1987), p. 18.

p. 59: Larry Wilson, *Changing the Game—The New Way to Sell* (New York: Simon & Schuster, 1987), p. 5.

p. 83: D. R. Spitzer, "30 Ways to Motivate Employees to Perform Better," *Training/HRD*, March 1980, p. 51.

p. 133: Chris Lee, "Ethics Training: Facing the Tough Questions," *Training*, March 1986, p. 31.

p. 149: Dudley Bennett, *TA and the Manager* (New York: American Management Associations, 1976), p. 18.

p. 180: Jan Hartman, "How to Learn from Success and Failure," *New Dimensions*, April/May 1984, p. 5.

p. 202: Janet G. Elsea, *The Four-minute Sell*, (New York: Simon & Schuster, 1984), p. 9.

p. 215: Judith Martin, "Low income is not low class," *Roanoke Times & World-News*, March 13, 1988, p. E-10.

p. 229: "Living with Uncertainty," *The Royal Bank Letter*, Vol. 68, No. 1, March/April 1987, p. 1.

p. 236: Craig Brod, *Technostress: The Human Cost of the Computer Revolution* (Reading, Mass.: Addison-Wesley, 1984), p. xx.

Figure Credits

Figure 2.1: From *The Innovative Organization: Productivity Programs in Action*, copyright 1982, Pergamon Press, Inc., which appeared in *Thriving on Chaos: Handbook for a Management Revolution* by Tom Peters. Copyright © 1987 by Excel, a California Limited Partnership. Reprinted with permission of Pergamon Press, Inc., and Alfred A. Knopf, Inc.

Figure 4.3: Reprinted by permission of *Harvard Business Review*. An exhibit from "One More Time: How Do You Motivate Employees?" by Frederick Herzberg, January-February 1968. Copyright © 1968 by the President and Fellows of Harvard College; all rights reserved.

Figure 5.1: Adapted from Richard I. Evans, *Dialogue with Gordon Allport* (Praeger Publishers, New York, 1981). Copyright © 1971 by Richard I. Evans and 1981 by Praeger Publishers. Used with permission.

Figure 5.2: Adapted by permission of publishers, from *Managerial Values and Expectations*, by Warren H. Schmidt and Barry Z. Posner, an AMA Survey Report, p. 17 © 1982. American Management Association, New York. All rights reserved.

To Vera, Lynne, Mark, Monique, Michelle, and Colleen
Barry L. Reece

To Matthew and Patrick
Rhonda Brandt

Contents

5

6

7

Preface

The past decade will be remembered as a period of significant change in the workplace. One of the most important developments has been the increased importance of interpersonal skills in almost every type of organization. Employers want to hire persons who can work effectively in teams and who are able to represent the employer favorably to clients, customers, and members of the public. They want employees who possess the ability to communicate effectively and in a pleasant manner.

Human Relations: Principles and Practices is an introduction to the important human side of today's work world. Based on the premise that the practice of good human relations is essential to career success, the text focuses on the skills a person needs in order to function effectively while working with people. By studying the concepts and strategies presented here, the reader can learn to become a well–rounded "total person," one who can adjust quickly to the demands of work and make wiser choices when people-related problems arise.

The "total person" approach to human relations is the central theme of *Human Relations: Principles and Practices*. We take the position that human behavior at work is influenced by many interdependent traits such as physical fitness, emotional control, values orientation, self-awareness, nutrition, self-concept, and personal appearance. A major goal of this text is to help the reader develop a balanced blend of these important traits. It is our strong belief that if the whole person can be improved, significant benefits occur to the employer and the employee.

Our aim has been to present the material in a non-technical, interesting, and readable style. This is achieved, in part, by including a large number of real-world examples of how human relations principles and practices described in the book are being applied in a variety of contemporary organizational settings. These examples have been obtained from relatively small companies such as Celestial Seasonings, as well as from large firms such as Pitney Bowes, Marriott Corporation, Hewlett-Packard, and Quaker Oats. Students preparing for a variety of careers will find the content practical and relevant.

CHAPTER ORGANIZATION

Human Relations: Principles and Practices is comprised of nine chapters. Chapter 1 provides a strong rationale for the study of human relations and reviews the historical development of this field. It also includes a detailed discussion of the major forces influencing behavior at work, as well as a description of seven broad themes that emerge from a study of human relations. These themes are: communication, self-acceptance, self-awareness, motivation, trust, self-disclosure, and conflict management.

Chapters 2–5 reflect the basic fact that our effectiveness in dealing with others depends in large measure on our self-awareness and self-acceptance. We believe that by building a positive self-concept and by learning to explore inner attitudes, motivations, and values, the reader will learn to be more sensitive to the way others think, feel, and act.

Chapters 6–8 feature a variety of practical strategies that can be used to develop and maintain good relationships with coworkers, supervisors, and managers. These chapters, on learning to achieve emotional control, positive reinforcement, and positive first impressions, discuss the importance of these concepts in the workplace and help the reader develop skills in these areas.

Chapter 9 deals with the special human relations challenge presented by work-related changes. It describes ways we can cope more effectively with personal and professional life changes.

SPECIAL FEATURES

Human Relations: Principles and Practices includes several special features that enhance the teaching/learning process. Each chapter opens with a preview of major topic areas and an opening vignette that builds reader interest in the material. Numerous Thinking/Learning Starters within each chapter give students a chance to reflect on the material and relate their own experiences to the concepts discussed. A series of thought-provoking quotes from a variety of authors, leaders in business, and scholars, called Total Person Insights, appears in every chapter. The chapters close with a list of key terms and a series of review questions designed to reinforce the reader's understanding of important ideas. If students are interested in pursuing a particular subject in greater detail, a list of suggested readings is also offered at the end of each chapter.

Each chapter features two case problems based on actual human relations situations. The majority of these cases deal with current situations in real organizations. Some cases focus on an employee problem within the context of a specific organization. Other cases focus on a human relations problem that may require a change in organizational policies or procedures.

ACKNOWLEDGMENTS

Many people have made contributions to *Human Relations: Principles and Practices*. The text has been strengthened as a result of numerous helpful comments and recommendations. We extend special appreciation to the following persons.

James Aldrich
North Dakota State School of Science

Garland Ashbacher
Kirkwood Community College

Rhonda Barry
American Institute of Commerce

C. Winston Borgen
Sacramento Community College

Lawrence Carter
Jamestown Community College

Michael Dzik
North Dakota State School of Sciences

John Elias
University of Missouri

Mike Fernstead
Bryant & Stratton Business Institute

M. Camille Garrett
Tarrant County Junior College

Roberta Greene
Central Piedmont Community College

Sue Hahn
South Hills Business School

Sally Hanna-Jones
Hocking Technical College

Carolyn K. Hayes
Polk Community College

Marlene Katz
Canada College

Robert Kegel, Jr.
Cypress College

Vance A. Kennedy
College of Mateo

Deborah Lineweaver
New River Community College

Russ Moorhead
Des Moines Area Community College

Erv J. Napier
Kent State University

Barbara Ollhoff
Waukesha County Technical College

Leonard L. Palumbo
Northern Virginia Community College

Naomi W. Peralta
The Institute of Financial Education

William Price
Virginia Polytechnic Institute and State University

Jack C. Reed
University of Northern Iowa

J. Douglas Shatto
Muskingum Area Technical College

V. S. Thakur
Community College of Rhode Island

Linda Truesdale
Midlands Technical College

Wendy Bletz Turner
New River Community College

Burl Worley
Allan Hancock College

We would also like to thank Dr. Denis Waitley and Mr. Charles Haefner for helping us develop a fuller understanding of human relations, and Lynne Reece for her significant contribution to this text in the areas of manuscript and literature review.

Over 100 business organizations, government agencies, and nonprofit institutions provided us with the real-world examples that appear throughout the text. We are grateful to the following organizations that allowed us to conduct interviews, observe workplace environments, and use special photographs and materials: Lowe's Companies, Inc., Deere & Company, Marriott Corporation, Wal-Mart Stores, King Soopers, Leggett Stores, Rockwell International Corporation, and Dominion Bank.

B. L. R
R. B.

Human Relations

Principles and Practices

Chapter 1

Introduction to Human Relations

CHAPTER PREVIEW

After studying this chapter, you will be able to

1. Understand how the study of human relations will help you succeed in your chosen career.

2. Explain the nature, purpose, and importance of human relations in an organizational setting.

3. Identify the reasons why human relations is receiving more attention in the workplace.

4. Identify the major forces influencing human behavior at work.

5. Review the historical development of the human relations movement.

6. Identify the seven basic themes emerging from a study of human relations.

Each year *Fortune* magazine conducts a nationwide poll of over 8,000 corporate executives, corporate directors, and financial analysts to determine America's most admired large corporation. In 1989 Merck & Co., Inc. won the number one rating for the third year in a row. What makes this pharmaceutical company so special? One of the company's major strengths is its awareness of the changing makeup of the work force. Merck has been a pioneer in setting up flexible work schedules, day care centers, and parental leave for both men and women. The company was cited in a survey conducted by *The Wall Street Journal* as one of the best employers for women and parents.[1]

Merck's ranking among major U.S. corporations is based in large part on the firm's ability to attract, develop, and keep talented people. It is a company that deemphasizes rank and title. There are no executive lunch-rooms, and managers have adopted an open-door policy.[2]

Merck and Company is not an isolated success story. Organizations throughout the United States are discovering and rediscovering the benefits that can be achieved when they improve the quality of work life. A growing number of organizations, from hospitals to hotels, are giving greater attention to the human side of enterprise. Most of the organizations that survive and prosper over a long period of time maintain a proper balance between concern for production and concern for people.

These employees of Merck & Co. are working as a team to achieve their project goals. Merck & Co. Inc.

THE NATURE, PURPOSE, AND IMPORTANCE OF HUMAN RELATIONS

Many of America's best-managed organizations are going beyond being "nice to people" to genuinely helping them come alive through their work. Managers have learned that the goals of worker and workplace need not conflict.[3] This chapter focuses on the nature of human relations, its development, and its importance to the achievement of individual and organizational goals.

Human Relations Defined

The term *human relations* in its broadest sense covers all types of interactions among people—their conflicts, cooperative efforts, and group relationships. It is the study of *why* our beliefs, attitudes, and behaviors sometimes cause interpersonal conflict in our personal lives and in work-related situations. The study of human relations emphasizes the analysis of human behavior, prevention strategies, and resolution of behavioral problems.

Knowledge of human relations does not, of course, begin in the classroom. Although this may be your first formal course in the subject, your "education" in human relations actually began with your family, friends, and early employment experiences. You learned what was acceptable and what was not. You tested your behavior against that of others, formed close relationships, experienced conflict, developed perceptions of yourself, and discovered how to get most of your needs met. By the time you reached college age, you had probably formed a fairly complex network of relationships and had a pretty good idea of who you were.

However, behavior sometimes allowed at home or school cannot always be used as a reliable guide to human relations on the job. For example, a tendency to "do your own thing" without regard for the impact of your conduct on others could limit your chances for success or advancement in an organization that values teamwork.

The Importance of Human Relations

One of the most significant developments of the past decade has been the increased importance of interpersonal skills in almost every type of work setting. In the minds of many employers, interpersonal skills represent an important category of "basic skills" the worker is expected to bring to the job. Technical ability is often not enough to achieve career success. Studies indicate that many of the people who have difficulty obtaining or holding a job, or advancing to positions of greater responsibility, possess the needed technical competence but lack interpersonal competence.

Many of today's jobs require a blend of technical skills and human relations skills.
Lorraine Rorke/The Image Works

Several trends in the workplace have given new importance to human relations. Here we will discuss a few of the major trends.

- The labor market has become a place of churning dislocation caused by the heavy volume of mergers, buyouts, and business closings due to economic volatility. These activities have been accompanied by thousands of layoffs and the elimination of hundreds of product lines.[4] Some 20 million Americans leave their jobs each year, half involuntarily. About 10 million workers change careers each year.[5] As America attempts to cope with rapid technological change and new competition from multinational companies, there is every reason to believe we will see more, not less, volatility in the labor force. In many respects, interpersonal skills represent the critical "transferable skills" needed in an ever changing labor market.

- Organizations are developing an increasing orientation toward service to clients, patients, and customers. As the authors of *Service America* note, we now live in a new economy, a service economy, where relationships are becoming more important than physical products. Restaurants, hospitals, banks, public utilities, colleges, airlines, and retail stores all have the problem of gaining and retaining the patronage of their clients and customers. In a service-type firm there are thousands of "moments of truth," those critical incidents in which customers come into contact with the organization and form their impressions of its quality and service.[6] Employees must not only be able to get along with customers, they must project a favorable image of the organization they represent. J. W. Marriott, Jr., president of Marriott Corporation, believes that the success of his company depends on positive employee attitudes. He says, "It takes happy employees to make happy customers."[7]

- The work force is tending to become organized into teams in which each specialized employee plays a part. If the people in these jobs cannot work effectively as a team, the goals of the organization will suffer. The new Gen Corp Automotive plant at Shelbyville, Indiana, provides a good example of the team approach. The plant is organized into about twenty-five teams of twelve to fifteen production workers who report to a team leader. The workers, called "associates," are cross-trained so they can perform the jobs of fellow workers if necessary.[8]

- Diversity has become a prominent characteristic of today's work force. By the year 2000 about 80 percent of the entry-level employees will be women and immigrants.[9] The work force is also aging; in the future we will see increased employment of the over-sixty-five population. Within this heterogeneous work force we will find a multitude of values, expectations, and work habits. This mixed work force will be looking for a variety of rewards.

- A new breed of supervisory-management personnel will be needed to match the new generation of workers. The current generation of workers is better educated, better informed, and has higher expectations than did previous generations. There is a new attitude that psychologists describe as a **feeling of entitlement** among younger workers. They seek jobs that give not only a sense of accomplishment but also a sense of purpose, jobs that provide meaningful work.[10] Today's supervisors and managers must shift from manager-as-order-giver to manager-as-facilitator. John Naisbitt, author and consultant, notes that "we are moving from the manager who is supposed to have all the answers and tells everyone what to do, to a manager whose role is to create a nourishing environment for personal growth."[11] We must think of today's manager as teacher, mentor, resource, and developer of human potential.

It is safe to say that no line of work, organization, or industry will enjoy immunity from these trends. Today's employee must be adaptable and flexible, able to achieve success within a climate of change. It is important to develop those interpersonal skills—courtesy, sensitivity, a positive attitude, ability to cope with conflict—that are valued by all employers.

The Influence of Behavioral Science on Human Relations

The field of human relations draws on the behavioral sciences—psychology, sociology, and anthropology. Basically, these sciences focus on the *why* of human behavior. Psychology attempts to find out why *individuals* act as they do, and sociology and anthropology are concerned primarily with *group* dynamics and social interaction. Human relations differs from the behavioral sciences in one important respect. Although also interested in the why of human behavior, human relations goes further and looks at what can be done to anticipate problems, resolve them, or even prevent them from happening. In other words, the field of human relations emphasizes knowledge that can be *applied* in practical ways to problems of interpersonal relations in an organization.

Human Relations and the "Total Person"

The material in this book will focus on human relations as the study of *how people satisfy both personal growth needs and organizational goals in their personal career.* We believe, as do most authors in the field of human relations, that such human traits as physical fitness, emotional control, self-awareness, self-esteem, and values orientation are interdependent. Although some organizations may occasionally wish they could employ only a person's skill or brain, all that can be employed is the whole or **total person.**[12] One's separate characteristics are part of a single system making up a whole person. Work life is not totally separate from home life, and emotional conditions are not separate from physical conditions. The quality of one's work, for example, is often related to physical fitness and nutrition.

Many organizations are beginning to recognize that if the whole person can be improved, significant benefits accrue to the firm. They are establishing employee development programs that address the total person, not just the employee skills needed to perform the job. These programs include such topics as stress management, assertiveness training, physical fitness, problem solving, and personal attitude development. A few examples follow:

Item: Hoffman-La Roche, Inc., a New Jersey-based firm, sponsors a fully developed corporate child-care program. This program was the outgrowth of a staff survey indicating that employees wanted to minimize baby-sitting arrangements as much as possible.

Item: Pitney Bowes established a career planning workshop to help employees form and chart their long-term career goals inside or outside the firm. This program enables employees to develop the skills needed to manage their careers.

Item: IBM initiated a new "flexibility" program which offers employees unpaid leaves of up to three years to care for a new baby or an elderly parent.

Northwest Mutual is interested in the "total person." Employees can obtain nutritious meals at the company's four-star cafeteria.
Northwestern Mutual Life

Item: The Northwestern Mutual Life Insurance Company is taking care of the physical and mental needs of its employees. In the company's four-star-rated cafeteria (lunch is free), the daily menu reports how many calories each item contains. More than 1,300 paintings hanging throughout the building contribute to a more human work environment.[13]

Some of the results of these programs may be difficult to assess in terms of profit and loss. For example, does the person in good physical health contribute more? If an employee is under considerable stress, does this mean he or she will have more accidents on the job? Specific answers vary, but most human relations experts agree that an employee's physical and mental well-being have a definite impact on job performance and productivity. Robert Pike, a noted management consultant, has stated:

> The greatest resource we have in our companies today is the human resource. . . . By helping people develop the tools to reduce and resolve personal conflicts, by assisting them to become more aware of what attitudes they have, and by helping them to experience the results that improved attitudes can provide, we can help build better people, a more productive company, and make a positive contribution to our community.[14]

The Need for a Supportive Environment

John W. Humphrey, Chief Executive Officer of the Forum Corporation, says, "These days, the only sustainable competitive advantage in any business is

---

TOTAL PERSON INSIGHT

66 To me, there's no essential difference between the way we spend time in work and the way we spend the rest of our lives. Time is time; our working life adds up—in a few short decades—to be our life itself. 99

Marsha Sinetar

---

people, not product."[15] Unfortunately, not every chief executive or manager attributes the same importance to people or people problems. Some people do not believe that total person training, job enrichment, motivation techniques, or career development help increase productivity or strengthen worker commitment to the job. It is true that when such practices are tried halfheartedly or without full management support, there is a good chance they will fail. Such failures often have a demoralizing effect on employees and management alike. "Human relations" may take the blame, and management will be reluctant to try other human relations techniques or approaches in the future.

A basic assumption of this book is that human relations, when applied in a positive and supportive environment, can help individuals achieve greater personal satisfaction from their careers and help increase an organization's productivity and efficiency. In the subsequent chapters of the book, we will examine the impact of an individual's values, attitudes, appearance, motivation, and communication style on interpersonal relations in the workplace. We will also take a look at group interaction and the special human relations challenges that organizations encounter in today's complex environment.

Myths and Misconceptions

Now that you know what human relations *is*, it may be helpful to explore what it *is not*.

It is not concerned with personality or character development in order to give you the power to manipulate people. Nor does human relations offer the ultimate formula to solve the people problems you are likely to encounter. In dealing with others, you will often find that there is seldom a clear-cut "right" or "wrong" way to handle problem situations. In one plant, for example, the night superintendent found that workers on the first shift settled their disputes themselves. They viewed his efforts to arbitrate as an interference. The second shift, however, expected their superintendent to settle disagreements and brought him all their disputes. Their view of a good manager was someone who knew how to arbitrate.

Human relations *can* help you develop appropriate solutions to problems by giving you a good grasp of behavior concepts—with regard to both your own behavior and that of others. Texts such as this one can provide a good grounding in the fundamentals of human relations and offer guidelines and suggestions for modifying behavior and enhancing group interaction. But human relations skills do not guarantee quick changes. Unlike characters in a movie, people in real life do not alter their behavior overnight. Even when everyone agrees a change needs to be made, it still takes time and effort. You may have experienced this fact yourself in trying to break an old habit or develop a new one. Unless people are willing to *work* at change, no solution—no matter how good—will be effective. Take the opportunity to assess your human relations skills in light of the information in this book and to make changes you feel are necessary.

It is also a popular belief among some people that human relations is nothing more than good common sense. Everyone knows that you give praise where it is due, acknowledge a job well done, and listen to what employees have to say. Yet research studies conducted over the years tell a different story. These studies indicate that many employees do not feel they are given adequate recognition for work well done and that management often fails to listen to employees' suggestions, concerns, and grievances. Apparently, common sense is not enough to ensure good human relations on the job.

THINKING/LEARNING STARTERS

1. How can the study of human relations be helpful to you? In what ways can it contribute to your career goals?
2. What is your reaction to the opinion that human relations is nothing more than common sense?
3. Do you believe the trends in the work force described in this chapter will continue throughout the 1990s?

FORCES INFLUENCING BEHAVIOR AT WORK

A major purpose of this text is to increase your knowledge of factors that influence human behavior in a variety of work settings. An understanding of human behavior at work begins with a review of the major forces that influence the worker. Figure 1.1 shows the five forces that affect every employee, regardless of the size of the organization.

Organizational Culture

Every organization, whether a manufacturing plant, retail store, hospital, or government agency, is unique. Each has its own culture. **Organizational cul-**

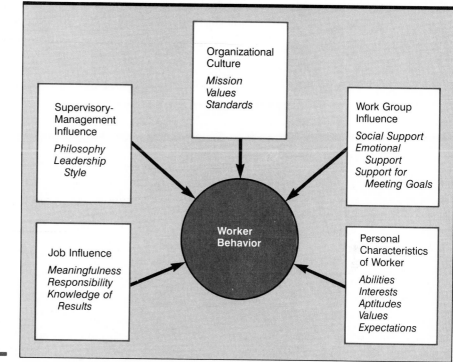

Figure 1.1
Major Forces Influencing
Worker Behavior

ture is a collection of beliefs, behaviors, and work patterns held in common by the workers employed by a specific firm. Most organizations over a period of time tend to take on distinct norms and practices. At Maytag Company, for example, a commitment to high-quality products has been instilled in every member of the work force. Maytag machines rank at the top in industry comparisons, and this fact builds pride in the workers. Polaroid Corporation places a great emphasis on equal employment opportunity. About one out of every five of its hourly employees is a member of a minority.

An organization's culture is an outgrowth of the philosophy and goals of those who join together to create it. Some organizations are cold and impersonal, and place major emphasis on achieving productivity goals regardless of the human costs. Other organizations are warm, friendly, and supportive of employee needs. Which organizational climate is more effective? The human-oriented climate is usually best in the long run. People tend to be more productive when they are part of an organization with a culture that inspires personal growth and development, and builds and maintains a sense of personal worth. These, after all, are the basic rewards of work.

Jay Hall, author of *The Competence Process,* says that when people lose access to the basic rewards of work, they are deprived of self-respect and become less productive. He further states that work is the context of individual competence, and the organization creates the context for work.

People come to the organization, capable and desirous of working compe-
tently. Managers then supply them with the policies and ground rules, standards and objectives, which will characterize their work. People supply the
capacity and managers supply the context. Often the two collide because the
context for doing work reflects few of the reasons people work at all.[16]

Supervisory-Management Influence

Supervisory-management personnel are in a key position to influence employee behavior. It is not an exaggeration to say that supervisors and managers are the spokespersons for the organization. They establish its image in
the eyes of employees. Each employee develops certain perceptions about
the organization's concern for his or her welfare. These perceptions, in turn,
influence such important factors as productivity, customer relations, safety
consciousness, and loyalty to the firm. Effective managers are aware of the
organization's basic purposes, why it exists, and its general direction. They
are able to communicate this information to workers in a clear and positive
manner.

Supervisory-management personnel hold the key to both outlook and
performance. They are in a unique position to unlock the internal forces of
motivation and help employees channel their energies toward achieving the
goals of the organization. Today, managers need to use both logic and intuition, recognize both facts and feelings, and be both technically competent
and emotionally caring.[17]

Although it is up to supervisors and managers to develop the firm's values and guiding principles at every level of the organization, this process
can be very challenging. When Lee Iacocca became the chief executive officer at Chrysler Corporation, he launched a campaign to improve quality.
But a major change in culture does not happen overnight. Iacocca recalls the
problems the company faced at one particular plant:

> You have to change your basic culture to get better quality. One of our most
> expensive and highly automated plants gives us the most trouble. Maybe it is
> lousy management, maybe a lousy work force, maybe a combination of the
> two. It may be personality clashes, whatever, but it permeates down, and the
> guys don't do their job right.[18]

Work Group Influence

In recent years behavioral scientists have devoted considerable research to
determining the influence of group affiliation on the individual worker.
They are particularly interested in group influence within the formal structure of the organization. This research has identified three functions of
group membership.[19] First, it can satisfy *social needs*. Many people find the
hours spent at work enjoyable because coworkers provide the social support
they need. Second, the work group can provide the *emotional support* needed

> **TOTAL PERSON INSIGHT**
>
> **66** . . . jobs do a lot more than merely provide income. They provide the opportunity to learn and enhance skills, to have some control over one's fate and, perhaps most important, to gain a sense of self-worth, a sense of carrying one's own weight. **99**
>
> William Raspberry

to deal with pressures and problems on the job. Finally, the group provides *assistance in meeting goals.* A cohesive work group lends support to all individuals as they seek to meet the goals of the work unit. An effective work group is often described as one that maintains a balance between group productivity and the satisfaction of individual needs.

Job Influence

Some workers find their jobs to be a source of enormous personal satisfaction. Charles Jordan, director of design for General Motors Corporation, is one of these people. He has been quoted as saying, "I've got the best job in the world. I love cars and I'm living in the future." In reference to his position, he says, "It never quite seems like work!"[20] Unfortunately, not everyone receives this much satisfaction from work. Many workers perceive their jobs to be meaningless and boring because there is little variety to the work. Some autoworkers complain that their work is noisy, dirty, and monotonous. In some southern textile plants, workers still labor in the heat on noisy equipment to produce cotton cloth and other materials. And many electronic data processing terminal operators say the tedious work causes them physical and mental anguish.

Job satisfaction tends to increase when there is compatibility between the wants and needs of the employee and job characteristics. To be completely satisfying, a job must provide three experiences for a worker: meaningfulness, responsibility, and knowledge of results.[21] Throughout the past two decades, there has been a gradual increase in job satisfaction among American workers. One factor that appears to be contributing to this positive trend is improved organizational practices dealing with human relations.

Personal Characteristics of the Worker

Every worker brings to the job a combination of abilities, interests, aptitudes, values, and expectations. Worker behavior on the job is most frequently a reflection of how well the work environment accommodates the unique characteristics of each worker. For more than half a century, work researchers and theorists have attempted to define the ideal working conditions that would maximize worker productivity. These efforts have met with partial success, but some unanswered questions remain.

Identifying the ideal work environment is difficult because the work force is gradually changing. The challenge is to monitor changes closely and attempt to respond to the evolving needs of workers. Today many management and union leaders fail to realize that a philosophy and organization of work that was appropriate for the 1960s and 1970s may not be appropriate for the 1980s and 1990s. Coming into the workplace today is a new generation of workers with value systems and expectations about work that are very different from those of previous generations. Today's better-educated and better-informed workers value identity and achievement. They also have a heightened sense of their rights.

This review of the five major forces that influence employee behavior at work helps us understand the complex nature of interpersonal relations. It also helps us develop greater awareness of why people-oriented problems surface with such frequency in organizational settings.

DEVELOPMENT OF THE HUMAN RELATIONS MOVEMENT

Problems in human relations are not new. All cooperative efforts carry the potential for people-oriented conflicts. However, it is only within the past few decades that management, researchers in behavioral sciences, and industry experts have recognized that human relations problems can have considerable impact on organizational productivity. During this period, the human relations movement has matured into a distinct and important field of study.

Although it is difficult to pinpoint exactly when the human relations movement began, most researchers and historians agree that it emerged in about the mid-1800s. In the beginning, the focus was mainly to improve efficiency, motivation, and productivity. But over time, human relations research became more involved with a redefinition of the nature of work and the gradual perception of workers as complex human beings. The change reflected a shift in values from a concern with things to a greater concern for people.

Impact of the Industrial Revolution

Prior to the Industrial Revolution, most work was performed by individual craftworkers or members of craft guilds. Generally, each worker saw a project through from start to finish. Skills such as tailoring, carpentry, or shoe-

*This craftsman was able to perform every step in the produc-
tion of a shoe.*
Culver Pictures

*Each of these factory workers is responsible for only one or two
steps in the shoe manufacturing process.*
Culver Pictures

making took a long time to perfect and were often a source of pride to an
individual or a community. Under this system, however, output was limited.

The Industrial Revolution had a profound effect on the nature of work
and the role of the worker. Previously, an individual tailor could make only
a few items of clothing in a week's time; factories could now make
hundreds. Employers began to think of labor as another item in the manufacturing equation, along with raw materials and capital. One author described the situation this way:

> The rise of industrialization led to a narrow definition of man as an economic
> unit. In the early stages of the industrial era, the individual was reduced to
> an interchangeable part in highly structured work situations.[22]

Individuals no longer worked for themselves but sold their labor in the marketplace. As farmers and other rural workers sought employment in the factories and shops, cities became congested urban centers where the labor
supply was cheap and plentiful.

Employers at that time did not realize how workers' needs affected production. As a result, few owners or managers gave any thought to working conditions, health and safety precautions, or worker attitudes and motivation. Hours were long and the pay was low.

Taylor's Scientific Management

Around the turn of the century, Frederick Taylor and other researchers interested in industrial problems introduced the concept of **scientific management**. They believed that productivity could be improved by breaking a job down into isolated, specialized tasks and assigning workers to each of those tasks. The development of scientific management coincided with the revolutionary concept of mass production. Needless to say, Taylor's theories became immensely popular among business owners and managers. Eventually, they helped pave the way for the assembly line.

Taylor's work was sharply criticized by those who felt it exploited more than helped the workers. More than ever, employees were treated as a commodity, as interchangeable as the parts they produced. Taylor originally felt that by increasing production, the company would end up with a larger financial pie for everyone to share. Management would earn higher bonuses; workers would take home more pay. He did not foresee that his theories could be applied in ways that dehumanized the workplace even further.

Testing and the Emerging Individual

As scientific management gained wide acceptance, employers and managers found themselves assessing each worker's unique capabilities to match the right person with the right job. Some workers seemed skilled at intricate, detailed work, whereas others could handle heavy machinery. Still others showed a knack for supervising work crews and achieving company goals. If managers could test for the specific skills they needed, they could improve their hiring practices and increase efficiency and output. Many employers believed they had found the answer to their production problems. The concept of testing for skills and abilities made scientific management seem even more "scientific."

But the popularity of testing as a way to solve labor-management problems had an interesting and unexpected side effect. As more and more organizations developed and administered tests, evidence began to accumulate that an individual's performance was influenced by the level of personal motivation. In addition, workers' job performances did not always match their test scores. Some exceeded their potential, and others fell consistently below it. Apparently something more complex influenced people's performance on the job.

The Hawthorne Studies

Elton Mayo and his colleagues accidentally discovered part of the answer while conducting research in the mid-1920s at the Hawthorne Western Electric plant located near Chicago. Their original goal was to study the effect of illumination, ventilation, and fatigue on production workers in the plant. Their research became known as the **Hawthorne studies** and has become a landmark in the human relations field.

For one part of their research, Mayo and his colleagues selected two groups of employees doing similar work under similar conditions and kept output records for each group. After a time, the researchers began to vary the intensity of light for one group while keeping it constant for the other. Each time they increased the light, productivity rose. To determine if better illumination was responsible for the higher outputs, they began to dim the light. *Productivity continued to rise.* In fact, one of the highest levels of output was recorded when the light was scarcely brighter than the full moon! The researchers realized some other influence was at work.

In talking with employees, Mayo made two important discoveries. First, all the attention focused on the test group made them feel more important. For the first time, they were getting feedback on their job performance. In addition, test conditions allowed them greater freedom from supervisory control. Under these circumstances, morale and motivation increased and productivity rose. Mayo repeated his experiments over several years, always with the same results. Group morale and motivation seemed to override the effects of fatigue, illumination, and ventilation.

Second, Mayo found that the interaction of workers on the job created a network of relationships called an **informal organization.** This organization exerted considerable influence on workers' performance and could, in some cases, countermand orders handed down through the formal or managerial structure. For example, if management wanted to increase production, the workers could decide among themselves not to speed up the work. Thus, the informal organization could affect the rate of output substantially.

Although the Hawthorne studies have been criticized for flawed research methodology,[23] this research can be credited with helping change the way management viewed workers. The assembly line had streamlined the work, and testing procedures could isolate and identify some abilities and skills. But studies such as Mayo's revealed that the average worker represented a complex combination of needs, values, and attitudes.

From the Depression to the 1980s

During the Depression interest in human relations research waned as other ways of humanizing the workplace gained momentum. During that period, unions increased their militant campaigns to organize workers and force employers to pay attention to such issues as working conditions, higher pay,

---

TOTAL PERSON INSIGHT

66 As concern for people inches toward parity with concern for getting the job done, managers will have to exercise greater skills in dealing with people. They will need to express and accept emotions, nurture and support colleagues and subordinates, and promote interactions between bosses and subordinates and between leaders and members of the work team. These behaviors are desirable not only for their own sake, but because they can increase organizational effectiveness and efficiency. 99

Alice Sargent

---

shorter hours, and protection for child laborers. When Congress passed the Wagner Act, businesses were required by law to negotiate contracts with union representatives. Other labor laws passed in the 1930s outlawed child labor, reduced the hours women worked, and instituted a minimum wage for many industries.

Through World War II and the years of postwar economic expansion, interest in the human relations field was revived. Countless papers and research studies on worker efficiency, group dynamics, organization, and motivational methods were published. Douglas McGregor introduced his Theory X, a rather pessimistic, authoritarian view of human behavior, and Theory Y, a more positive, optimistic view. Abraham Maslow, a noted psychologist, devised a "hierarchy of needs," stating that people satisfied their needs in a particular order. Both theories had considerable influence on the study of motivation and will be explored in detail in Chapter 4.

Since the 1950s, theories and concepts regarding human relations have focused more and more on an understanding of human interaction. Eric Berne in the 1960s revolutionized the way people think about interpersonal communication when he introduced transactional analysis with its "Parent-Adult-Child" model. At about the same time Carl Rogers published his work on personality development, interpersonal communication, and group dynamics. In the early 1980s, William Ouchi introduced the Theory Z style of management, which is based on the belief that worker involvement is the key to increased productivity.

There is no doubt that management consultants Tom Peters and Robert Waterman also influenced management thinking regarding the importance of people in organizations. Their best-selling book *In Search of Excellence*, published in 1982, explained what makes America's best-run companies successful. It featured eight attributes of excellence. One of these attributes, "productivity through people," emphasized that excellent companies treat the worker as the root source of quality and productivity.[24] In *A Passion for*

Excellence (with Nancy Austin), published in 1985, and *Thriving on Chaos,* published in 1987, Peters has continued to stress the importance of people and relationships in organizations.

We will explore these and other concepts throughout the book.

THINKING/LEARNING STARTERS

1. What do you personally find to be the basic rewards of work?
2. The book *In Search of Excellence* cites "productivity through people" as an attribute of excellent companies. Do you agree or disagree with this view?
3. What degree of worker involvement have you experienced in places that you have worked?

MAJOR THEMES IN HUMAN RELATIONS

Several broad themes emerge from the study of human relations. They are communication, self-acceptance, self-awareness, motivation, trust, self-disclosure, and conflict management. These themes reflect the current concern in human relations with the twin goals of personal growth and development and the satisfaction of organizational objectives. To some degree, the themes overlap and most are discussed in more than one chapter of this book.

Communication

It is not an exaggeration to describe communication as the "heart and soul" of human relations. **Communication** is the means by which we come to an understanding of ourselves and others. In order to continue to grow and develop as persons, we must communicate. John R. Diekman, author of *Human Connections,* says that ". . . if we are going to do anything constructive and helping with one another, it must be through our communication."[25] Communication is the *human* connection. That is why the subject is covered in more than one section of this book. Chapter 6 introduces transactional analysis, an important and practical theory of communication. A major goal of this chapter is to help you achieve complementary transactions more frequently when you communicate with other people. Chapter 7 offers ways to use positive reinforcement to improve relationships and reward behavior. Various forms of written and verbal reinforcement are discussed.

Self-Acceptance

The degree to which you like and accept yourself is the degree to which you can genuinely like and accept other people. **Self-acceptance** is the foundation of successful interaction with others. In a work setting, people with high self-esteem tend to cope better with change, accept responsibility, tolerate differences, and generally work well as team members. On the other hand, low self-esteem can create barriers to good interpersonal relations. Self-acceptance is crucial, not only for your relationships with others, but for setting and achieving your goals. The more you believe you can do, the more you are likely to accomplish. Chapter 3 explains why high self-esteem is essential for effective human relations and success at work. This chapter also offers many suggestions on ways to help you build high self-esteem.

Self-Awareness

Do you fully understand how your behavior influences others? Are you fully aware of the reasons why you have formed certain attitudes toward others? Do you know what is most important to you in life? With increased levels of self-knowledge comes **self-awareness,** an understanding of who you are and how your behavior influences other people.

On and off the job, your decisions regarding what is appropriate behavior are based in large part on your self-awareness. As you learn more about the impact of your behavior on other people, you can make more appropriate decisions. Accurate self-knowledge is essential for developing positive personal relationships, managing others effectively, and setting appropriate life goals and career paths for oneself.[26] The concept of self-awareness surfaces in several chapters.

Motivation

Human relations researchers no longer talk about **motivation** simply in terms of reward and punishment but rather as the drive to satisfy needs. Most employees tend to work best when they feel the organization is meeting their needs for growth and development. As a result, motivation is likely to be high where employees and management support and influence one another in positive ways.

Chapter 4 will explore the complex drives of human beings and examine the theory and practice of motivation strategies. Chapter 5 will help you identify the priorities and values in life that motivate you. In addition, Chapter 7 discusses how worker performance can be influenced by positive reinforcement, a form of external motivation.

Trust

Good relationships, whether among coworkers or between employer and employee, are based on **trust.** Without trust, most human relationships will degenerate into conflict. William Ouchi, author of *Theory Z*, a popular book about how American business can meet the Japanese challenge, recognizes trust as a key to long-term personal and organizational success. He said, "To trust another is to know that the two of you share basic goals in the long-run so that left to your own devices, each will behave in ways that are not harmful to the other."[27] When a climate of trust is present, frank discussion of problems and a free exchange of ideas and information are encouraged. The concept of trust receives attention in several chapters.

Self-Disclosure

Self-disclosure and trust are two halves of a whole. The more open you are with people, the more trust you build up. The more trust in a relationship, the safer you feel to disclose who you are. Self-disclosure is also part of good communication and helps eliminate unnecessary guessing games. Managers who let their subordinates know what is expected of them help those employees fulfill their responsibilities. The need of individuals to verbalize the thoughts and feelings they carry within them is discussed in several parts of the book.

Conflict Management

Conflict management in human relations refers primarily to conflicts *within* an organization, although it can also mean disputes among organizations or between an organization and the public. It is true that whenever people work together, some conflict is inevitable. But disputes, personal clashes, and disagreements left unresolved can hurt an organization's operations and reduce its effectiveness as a provider of goods or services. Conflict tends to obstruct cooperative action, create suspicion and distrust, and decrease productivity. The ability to anticipate or resolve conflict can be an invaluable skill. The issue of conflict management is a major topic in Chapter 6. This topic also surfaces in several other chapters.

THINKING/LEARNING STARTER

Now that you have had an opportunity to read about the seven themes of human relations, what do you consider your strongest areas? In which areas do you feel you need improvement? Why?

HUMAN RELATIONS: WHERE TO BEGIN

Right now you may be thinking: "Human relations is an important subject, but can it really be *taught?* Isn't getting along with others a matter of experience, something you learn through trial and error?" Experience is undoubtedly an important part of the learning process, but as a teaching method it has certain drawbacks. After all, you can learn an important lesson by being fired, but you will have to find another job before you can apply your new-found knowledge.

A basic course in human relations cannot give you a foolproof set of techniques for solving every people-related problem that might arise. It can, however, give you a better understanding of human behavior in groups, help you become more sensitive to yourself and others, and enable you to act more wisely when problems occur. You may even be able to anticipate conflicts or prevent small problems from escalating into major ones.

Many leaders feel that courses in human relations are important because very few workers are responsible to themselves alone. They point out that most jobs today are interdependent. If people in these jobs cannot work effectively as a team, the efficiency of the organization will suffer. Many young, inexperienced workers, leaving school for their first job, are surprised to learn that their attitudes, behavior, and personality matter just as much if not more than their technical or business skills.

SUMMARY

Human relations is the study of how people fulfill both personal growth needs and organizational goals in their careers. Many organizations are beginning to realize that an employee's life outside the job can have a significant impact on work performance, and some are developing training programs in human relations that address the total person. Increasingly, organizations are discovering that many forces influence the behavior of people at work.

Human relations is not a set of foolproof techniques for solving people-related problems. Rather it gives people an understanding of basic behavior concepts that may enable them to make wiser choices when problems arise, to anticipate or prevent conflicts, and to keep minor problems from escalating into major ones.

The development of the human relations movement has involved a redefinition of the nature of work and the gradual perception of managers and workers as complex human beings. Two landmarks in the study of motivation and worker needs are Frederick Taylor's work in scientific management and Elton Mayo's Hawthorne Studies. Many industry leaders predict an increased emphasis on human relations research and application. The reasons for this trend include higher educational levels of employees and managers, worker organizations pressing for attention to employee concerns, a weakening of the traditional work ethic, and increased federal legislation affecting organizations.

Seven major themes emerge from a study of human relations: communication, self-acceptance, self-awareness, motivation, trust, self-disclosure, and conflict management. These themes reflect the current concern in human relations with the twin goals of personal growth and the satisfaction of organizational objectives.

KEY TERMS

human relations	communication
feeling of entitlement	self-acceptance
total person	self-awareness
organizational culture	motivation
scientific management	trust
Hawthorne studies	self-disclosure
informal organization	conflict management

REVIEW QUESTIONS

1. Given the information provided in this chapter, provide a personal definition of human relations. 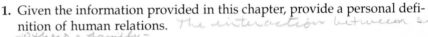 *The interaction between self + Others - family -*

2. List and describe the major trends which have given new importance to human relations.

3. Describe the total-person approach to human relations. Why is this approach becoming more popular?

4. List and describe the five major forces influencing human behavior at work.

5. In what ways can training in human relations benefit an organization?

6. How did Taylor's work help usher in the modern assembly line? Why was his work criticized by some researchers and not by others?

7. Mayo's research indicated that workers could influence the rate of production in an organization. What discoveries did he make that led to this conclusion?

8. IBM and some other large companies are now offering employees unpaid leaves to care for a new baby or an elderly parent. Should this policy be adopted by other organizations?

9. What seven themes emerge from a study of human relations? Describe each one briefly.

10. Re-read the Total Person Insight on page 9 and then indicate what you feel is the meaning of this quotation by Marsha Sinetar.

████   ██ CASE 1. 1

The Human Factor at Hallmark

Hallmark Cards Inc., the world's largest greeting card company, has been recognized by the authors of *The 100 Best Companies to Work for in America* and *A Great Place to Work*. Why is this company receiving such positive acclaim? One reason is Hallmark's policy of no layoffs, even in the face of strong competition.

Hallmark, founded in 1910, has been a pioneer in employee benefits. The list of benefits includes adoption assistance of up to $1,000, interest-free loans of up to $1,000 for unexpected emergencies, free refreshments during breaks, a physical-fitness building, and low-interest $2,500-a-year college loans for children of employees.[1] The company also offers employees a profit-sharing program. Each year the company sets aside a portion of corporate profits and puts it into an employee fund.

One tradition that demonstrates the familylike atmosphere at Hallmark is the anniversary party given to employees with twenty-five years of experience with the company. The employee may invite any of his or her friends throughout the company. It is not unusual for two hundred or more people to attend this special event.[2]

In recent years Hallmark has used the team approach to improve productivity. Artists, writers, and marketers work in teams to create various types of greeting cards. Under the teamwork system, artists are producing 15 percent more designs than they did two years ago.[3]

Sources: Robert Levering, Milton Moskowitz, and Michael Katz, *The 100 Best Companies to Work for in America* (New York: New American Library, 1985), pp. 139–141; Robert Levering, *A Great Place to Work* (New York: Random House, 1988), p. 180; *Gaining the Competitive Edge* (Alexandria, Va.: American Society for Training and Development, 1988), p. 14.

Questions

1. Hallmark appears to be a very employee-oriented company. What aspects of this company's culture contribute to this loyalty?

2. Hallmark is in the greeting card business. Would the policies and procedures at this company work in other industries such as banking? retailing? auto manufacturing? Why or why not?

---

[1] Robert Levering, Milton Moskowitz, and Michael Katz, *The 100 Best Companies to Work for in America* (New York: New American Library, 1985), p. 139.

[2] Robert Levering, *A Great Place to Work* (New York: Random House, 1988), p. 180.

[3] *Gaining the Competitive Edge* (Alexandria, Va.: American Society for Training and Development, 1988), p. 14.

■ CASE 1.2

Culture Shock

The behavior of employees within an organization is determined more by the organization's culture than by directives from management or by other factors, according to Morty Lefkoe, president of a Connecticut-based consulting firm. His company specializes in helping corporations reshape their cultures. He notes that when an organization attempts to implement a new way of doing things that is inconsistent with its culture, it most often fails.[1] In other words, if the policy or practice is not in harmony with the firm's culture, it is likely to be rejected by employees.

The strong influence of culture on employee behavior has created problems for many companies involved in mergers. In recent years there have been a record number of mergers, and many of these have created a "clash of cultures." One example of this situation is the merger of Scandinavian Airlines System (SAS) and Continental Airlines. SAS is an airline that has developed a commitment to excellent customer service. It pays a great deal of attention to the real needs of the customer.[2] Continental had not, in the past, given customer service such a high priority. Employees from both airlines are now attending seminars, and company officials hope Continental employees will pick up SAS's way of doing business.[3]

Sources: Morty Lefkoe, "Why So Many Mergers Fail," *Fortune,* July 20, 1987, pp. 113–114; "Culture Shock at 39,000 Feet," *Fortune,* November 7, 1988, p. 11; Karl Albrecht and Ron Zemke, *Service America* (Homewood, Ill.: Dow Jones-Irwin, 1985), pp. 19–30.

Questions

1. If you were an employee of SAS or Continental, what concerns would you have at the time the merger was announced?

2. In your opinion, will a series of employee seminars resolve problems created by the "clash of cultures"?

3. What steps should top management take to develop support among Continental employees for SAS's strong service orientation?

SUGGESTED READINGS

Albrecht, Karl, and Ron Zemke. *Service America.* Homewood, Illinois: Dow Jones-Irwin, 1985.

[1] Morty Lefkoe, "Why So Many Mergers Fail," *Fortune,* July 20, 1987, p. 113.

[2] Karl Albrecht and Ron Zemke, *Service America* (Homewood, Ill.: Dow Jones-Irwin, 1985), pp. 19–30.

[3] "Culture Shock at 39,000 Feet," *Fortune,* November 7, 1988, p. 11.

Editors of *Harvard Business Review. Harvard Business Review—On Human Relations.* New York: Harper & Row, 1979.

Hall, Jay. *The Competence Connection.* The Woodlands, Texas: Woodstead Press, 1988.

Hall, Jay. *The Competence Process.* The Woodlands, Texas: Teleometrics International, 1980.

Levering, Robert. *A Great Place to Work.* New York: Random House, 1988.

Levering, Robert, Milton Moskowitz, and Michael Katz. *The 100 Best Companies to Work for in America.* New York: New American Library, 1985.

Naisbitt, John. *Megatrends—Ten New Directions Transforming Our Lives.* New York: Warner Books, 1982.

Naisbitt, John, and Patricia Aburdene. *Re-inventing the Corporation.* New York: Warner Books, Inc., 1985.

Pascarella, Perry. *The New Achievers.* New York: The Free Press, 1984.

Peters, Thomas, and Robert Waterman, Jr. *In Search of Excellence: Lessons from America's Best-Run Companies.* New York: Harper and Row, 1982.

Sargent, Alice G. *The Androgynous Manager.* New York: American Management Associations, 1980.

NOTES

1. Sal Villolino, "The Most Admired Company in America," *Human Resource Executive,* April 1988, p. 17.

2. Ibid., p. 38.

3. Perry Pascarella, *The New Achievers* (New York: The Free Press, 1984), p. x.

4. Patricia Galagan, "Here's the Situation," *Training and Development Journal,* July 1987, p. 21.

5. Richard I. Kirkland, Jr., "Why America Creates the Most Jobs," *Fortune,* December 21, 1987, p. 178.

6. Karl Albrecht and Ron Zemke, *Service America* (Homewood, Ill.: Dow Jones-Irwin, 1985), p. 31.

7. *Marketing and Distributive Educator's Digest,* Vol. 7, No. 1, Fall 1981, p. 28.

8. "Workers' Voices Heeded," *Roanoke Times & World-News,* January 1, 1989, p. D-1.

9. Galagan, "Here's the Situation," p. 21.

10. Craig Brod, *Technostress* (Reading, Mass.: Addison-Wesley, 1984), p. 35.

11. John Naisbitt, "New Way of Doing Business Looming for U.S. Industry," *The Charlotte Observer,* January 6, 1985, p. 60.

12. Keith Davis, *Human Behavior at Work* (New York: McGraw-Hill, 1981), p. 12.

13. Robert Levering, Milton Moskowitz, and Michael Katz, *The 100 Best Companies to Work for in America* (New York: New American Library, 1985), pp. 250–251.

14. Robert W. Pike and Frank Plasha, "Total Person Training," *Personnel Administrator,* April 1975, p. 35.

15. "Who Wins and Why," *INC.,* April 1987, p. 103.

16. Jay Hall, *The Competence Process* (The Woodlands, Texas: Teleometrics International, 1980), p. 39.

17. Alice G. Sargent, *The Androgynous Manager* (New York: AMACOM, a division of American Management Associations, 1980), p. viii (introduction by Elsa Porter).

18. "Iacocca," *Fortune,* August 2, 1988, p. 41.

19. D. R. Hampton, C. E. Summer, and R. A. Webber, *Organizational Behavior and the Practice of Management* (Glenview, Ill.: Scott, Foresman, 1973), p. 215.

20. "Tabletop Production Line," *Road & Track*, October 1982, p. 122.

21. Roy W. Walters, "Improving Man/Machine Interface for Greater Productivity," *BNAC Communicator*, Summer 1982, p. 13.

22. Pascarella, *The New Achievers*, p. 10.

23. For a detailed examination of the Hawthorne criticisms and the legacy of the Hawthorne research, see David A. Whitsett and Lyle Yorks, *From Management Theory to Business Sense* (New York: American Management Associations, 1983).

24. Thomas J. Peters and Robert H. Waterman, Jr., *In Search of Excellence* (New York: Harper & Row, 1982), p. 14.

25. John R. Diekman, *Human Connections* (Englewood Cliffs, N.J.: Prentice-Hall, 1982), p. xii.

26. Robert Bolton and Dorothy Grover Bolton, *Social Style/Management Style* (New York: American Management Associations, 1984), p. 4.

27. "William Ouchi on Trust," *Training and Development Journal*, December 1982, p. 71.

Chapter 2

Your Attitudes

CHAPTER PREVIEW

After studying this chapter, you will be able to

1. Understand the impact of employee attitudes on the success of individuals as well as organizations.

2. List and explain the ways people acquire attitudes.

3. Identify ways to change your attitudes.

4. Identify ways to help others change their attitudes.

5. Understand what adjustments organizations are making to produce positive employee attitudes.

Stew Leonard, owner of Stew Leonard's, the "world's largest dairy store," in Norwalk, Connecticut, credits his success to a change of attitude that he made shortly after the store opened. He was standing at the entrance of the store when a customer came up and said in an angry voice, "This eggnog is sour." He took the half-gallon carton, opened it, and tasted it. He then looked the customer in the eye and said, "You're wrong, it's perfect." And to prove he was right he added, "We sold over 300 half-gallons of eggnog this week, and you're the only one who complained." The angry customer demanded her money back and said, "I'm never coming back to this store again!"

That evening Leonard reflected on the incident and came to the conclusion that he had made a mistake. First, he had not listened to the customer.

Stew Leonard's attitude toward his customers, prominently displayed on a rock outside the front door of his dairy store, has brought him success.
Dave LaBianca

Second, he had humiliated her by saying that 300 other customers had not complained. He decided that the success of his small store would depend on good customer service that would generate repeat business. He decided to adopt two basic store policies which have been chiseled into a 6,000-pound rock next to the front door of his store. The simple message reads

> RULE 1 — THE CUSTOMER IS ALWAYS RIGHT.
> RULE 2 — IF THE CUSTOMER IS EVER WRONG, RE-READ RULE 1.

Today, thousands of customers walk past that rock every week as they enter his dairy store. Stew Leonard takes pride in the fact that 99 percent of these people are repeat customers.[1]

The beneficial power of individual and organizational attitudes is often not measurable. But the correlation between positive attitudes and high performance, low turnover, and increased productivity exists in most organizations.

WHAT IS AN ATTITUDE?

Most psychologists define an **attitude** as any strong belief or feeling toward people and situations. We have favorable or unfavorable attitudes toward ethnic groups, rich people, poor people, and other groups. We have strong or moderate attitudes toward welfare, labor unions, religion, politics, and other social issues. Attitudes are not quick judgments we make casually and can easily change. Since we acquire them throughout our lives, they are deeply ingrained in our personalities. We are very much in favor of those things toward which we have a positive attitude. And we are very much against those things toward which we have a negative attitude.

Dr. Jerome Kagan, Harvard professor and author, explains, "It is this 'for' or 'against' quality that distinguishes attitudes from more superficial and less influential opinions."[2] The point of view that more women seem to be entering management-level positions in organizations is an opinion. However, the belief that women should have equal pay and equal access to top-level jobs is an attitude backed by strong emotions.

People possess both positive and negative attitudes. And it is generally agreed that in human relations positive attitudes bring positive results just as negative attitudes bring negative results. People who are optimistic about their future and display a positive attitude toward others are usually sur-

"Sally, I'd like to talk to you about your attitude."
Reprinted from *The Saturday Evening Post* © 1988 BFL&MS, Inc. INDPLS.

rounded by friends who possess similar attitudes. Those who are pessimistic and have a negative attitude toward other people usually have few friends, and those few are apt to be negative thinkers as well.

People shape their attitudes about you by what they see and hear. They interpret your attitudes through your behavior. How you feel about something is usually no secret to friends and acquaintances. Office workers who turn out letters filled with typographical errors will no doubt be viewed as people who don't care about their work. Salespeople who always meet or exceed their established quotas will very likely be seen as ambitious and conscientious. They attract people with the same commitment and attitude toward their work.

Attitudes represent a powerful force in any organization. An attitude of trust, for example, can pave the way for improved communication and greater cooperation between an employee and a supervisor. A sincere effort by management to improve working conditions, when filtered through attitudes of suspicion and cynicism, may have a negative impact on employee-management relations. These same actions by management, filtered through attitudes of trust and hope, may result in improved worker morale. As another example, a caring attitude displayed by an employee can increase customer loyalty and set the stage for repeat business.

HOW ATTITUDES ARE FORMED

Throughout life you are constantly making decisions and judgments that help formulate your attitudes. These attitude decisions are often based on behaviors your childhood authority figures told you were right or wrong, childhood and adult behaviors for which you were rewarded or punished, role models you selected, and the various environmental and corporate cultures you chose to embrace.

Socialization

The process through which people are integrated into a society by exposure to the actions and opinions of others is called **socialization**.[3] As a child you interact with your parents, family, teachers, and friends. Children often feel that statements made by these authority figures are the "proper" things to believe. For example, if a parent declares, "People who live in big, expensive houses are either born rich or are crooked," the child is likely to hold this attitude for many years.

Rewards and Punishment

Attitude formation is often related to rewards and punishment. People in authority will generally encourage certain attitudes and punish others. Naturally, individuals will tend to develop attitudes that minimize punishments and maximize rewards. A child who is praised for sharing toys with playmates is likely to repeat the behavior. As an adult, your attitudes will continue to be shaped by rewards and punishment at work.

The Liebert Corporation, a Columbus, Ohio-based manufacturer, uses rewards to improve employees' attitudes toward attendance. The company gives hourly employees three shares of company stock for each year of perfect attendance and two free movie tickets for each unblemished quarter.[4] Flexcon Company, a specialty paper firm located in Spencer, Massachusetts, is using rewards to help employees quit smoking. The third Thursday of every month, the company puts $30 gift certificates into the pay envelopes of workers who have quit smoking or who are nonsmokers and have not

---

TOTAL PERSON INSIGHT

❝ Your attitudes can be the lock on, or the key to, your door of success. ❞

Dr. Denis Waitley

started smoking. The company also gives $15 certificates to employees who reduce their smoking. Many employees have quit smoking or cut down as a result of the program.[5]

Role Model Identification

Most young people would like to have more power, status, and popularity. These goals are often achieved through identification with a role model. A **role model** is that person you most admire and would most like to emulate. Young children are most likely to identify their parents as their role models. During later stages of development, television stars and sports heroes may replace parents as role models. As you might expect, such people can exert considerable influence—for better or for worse—on developing attitudes.

The media have a tremendous influence on people's selection of role models. By the time they graduate from high school, most young adults will have spent 50 percent more time in front of a television than in a classroom or having quality experiences with parents, family, or friends.[6] Many television programs are dominated by crime, violence, and stereotyped or deviant characters and life situations. At the other extreme, other programs present beautiful superheroes with superhuman abilities. With this constant reinforcement from fictional negative and positive role models, it is sometimes difficult for young people to sort out which behaviors and attitudes are acceptable in the real world.

Role models at work can have a major influence on employee attitude development. The new salesperson in the menswear department naturally wants help in adjusting to the job. So does the new dental hygienist and the recently hired auto mechanic. These people will pay special attention to the behavior of coworkers and managers. Therefore, if a worker leaves the job early and no negative consequences follow, new employees may develop the attitude that staying until quitting time is not as important as they had thought. If a senior employee is rude to customers and suffers no negative consequences, the new employee may imitate this attitude and behavior.

In most organizations, supervisory and management personnel have the greatest impact on employee attitudes. The supervisors' attitudes toward safety, cost control, accuracy, dress and grooming, customer relations, and the like become the model for subordinates. Employees will pay more attention to what their supervisors do than to what they say.

If supervisors want to shape employee attitudes, they must demonstrate the kind of behavior they want others to develop. Albert Schweitzer, the French philosopher and Nobel Peace Prize winner, was right on target when he said: "Example is not the main thing in influencing others, it is the only thing."

Organizations are realizing the importance of the interconnectedness between employees' work and other apects of their lives.
© Charles Gatewood/The Image Works

Barabara A. Meyer points out that one may not always be conscious of the fact that he or she is serving as a role model to another person:

> Most of us do not recognize ourselves as role models, yet we project behavior which people use as a pattern for their own conduct. Everyone who serves as a role model also teaches, since the followers first learn behavior or ideas and then manifest them in their own lives.[7]

Cultural Influences

Culture is everything in our surroundings that is made by human beings. It consists of tangible items (such as foods, furniture, buildings, clothing, and tools) and intangible concepts (such as education, welfare, and laws). Culture also includes the values and a broad range of behaviors that are acceptable within a specific society.[8]

People strive to define themselves in every culture. And the definition varies from culture to culture. If you ask an adult living in Japan, "Who are you?" that person is likely to respond, "I'm an employee of Sony Corporation." In Japanese culture, people are likely to be defined by the organization for which they work. In the United States, one's job and employer are somewhat less likely to be the major source of identity. For instance, a young woman who spends hours each week trying to improve the environment may define herself as an environmentalist. The fact that she works as a department supervisor at a local supermarket may be incidental to how she defines herself.

Many organizations today are striving to define their own corporate culture. Generally speaking, **corporate culture** represents the set of attitudes that form the basis on which corporate decisions are made. If employees do not adopt the attitudes represented by their organization's corporate culture, they may find they feel like misfits.

TABLE 2.1   A Statement of Corporate Culture

Our Quest for Excellence

We believe that in order to make this world a better place in which to live, we must be totally dedicated to the endless quest for excellence in the important tasks which we endeavor to accomplish.

Our Products

We believe in marketing and selling healthful and naturally oriented products that nurture people's bodies and uplift their souls. Our products must be superior in quality, of good value, beautifully artistic, and philosophically inspiring.

Our Consumers and Customers

We believe that our past, current, and future successes come from a total dedication to excellent service to those who buy our products. Satisfying our customer and consumer needs in a superior way is the only reason we are in business, and we shall proceed with an obsession to give wholeheartedly to those who buy our products. Our customers and consumers are king, and we are here to serve them.

Our Growth

We believe in aggressive, steady, predictable and well planned growth in sales and earnings. We are intent on building a large company that will flourish into the next century and thereafter.

Dignity of the Individual

We believe in the dignity of the individual, and we are totally committed to the fair, honest, kind, and professional treatment of all individuals and organizations with whom we work.

Our Employees

We believe that our employees develop a commitment to excellence when they are directly involved in the management of their areas of responsibility. This

Table 2.1 *(continued)*

team effort maximizes quality results, minimizes costs, and allows our employees the opportunity to have authorship and personal satisfaction in their accomplishments, as well as sharing in the financial rewards of their individual and team efforts.

We believe in hiring above average people who have a "hands on" approach to work and quest for excellent results. In exchange, we are committed to the development of our good people by identifying, cultivating, training, rewarding, retaining, and promoting those individuals who are committed to moving our organization forward.

Our Environment

We believe in fostering a working environment which promotes creativity and encourages possibility thinking throughout the organization. We plan our work to be satisfying, productive, and challenging. As such, we support an atmosphere which encourages intelligent risk taking without the fear of failure.

Our Dream

Our role at Celestial Seasonings is to play an active part in making this world a better place by unselfishly serving the public. We believe we can have a significant impact on making people's lives happier and healthier through their use of our products. By dedicating our total resources to this dream, everyone profits: our customers, consumers, employees, and shareholders. Our actions are building blocks in making this world a better place now and for future generations.

Source: Reprinted with the permission of Celestial Seasonings, Inc.

One important element in the culture of many contemporary organizations is *quality*. For many years, Zenith Radio Corp. has had as its motto "The Quality Goes in Before the Name Goes On." Because customers today expect perfection in the products and services they buy, organizations realize that the *attitude of wanting to produce a quality product* must be present in every employee.

Jerry Junkins, chairman, CEO, and president of Texas Instruments, Inc., says, "A continuous process, total quality means that the customer is always number one, a task can always be improved, and all employees must be involved."[9] Robert H. Paquette, president of Vitramon, Inc., agrees. "The key to the highest standards of workmanship and reliability lies in a team attitude toward achieving a quality level."[10]

Zitel Corporation takes their commitment to quality one step further and directly relates it to the attitude the organization maintains toward its employees. Jack King, CEO and president, declares, "Quality is caring. Caring that your customer benefits from using your products and being associated with your company. Caring that your products and services are better than expected or need to be. Caring enough to share in the success and problems of our coworkers as though they were our own."[11]

As adults the organizations we choose to work with will have a strong influence on the formation and maintenance of our personal attitudes.

THINKING/LEARNING STARTERS

1. Identify at least one thing you feel strongly about. Do you know how you acquired this attitude? Is it shared by any particular group of people? Do you spend time with these people?
2. Think of an attitude with which you strongly disagree. What cultural conditioning may have caused it? You obviously feel negatively toward it, but can you think of any positive value it may have?

That abortion is OK →

None whats soever

HOW TO CHANGE ATTITUDES

If you begin to notice that successful people will not associate with you, that you've been overlooked for a promotion you thought you should have had, or that you go home from work depressed and a little angry at the world, you can almost always be sure you need an attitude adjustment.

Unfortunately, people do not easily adopt new attitudes or discard old ones. It is difficult to break the attachment to emotionally laden beliefs. Yet attitudes can be changed. There may be times when you absolutely hate a job, but you can still develop a positive attitude toward it as a steppingstone to another job you actually do want. There will be times as well when you will need to help colleagues change their attitudes so that you can work with them more effectively. Knowing how to *intentionally* change attitudes in yourself and others can be essential to effective human relations—and your success—in an organization.

Changing Your Own Attitude

You are constantly placed in new situations with people from different backgrounds and cultures. Each time you go to a new school, take a new job, get a promotion, or move to a different neighborhood, you may need to alter your attitudes in order to cope effectively with the change.

In all these situations, it may help to realize that outside elements, such as the economy, your supervisor, the traffic, and the weather, are out of your control. At the same time, one thing you *can* control is your attitude toward these things and people. If you allow yourself to dwell on negative thoughts or attitudes, you can expect to exhibit negative, self-destructive behaviors. When you screen your thoughts to accentuate the positive, you will find your world a much more pleasant place to be. When you are happy and feel in control of your life, other people enjoy working with you.

Being able to control your attitudes is a powerful human relations skill that usually involves certain basic changes.

1. *Alter your thinking.* Become aware of your negative attitudes toward people and situations. Decide if these attitudes are valid or if you have been socialized into holding them. If they are a result of socialization, they may deserve to be reexamined.

   A study completed by Charlotte Decker Sutton and Kris Moore and published in the *Harvard Business Review* describes a "revisit" of executive men and women twenty years after the study was initially conducted. Slightly more than half the women in the original study reported that they would be comfortable working for another woman. Twenty years later, *the survey results were the same.* Twenty years ago, less than 10 percent of the men in the survey reported that they would be comfortable working for a woman. In the "revisit," almost 50 percent reported that they would be comfortable in this situation.[12]

   Many conclusions can be, and have been, drawn from this study. It does illustrate that some people hang on to their attitudes and some are able to let them go when they are no longer appropriate.

2. *Think for yourself.* Determine your own attitudes and reasons for having them. Peer pressure and family ties are strong influences, but you can

be your own judge when and if you choose to be. Buckminster Fuller, the respected architect and inventor, stated that learning to think for himself was the turning point in his life. He discovered at age thirty-two that he needed to become more of an independent thinker and stop relying on others to influence every aspect of his life. Once he made the decision to think for himself, he became highly motivated to discover what he described as the "operating principles" of the world.[13]

3. *Keep an open mind.* We often make decisions and then refuse to consider any other point of view that might lead us to question our beliefs. Many times our attitudes persist even in the presence of overwhelming evidence to the contrary—especially when emotions are involved. A classic example reached headlines around the world when Senator Gary Hart, 1988 presidential hopeful, gathered tremendous support for the Democratic nomination based on a platform of truth, justice, and honor. Then the *Miami Herald* published a story about and pictures of Senator Hart's liaison with a young woman. He withdrew his bid for the nomination as he realized that people across the country were reacting negatively to this news. Yet within a month, a strong faction of supporters gathered enough momentum for Hart to seriously consider reentering the race. These supporters still believed Gary Hart could run on his original platform, despite ample evidence to the contrary.

For generations, James Allen, the famous Harvard psychologist, has been known for this discovery: By changing the inner attitudes of your mind, you can change the outer aspects of your life.[14] Each generation seems to have to rediscover this truth for itself.

Helping Others Change Their Attitudes

It is true that you are really only in control of your own attitudes. You can bend and flex and alter these as often as you find it beneficial, but there are times when you need to stand firm and maintain your position regarding a situation. At that point you may want to help other people change their attitudes. Unfortunately, you cannot hand your colleagues "a ready-made box of attitudes." But often you can help produce an atmosphere in which they will want to change their thinking.

Many people attempt to beg, plead, intimidate, or even threaten others into adopting new attitudes. There are, however, two more powerful techniques that will *lead* other people to adopt the attitudes you wish them to. These two techniques involve (1) affecting the consequences people receive after altering their behavior toward the attitude you want them to embrace; and (2) changing the conditions that surround the situation.

Consequences When people participate in an activity that is followed by positive **consequences**, they have the tendancy to repeat the activity. By the same token, people are likely to avoid things that are followed by negative consequences.

Assume you are the team leader for your division of an organization. Your supervisor has told you that there must be a 10 percent cut in operating expenses. Your attitude is that suggestions from your staff are important in formulating a plan to carry this out. You want to produce an atmosphere in which everyone is willing to share his or her thoughts and ideas. Not only will employees feel their contributions are valued, but they will also be committed to the courses of action decided upon.

You call a meeting to discuss the issue of operating expenses with your fellow employees. Soon a person seated across the table speaks up and says, "I think we can all reduce the length of our long-distance telephone calls. I know I talk too long to established customers." You write this down and perhaps smile or in some other way indicate that you appreciate the input. Soon everyone is eager to share ideas.

Suppose you had reacted differently to the first person's suggestion. What if you had frowned and said, "Look, we've talked about that problem before. I'm looking for fresh ideas!" Probably members of the group would have been reluctant to speak up. If the risk of encountering negative consequences is too great, people will avoid sharing their ideas.

A simple rule applies in shaping attitudes: Whenever an experience is followed by positive consequences, it is more likely to be repeated in the future. If you want people to arrive for work on time, reward this behavior in some way. If operating expenses are too high, look for ways workers are willing to cut costs, and then reward those who manage to reduce expenses. As a rule, people will willingly do things that bring about positive consequences for themselves.

It is important to look at consequences through the eyes of the person you are trying to influence, rather than just your own. Robert Mager, a nationally known authority in the field of training and development, says the following:

> It doesn't matter what I might seek out or avoid: it is what is positive or aversive to the person whose behavior I am trying to influence that counts. And this, incidentally, is one reason we don't succeed more often than we do in the area of human interaction. We try to influence others by providing consequences that are positive to us but not to them.[15]

Conditions If you want to help another person develop a favorable attitude toward a situation, create and accentuate the positive **conditions** surrounding it. Imagine you are an employee of a fast-food restaurant. You like your job and want to keep it and perhaps move into a management position. One of your fellow employees, Monique, came to work five weeks ago and has had problems adjusting to her job ever since. From the first day, she found the job frustrating. The manager simply didn't seem to care whether she succeeded or failed. He spent about five minutes with her going over the proper way to process a customer's order and then assigned her to a counter station. Soon she found there were many customers' questions she couldn't answer and she had trouble operating the computerized cash register. At the end of her shift, the manager said, "If you don't get with it, I'm going to replace you. We only give instructions once around here."

Monique has finally learned how to handle orders quickly, but she finds other aspects of the job to be unpleasant. She notices there is little cooperation among her fellow employees. The people who work on her shift do not work as a team. Also, she feels the people she works with, including supervisors, do not take pride in their work. She wants to quit.

As a fellow employee, you have two choices. You can choose to adopt Monique's negative attitudes about the poor training procedures, the lack of teamwork, and employee cooperation. Chances are she will quit and you will, too. Or, you can choose to do something about the situation and help Monique develop a positive attitude.

It is interesting to note that all the conditions that have made work unpleasant for Monique could have been changed. The manager could have displayed a caring attitude toward her. He could have given her adequate training before she actually began working with customers, and could have offered her constructive suggestions concerning her performance.

But perhaps you as a fellow employee could have a powerful impact on Monique's attitude. To the extent you can help eliminate the conditions that she finds undesirable, you could help her change her attitude. In this case, you could

1. encourage fellow workers to help Monique feel at home.

2. avoid tactless comments that reduce her self-esteem.

3. make positive comments regarding the things she does right.

4. show that you take pride in your work.

5. be a good listener when Monique displays frustration.

THINKING/LEARNING STARTERS

1. Are you holding a grudge against someone? Describe the situation. What are the benefits of holding on to this attitude? What are the benefits of letting go of the attitude and moving on to a more productive atmosphere?

2. Think of a situation at work or home that is upsetting to you. How can you alter the situation to help change the other person's opinions? If it is absolutely impossible to change the situation, what will result if you change your attitude? Which direction is the best solution to the problem?

ORGANIZATIONS ARE MAKING ADJUSTMENTS

Many companies are realizing the effect an employee's attitude has on job performance and productivity. The factors of attitude and output cannot be separated. For generations, employers and labor unions focused on providing the salaries and fringe benefits necessary to keep their work force producing at top efficiency. Contemporary workers, however, rank money well down on their list of criteria for a satisfying job. When asked what they most want from their job, they typically respond: work with people who treat them with respect, interesting work, recognition for good work, the chance to develop skills, and so forth. Job security, high pay, and good benefits are not at the top of the list of criteria. As author and management consultant Peter Drucker says: "To make a living is not enough. Work also has to make a life."[16] Organizations are having to adjust to this change in worker attitudes.

People who display a positive attitude can pave the way for greater cooperation, trust, and communication at work.
Jean-Claude Lejeune/Stock, Boston

Quality of Work Life

Research indicates that satisfying work conditions can foster positive attitudes. Therefore, many organizations are creating work environments that consistently provide recognition, financial incentives, and opportunities for growth in all aspects of workers' personal and professional lives. This emphasis on the **quality of work life (QWL)** has been receiving increasing attention. As early as 1975, the Buick division of General Motors Corp. established a joint committee of labor, management, and community leaders to oversee Buick's QWL process. It proved to be a powerful, positive example for other organizations and communities throughout the nation.

The interconnectedness between the organization and other aspects of a worker's life—education, family health, the community—means that a company cannot sit back and complain about the lousy school system, how the women's movement is making it harder to transfer people, and the high cost of employee health bills, without becoming involved in the resolution of those problems. Companies understand the correlation between people and profit. It is important that they also realize that their interests and the interests of the people and community are increasingly the same.

Every year *Fortune* magazine publishes a list of the most powerful corporations in America, called "The Fortune 500." There is now a movement to research and publish "The Fortunate 500" list, which would comprise companies deemed to have the highest QWL. This movement reflects the increasing concern with the quality of work life in today's workplace.

The necessary adjustments of companies to the evolving needs of workers have been slow but steady. During the industrial period, companies needed to find or build massive buildings near transportation, natural resources, water, and clients. In the current information and electronics era, companies do not have these same restrictions. Progressive management teams are now looking to locate their organizations where their employees will be most happy and therefore most productive. They give attention to quality of life criteria such as good climate, good schools, cultural opportunities, recreational facilities, and opportunities for two-career couples.[17]

Self-Management

One of the most fundamental adjustments being made in organizations today is the movement away from an authoritarian hierarchy—where everyone has both a superior and an inferior—toward a system of **self-management**. The new management structure has taken on a variety of labels, such as lateral structure, lattice, and network. Basically, the structure involves the formation of *small teams in which people manage themselves*. A team is given full responsibility to produce the best-quality product or service possible, with maximum efficiency and without day-to-day supervision.

Within companies today, there is not the time, the personnel, or the resources to monitor people. As a result, it is far more practical for people to manage themselves. Thus the "self-management movement" was created.

Employers are beginning to realize that people cannot be supervised into getting the job done right. They have to bring the spirit of getting it right with them to the job, and the work environment must reinforce this attitude by providing workers the freedom to accomplish work in a way that exhibits their competence and effectiveness. People want the satisfaction of knowing that their work is respected. People usually perform better when they manage themselves.[18] Self-management structures allow this to happen.

Self-management may involve something as simple as giving a receptionist responsibility for ordering supplies, or it may mean redesigning an assembly line to provide production workers with more challenging and interesting work with total responsibility for quality control. One company that has achieved considerable success in the area of self-management is IBM. It has been experimenting with ways of expanding jobs so that workers exercise greater judgment, have more control over the flow of work, and perform a variety of tasks. These changes have resulted in increased worker morale and efficiency.

Volvo, the Swedish car manufacturer, initiated a major self-management program in the early 1970s. When a new assembly plant was built at Kalmar, Sweden, Volvo rejected the traditional conveyor assembly line in favor of special carriers that move automobiles in various states of completion among small assembly departments. The movement of carriers is worker controlled. Within each department, a team of fifteen to twenty-five workers is free to structure its tasks in any way its members see fit, provided their assigned output is achieved.[19] Has this departure from the auto industry's traditional practices influenced workers' behavior at the Kalmar plant? Yes, says Volvo's management, who point to reduced absenteeism, reduced turnover, and better-quality automobiles.

Throughout corporate America, there is increasing evidence that people are expected to manage themselves. There are numerous examples available, but perhaps the experiment at the Delco-Remy plant in Fitzgerald, Georgia, will clarify the self-management team approach. The Fitzgerald plant is entirely team based (see Figure 2.1). Operating and support teams are interlocked all the way to the top of the organization chart. Both productivity and quality improved dramatically when the former "supervisors" became coaches, teachers, and mentors helping employees strive for the same team goal. Each individual member of the team had a job that fit into the total plan, and each member had total responsibility for getting that job done correctly. The attitudes engendered by this level of trust, interdependency, and responsibility have been enormously beneficial to the company.

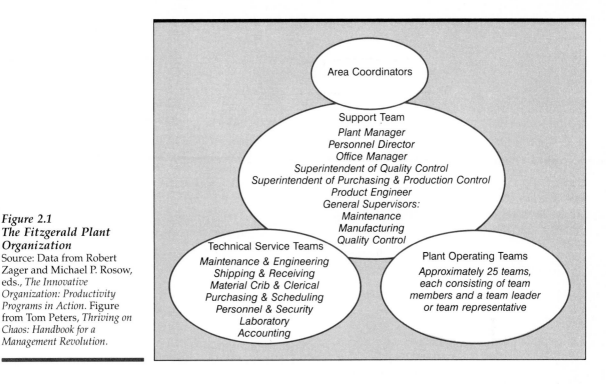

Figure 2.1
The Fitzgerald Plant
Organization
Source: Data from Robert
Zager and Michael P. Rosow,
eds., *The Innovative
Organization: Productivity
Programs in Action*. Figure
from Tom Peters, *Thriving on
Chaos: Handbook for a
Management Revolution*.

Some attempts at self-management, however, have not been successful. Programs sometimes fail because management does not prepare workers for a change in their jobs. The way in which a new program is introduced is of critical importance. If workers perceive the change as a gimmick developed by management, the program will likely not be a success. In addition, the introduction of a self-management program may have a negative impact on the morale of workers who have learned to cope with a lack of challenge and do not possess a strong desire to become involved in nonroutine work. Some employees value the security of a routine job and minimal responsibility more than the opportunity for variety in their work and greater responsibility. Chapters 4 and 5 deal with personal motivators and values.

SUMMARY

An attitude is defined as any strong belief toward people and situations. It is a state of mind supported by feelings. People possess hundreds of attitudes about work, family life, friends, coworkers, and the like.

Attitudes represent a powerful force in every organization. If the persons employed by a service firm display a caring attitude toward customers, the business will likely enjoy a high degree of customer loyalty and repeat business. If the employees of a manufacturing firm display a serious attitude toward safety rules and regulations, fewer accidents are likely to occur.

People acquire attitudes through early childhood socialization, rewards and punishment, role model identification, and cultural influences. Although many factors can influence the formation of an attitude, people do not easily adopt new ones or discard old ones. If you choose to, you can change your attitude by altering your thinking, thinking for yourself without undue pressure from your peers, family, and others, and keeping an open mind. You can help others change their attitudes by altering the consequences and conditions that surround the situation. Positive consequences and conditions produce positive attitudes.

Organizations are taking steps to improve the quality of work life of their employees in order to help them be more productive. Some organizations are adjusting their structures from authoritarian hierarchies to self-management teams in order to enhance individual attitudes toward greater job satisfaction.

KEY TERMS

attitude
socialization
role model
culture
corporate culture

consequences
conditions
quality of work life (QWL)
self-management

REVIEW QUESTIONS

1. Provide a concise definition of the term *attitude*.

2. It has been said that "attitudes represent a powerful force in any organization." What examples can you give to support this statement?

3. Describe how rewards and punishment can shape the attitudes of employees in an organization. Give at least one example.

4. How can selecting a positive role model within an organization help an individual reach his or her goals?

5. Describe the quality of work life elements that most often influence a person's feeling of satisfaction with his or her job.

6. Explain how consequences can influence the shaping of attitudes in an organization.

7. Robert Mager says that the conditions that surround a subject can play an important role in shaping attitudes. Provide at least one example to support Mager's statement.

8. How will QWL factors influence retention of good employees in an age when one-third of the population changes jobs every year?

9. Describe an organization that has implemented self-management teams. How do they differ from traditional supervisor/employee management structures?

10. Explain in your own words the meaning of Dr. Waitley's Total Person Insight on page 32.

■■■ CASE 2.1

Worker Involvement: Is It Worth It?

Iggesunds Bruk, a Swedish supplier of pulp, paper, lumber, chemicals, and steel, was selected to participate in a national research project attempting to assess the value of worker participation in the development of a new company plant. The organization of the project included the participation of worker representatives with managers on various planning committees. The representatives, who were paid for the time spent on committee work, were involved in the evaluation of different machines, the need for tools, and the layout of the work area.

When the project began, Iggesund had no prior experience with worker participation in management planning, nor had it experimented with job enrichment. Today, both management and workers are proud of the results and agree that the plant is different from what it would have been without the workers' involvement. The chief difference is the attention to personnel facilities and environmental controls, including enclosures to reduce machinery noise and a ventilation system to remove dirt and grease. Iggesund found, however, that worker participation increased the planning expenses by 46 percent and increased the total project costs by 7 percent. The additional meeting time added three months to the project.

Source: Extract from Knut Haganäes and Lee Hales, "Scandinavian Models of Employee Participation," *S.A.M. Advanced Management Journal,* Winter 1983, pp. 24–26. Reprinted by permission, Society for Advancement of Management, Cincinnatti, OH 45206.

Questions

1. As an executive, you want your firm to consider employee participation in the development of a new plant. Your colleagues have handed you the statistics on the increased expenses and project delays experienced by Iggesund. How would you counter these statistics to reaffirm your position?

2. What are the long-range benefits that might result from the changes implemented by the employee representatives?

3. What influence might the national attention that the Iggesund project received have had on the personnel involved in the study?

■■■■■■■■■■■■■■■■■■ ■ CASE 2.2

Johnson Wax's Worldwide Family Ties

Johnson Wax is identified by authors Levering, Moskowitz, and Katz as one of the 100 best companies to work for. It seems to be a dream company that has never had a layoff; gives employees an opportunity to express their views; and provides employees with a flexible health plan, recreational facilities, extensive insurance, and retirement and profit-sharing plans. The attitudes and morale of the employees reflect a strong commitment to the success of the organization. They feel they are part of a family.

While attending a meeting at the company's British plant near London, Samuel Johnson, chairman of the company, found that some of the employees were concerned about their future. Even though the British employees participate in a generous profit-sharing plan and work in comfortable, attractive facilities, they wondered how they fit into the big American company. Since Johnson Wax does 60 percent of its business outside the United States, Mr. Johnson recognized that something needed to be done to improve the morale of these people. He wanted to prove to them they were part of the "family."

He chartered a Boeing 747 jet and flew the entire British work force—480 people—to the United States. They were first taken to Racine, Wisconsin, site of corporate headquarters, where they toured the company's facilities, shopped, were feted at a company banquet, and were put up in hotels. One night during their stay, they were invited to dine in American employees' homes. Before flying back to Britain, they spent two days in New York City sightseeing and were treated to a complimentary dinner at the World Trade Center.

Sources: Robert Levering, Milton Moskowitz, and Michael Katz, *The 100 Best Companies to Work for in America* (New York: New American Library, 1985), pp. 173–177.

Questions

1. How do you think the attitudes of the British employees changed after visiting America? How do you think the experience affected the attitudes of the American employees?
2. Do you think it likely that the people of Racine, Wisconsin, changed their attitudes toward having Johnson Wax in town? Explain.

3. If Johnson Wax's budget had been low, in what specific ways could the company have accomplished an attitude adjustment in its British employees in a less expensive manner?

SUGGESTED READINGS

Buscaglia, Leo. *Living, Loving, and Learning.* New York: Holt, Rinehart, and Winston, 1982.

Clinard, Helen Hall. *Winning Ways To Succeed With People.* Houston: Gulf Publishing Company, 1985.

Deal, Terrence, and Allan Kennedy. *Corporate Cultures.* Reading, Mass.: Addison-Wesley, 1982..

Dyer, Wayne. *Gifts from Eykis.* New York: Simon & Schuster, 1983.

Mager, Robert F. *Developing Attitudes Toward Learning.* Belmont, Cal.: Fearon-Pitman, 1968.

Waitley, Dr. Denis. *The Winner's Edge: How to Develop the Critical Attitude for Success.* New York: Times Books, 1980.

Weising, Henrie, and Norman M. Lobsenz. *Nobody's Perfect—How to Give Criticism and Get Results.* Los Angeles: Stanford Press, 1981.

NOTES

1. Stew Leonard, "Love Your Customer," *Newsweek*, June 27, 1988, two unnumbered pages; Katharine Davis Fishman, "The Disney World of Supermarkets," *New York Magazine*, March 11, 1985; B. L. Ochman Public Relations, New York, "Stew Leonard's Fact Sheet."
2. Jerome Kagan, *Psychology: An Introduction* (New York: Harcourt Brace Jovanovich, 1984), p. 558.
3. Ibid., p. 548.
4. "Attendance Required," *INC.*, June 1985, p. 115.
5. "Cash for Clean Lungs," *INC.*, October 1984, p. 149.
6. Denis Waitley, *The Positive Parent* (Cedar Falls, Iowa: Advanced Learning, Inc., 1987), p. 16.
7. Barabara A. Meyer, "Role Modeling: Rewards and Responsibilities," *Delta Kappa Gamma Bulletin*, Vol. XLVIII–2, Winter 1982, p. 48.
8. William M. Pride and O. C. Ferrell, *Marketing*, 6th ed. (Boston: Houghton Mifflin Company, 1989), p. 139.
9. Peter Weiss, "Paying for Quality: The Tab Can Be High," *Purchasing Management*, September 12, 1988, p. 37.
10. Ibid., p. 21.
11. Ibid., p. 27.
12. Judith Briles, *Woman to Woman: From Sabotage to Support* (Far Hills, N.J.: New Horizon Press, 1987), pp. 175–176.
13. Phil Catalfo, "Buckminster Fuller—the 50-Year Experiment," *New Dimensions Foundation*, San Francisco, Cal., 1988 (audio tape).
14. James Allen, *As a Man Thinketh* (New York: Keenan Press, 1910).

15. Robert F. Mager, *Developing Attitudes Toward Learning* (Belmont, Cal.: Fearon-Pitman, 1968), p. 47.

16. Nancy W. Collins, Susan K. Gilbert, and Susan Nycum, *Women Leading: Making Tough Choices On the Fast Track* (Lexington, Mass.: The Stephen Greene Press, 1988), p. 1.

17. Naisbitt and Aburdene, *Re-Inventing the Corporation*, p. 88.

18. Ibid., p. 98.

19. Knut Haganäes and Lee Hales, "Scandinavian Models of Employee Participation," *S.A.M. Advanced Management Journal*, Winter 1983, pp. 23–24.

Chapter 3

Building High Self-Esteem

CHAPTER PREVIEW

After studying this chapter, you will be able to

1. Define *self-esteem* and discuss how it is developed.

2. Explain why high self-esteem is essential for effective human relations and success at work.

3. Understand the power of expectations.

4. Understand the impact of workers' self-esteem in an organizational setting.

5. Explain how, when, and why mentors are useful.

6. Identify ways to help build self-esteem.

*T*en years ago, I was at the bottom of the career ladder. I was a single mother raising two small children, going back to school at night while working full time as a receptionist. I really stretched myself — building my self-esteem, and going for goals I hadn't thought possible. My income went from $12,000 a year to more then $100,000 today. I'm living proof of the impact self-esteem has on income." The speaker is Connie Palladin, Ph.D., a career-development consultant in Palo Alto, California, and author of *The Believe in Yourself and Make It Happen Guide*. "I've seen the same process work with some of my clients," she continues. "As their self-esteem increased, they doubled or tripled their income in a few years. The more you look at it, the more you see that the link between self-esteem and success is incredibly strong." [1]

The right mental conditioning is critical for success. If you think negatively, you may set yourself up for failure. To be a winner, you must *expect* to win. People who believe they are worth $100,000 a year and deserve a loving family and a vacation home on the ocean may very well attain these goals, because they push their limits to achieve them. Someone who limits his or her expectations to a one-room apartment and an entry-level job probably won't try for more. The winner's edge, high self-esteem, is the basis for achievement in any organization.

SELF-ESTEEM DEFINED

"Love thy neighbor" is one of the world's best-known human relations principles. Yet most people forget that the phrase ends "as thyself." Those last two words are the foundation for accomplishing the first three. When you maintain your self-esteem, you feel confident and free to express yourself without being overly concerned with others' reactions. You work to fulfill your needs for achievement, strength, recognition, independence, and appreciation — to reach your greatest potential. If you maintain low self-esteem, you are plagued by doubts and anxieties that will limit your ability to achieve success.

Some social scientists believe that self-esteem is closely connected to students' performance in school. Students with low self-esteem tend to do less well than students with high self-esteem. [2] And some believe a person's low self-esteem can cause more serious problems throughout life. The California State Assembly established a twenty-five-member Task Force on Self-Esteem and Personal and Social Responsibility after hearing testimony that people with low self-esteem are more likely to exhibit violent behavior, discriminate against others, and abuse drugs. [3]

Some researchers are finding that generalizations about self-esteem and success can't be made as easily for females as they can for males, [4] while others are beginning to challenge the correlation between poor self-esteem and delinquency.[5] However, it is clear that low self-esteem can create barriers between friends, family, and business associates, leading to an inevitable breakdown in effective human relations. This is why Alfred Adler, a noted psychologist, has stated, "Everything begins with self-esteem, your concept of yourself."[6]

Self-esteem is the sum of self-confidence and self-respect. If you have high self-esteem, you feel competent and worthy. If you have low self-esteem, you feel incompetent and unworthy. If you have average self-esteem, you fluctuate between these feelings of competence and worthiness. Your measure of self-esteem is always a matter of degree. Your self-esteem reflects what you think and feel about yourself, not what someone else thinks or feels about you, even though you are always reevaluating yourself in light of others' comments about your behavior.

Your self-esteem includes your feelings about your adequacy in the roles you play in life, as a friend, brother or sister, daughter or son, employee or employer, student, researcher, leader, and so on. It includes the personality traits you believe you have, such as honesty, creativity, assertiveness, flexibility, and many more. Often your self-esteem derives from your physical characteristics and your skills and abilities. Are you tall, slender, short, or heavy? Do you like what you see in the mirror? Are you good at writing, fixing appliances, researching topics, playing the piano, or some other skill?

Although high self-esteem is the basis for a healthy personality, it does not mean becoming egotistical, that is, thinking and acting with only your own interests in mind. Genuine self-esteem is not expressed by self-glorification at the expense of others, or by the attempt to diminish others so as to elevate yourself. Arrogance, boastfulness, and the overestimation of your abilities reflect inadequate self-esteem rather than, as it might appear, too much self-esteem. Someone with an egotistical orientation to the world sees everything and everyone in terms of their usefulness to the person's own aims and goals. This attitude undermines good human relations; people become objects to be manipulated or used.

In an insurance office with five agents, a manager, and two secretaries, workers help one another achieve personal and company goals. Everyone gets along well with everyone else — except the number one salesperson. He has such a self-centered view of his work and himself that he expects other people in the office to drop everything and help him first. He leaves a stack of letters on the secretary's desk and tells her, "I need these typed by five." He ignores the fact that she is already hard at work on correspondence for three other agents. He tells the manager how an important client should be handled even though the manager has known the client for over ten years. He may or may not speak to the other agents — they are not as successful, and he has important calls to make, so why waste time? This person's self-esteem has passed beyond healthy self-confidence and has become a negative, egotistical personality trait. In terms of human relations, he has become a liability to the company, even though he is successful as a salesperson.

An individual with high self-esteem realizes the value of other people and the role they play in his or her success. Recognizing the difference between a person with high self-esteem and a person with an egotistical personality is important in developing and maintaining good human relations.

How Your Self-Esteem Develops

A Sunday school teacher once asked her class of small children, "Who made you?" Instead of giving the expected reply, an insightful child responded, "I'm not finished yet!" You are not born knowing who and what you are. You acquire your image of yourself over time by realizing your natural abi-

Positive feedback from an authority figure can have a powerful effect on a child's self-esteem.
© Alan Carey/The Image Works

lities and by constantly receiving messages about yourself from the people closest to you and from your environment.

Childhood   Your self-esteem is a reflection of your image of who you are. This image begins to form the minute you have the first conscious realization that you are a living, functioning being. Your family is the earliest source of information about yourself. An ancient Chinese proverb tells us, "A child's life is like a piece of paper on which every passer-by leaves a mark." Parents do not *teach* their children self-esteem. But they do leave negative or positive strokes on their slates:

- Bad boy! Bad girl!
- You're so lazy!
- You'll never learn.
- What's wrong with you?
- Why can't you be more like...
- It's all your fault.

- You're great!
- You can do anything!
- You're a fast learner.
- Next time you'll do better.
- I like you just the way you are.
- I know you did your best.

In most cases, you probably did not stop and analyze these messages; you simply accepted them as true and recorded them in your memory. As a result, your subconscious mind gradually developed a picture of yourself, whether accurate or distorted, that you came to believe as real.

> Everyone was once a child. Our experience today is filtered through the events and feelings of childhood, recorded in detail. We cannot have a feeling today that is "disconnected" from similar feelings recorded in the past, the most intense of which occurred to us in the first five years of life. This does not mean that today's feelings are not real, or that we are to discount them by claiming "they're just an old recording." We are today who we once were.[7]

The type of family discipline you grew up with probably had considerable effect on your self-esteem. Interestingly enough, some psychologists have found that children brought up in a permissive environment tend to develop *lower* self-esteem than those raised in a firmer and more demanding home. Parental discipline is one way of telling children that parents care about them and what they do. When someone cares about you, you tend to think more positively about yourself.

The strength of early parental positive feedback can have far-reaching effects in the course of a person's life. Irene Carpenter, the first woman elected a senior vice president in the ninety-year history of Citizens and Southern National Bank in Atlanta, recalls of her childhood: "My parents raised us to believe we could do anything we chose to do. . . . Many women in management do not start out with that concept of themselves. It has enabled me to overcome many of the obstacles I've encountered in the banking industry."[8]

The self-esteem formed in childhood lays the foundation for your attitudes toward work, your future success, your personal abilities, and the roles you play.

Adolescence   Infants love to look at their reflections. They are totally accepting of themselves. As an infant, you looked at pictures of yourself and other children and experienced joy. You probably didn't think, "I wish I looked like that baby," or, "That baby sure is ugly!" The worth of your own image was not dependent on or measured by the images of others. As you got older, however, and entered your teens, you probably started comparing yourself to other people. Typically you became less happy with who you were. You wished you were more like others you perceived as better, and you began to use put-downs as an equalizer. Teenagers often tear down others in order to build themselves up, trying to combat their doubts about themselves and their negative self-image. "Friends" add to the level of self-doubt by using "kidding" statements such as "Hi, Klutz!", "You're such a chicken.", or "You'll probably be late to your own funeral!" These negative images undermined your original strong self-acceptance. Their critical words may have been prompted by their own unmet needs and low self-esteem.

The media play a strong part in how adolescents see themselves. The beautiful people featured on TV and in the movies lead adolescents to use these unrealistic images to measure their own attributes and lifestyles. It is easy to feel deficient or diminished in comparison. Instead of seeing who you really are, you see who you are not and continually reinforce that negative image with your own inner thoughts, often referred to as **self-talk**. The propensity toward self-talk often follows teenagers into adulthood. The issue of self-talk is discussed later in this chapter, where you will discover how you can effectively improve your self-esteem by altering your self-talk.

The ages of twelve to eighteen are among the most crucial in developing and consolidating your feelings about yourself. During these years, you are moving away from the close bond between parent and child and are attempting to establish ideals of independence and achievement.[9] You must also deal with physical changes; relationships with peer groups; an emerging, often confusing identity; and the loss of childhood and assumption of some adult responsibilities. Is it any wonder that your self-esteem seemed to change not only day by day but hour by hour? In fact, many people never move beyond the image they had of themselves while in high school. Outwardly successful, they may still be trying to prove to their old classmates that they can "make it." For this reason, adolescent problems should not be underestimated, for it is in the resolution of these problems and conflicts that the self-esteem of the adult is born.

It is unfortunate that many teenagers look for their self-esteem everywhere except within themselves. Strong self-esteem is independent of the opinions of others or of external possessions. It comes mainly from an internal sense of worth. Because many adolescents (and adults) with low self-esteem judge their own value by comparing themselves with others, they have a desperate need for recognition and status. Therefore, they tend to value money and the things money can buy. During a role-playing incident between a teacher instructing a self-esteem unit and a teenage boy, the following exchange occurred.

The teacher asked: "What's your favorite car? Describe it."

"A Mustang with black interior," the student replied.

"Now imagine you just washed that car and drove it to school. I come along in a crane, swing a wrecking ball, and the whole thing shatters. Wham, and the door falls off. Wham, and the body is spread out like scrambled eggs. You are not insured. How would you feel inside?"

The student looked stricken.

"If that car is the *only* image you project," the teacher explains, "I have just destroyed you. I have taken away everything you represent. If you do not work from the inside out, somebody will come along at some point in your life — believe me — and take everything away."*

Adulthood   When you reach adulthood, your brain has a time-enforced picture of who you are, molded by people and events from all your past experiences. You have been bombarded over the years with positive and negative messages from your family, friends, strangers and the media. You may compare yourself to others, as was so common in adolescence, or you may focus on your own inner sense of self-worth.

As an adult, you are expanding the roles you play, taking on the role of wife or husband and even parent. Work experiences and your relationships with your coworkers and supervisors can have a major impact on your feelings about yourself. Doing a job well and being respected as a competent worker enhances your self-esteem. On the other hand, a difficult work situation that provides few opportunities to experience success can diminish your self-respect and inhibit your ability to learn and develop your skills. Thus, spouses, coworkers, friends, and professional colleagues are among those who will continue to influence your self-esteem throughout your life. In some cases, they may reinforce an already negative concept of yourself, whereas in others they may reaffirm the positive images you have built. Perhaps in your adult world you will be able to correct an outmoded, adolescent picture of your abilities and potential.

------

*Reprinted from *The Detroit Free Press*, December 5, 1985, by permission.

Dr. Denis Waitley, psychologist and well-known author and public speaker, discusses his changing self-esteem.

> I've had my own struggles with a poor self-image. Even though my parents told me I was special, my peer group in grammar school and junior high told me different. They offered me such labels as "buzzard beak," "beaver teeth," "Waitley Come Lately." ...During my plebe year at Annapolis the superlatives were, "Mr. Waitley, you couldn't lead a one-cadet parade," "You're so dense you couldn't lead a silent prayer!" or, "If your eyes were any closer together, we'd call you Cyclops." As I began to wear the labels others pinned on me, I began to play my own games....In response to a birthday gift I would say, "You shouldn't have gone to all this trouble for *me*." In response to a compliment, "Don't mention it. It was nothing." In response to a compliment on a great golf shot, "Yeah, bet I won't do that again!" After a seesaw career as a young adult, I finally learned to stop associating myself with external labels, negative self-talk, and humiliating self-presentation. In my early thirties, I began to talk affirmatively about my accomplishments and goals. I began to say "thank you" when other people would bestow any value upon me. I began to accept myself as a changing, growing, and worthwhile human being, imperfect but capable of becoming a Double Winner. And I began to feel good about myself.[10]

As an adult, you will be constantly adjusting the level of your self-esteem to the real world around you. It is important to be aware of how other people have influenced and will continue to influence your beliefs about yourself. You will need to learn how to protect your self-esteem against those who try to diminish or limit your potential and how to listen to those who will encourage and challenge you. Such knowledge can help you distinguish between what is helpful and what is destructive, what is true and what is false, and help you expand the range of what you believe you can be and do in the future.

Characteristics of People with High Self-Esteem

When several leaders were asked about the qualities exhibited by people with high self-esteem, they pointed out the following characteristics:

1. *They are future oriented and not overly concerned with past mistakes or failures.* They learn from their errors and are not immobilized by them. Every experience has something to teach — if you are willing to learn. A mistake can show you what doesn't work, what not to do. One consultant, asked whether he had obtained any results in trying to solve a difficult problem, replied, "Results? Why man, I've had lots of results. I know a hundred things that won't work!" The same principle applies to

---

TOTAL PERSON INSIGHT

❝ But if we never make mistakes, if we never look foolish, if we never take a risk, we'll never grow and we'll never experience the exhilaration that exists on the other side of those fears. We become self-limiting. ❞

Larry Wilson

---

your own progress. Falling down does not mean failure. Staying down does.

When Peter Ueberroth was only in his mid-twenties, he formed an air-shuttle company to provide service between Los Angeles and the Spokane, Washington, World's Fair. Within a year, because of a drop in the demand for charter service, his company failed and he was $100,000 in debt. Nevertheless, Ueberroth did not give up. He established another transportation company the following year. This new company provided central reservation services for the smaller hotels, airlines, and passenger ships that did not have their own representatives. Though he started with only $5,000 and one employee, this time Ueberroth's business grew. He took over several failing travel agencies and formed First Travel Corporation, now one of the largest travel companies in America. One success led to another. He agreed to head the 1984 Los Angeles Olympic games and helped turn a $300,000 debt into a $215 million surplus.[11]

2. *They are able to cope with life's problems and disappointments.* Successful people have come to realize that problems need not depress them or make them anxious. It is their attitude toward problems that makes all the difference. In his autobiography, Lee Iacocca recalls many disappointments. At the top of his list was the experience of being fired as president of Ford Motor Company after the firm had recorded two years of record profits. After being fired by Henry Ford he moved to Chrysler Corporation and brought the ailing company back from the brink of failure. Years later, he recalled the loss of his job at Ford: "A lot has happened since July 13, 1978. The scars left by Henry Ford, especially on my family, will be lasting, because the wounds were deep. But the events of recent years have had a healing effect. So you move on."[12]

3. *They are able to feel all dimensions of emotion without letting those emotions affect their behavior in a negative way.* This characteristic is one of the major reasons people with high self-esteem are able to establish and maintain effective human relations with the people around them. They realize emotions cannot be handled either by repressing them or by giv-

ing them free rein and lashing out at other people. You may feel better after such an explosion, but the people around you will not. Although you may not be able to stop feeling what you feel, you can control your thoughts and actions while under the influence of a particularly strong emotion. Robert Conklin, author of *How to Get People to Do Things*, suggests keeping the following statement in mind: "I can't help the way I feel right now, but I *can* help the way I think and act."[13] Remembering this principle can help you bring an emotionally charged situation under control.

4. *They are able to help others and accept help.* People with high self-esteem are not threatened by helping others to succeed, nor are they afraid to admit weaknesses. If you are not good at dealing with figures, you can bring in an accountant who will manage the records. If you see someone whose abilities are not being used to their fullest, you can suggest ways in which the person might develop his or her talents. An old adage in business goes, "First-rate people hire first-rate people. Second-rate people hire third-rate people." Individuals with secure self-esteem realize that in helping others succeed they benefit themselves as well.

5. *They are skilled at accepting other people as unique, talented individuals.* People with high self-esteem learn to accept others for who they are and what they can do. A relationship built on mutual respect for one another's differences and strengths can help both parties grow and change. It is not a relationship that limits or confines either person. Acceptance of others is a good indication that you accept yourself.

6. *They exhibit a variety of self-confident behaviors.* They accept compliments or gifts by saying "Thank you," without self-critical excuses, and without feeling obligated to return the favor. They can laugh at their situation, without self-ridicule. They let others be right or wrong, without attempting to correct or ridicule them. They feel free to express opinions, even if they differ from those of their peers or parents. They enjoy being by themselves without feeling lonely or isolated. They are able to talk about themselves to others without excessive bragging.

THINKING/LEARNING STARTERS

1. Can you recall two or three people from your childhood or adolescence who had a positive effect on your self-esteem? What did these people say or do? Were there any who had a negative effect on you? What did they say or do?
2. Identify at least two people who you feel exhibit the characteristics of people with high self-esteem. Explain what behaviors helped you identify them.

SELF-ESTEEM AND SUCCESS AT WORK

Your self-esteem is a powerful factor influencing your choice of career and how well you progress in that career. According to Richard Grote, president of Performance Systems Corp. in Dallas, "People take you at the value you put on yourself. If you believe in your own power, other people will believe you and treat you with the respect you've provided for yourself."[14]

In an organizational setting, workers with high self-esteem are inclined to form nourishing rather than destructive relationships. They tend to do more than what is strictly required on the job, and they are receptive to new experiences, to meeting new people, to accepting responsibility, and to making decisions. People who accept themselves can usually accept others, tolerate differences, share their thoughts and feelings, and respond to the needs of others. They do not perceive others as threats. Such people contribute to the well-being and productivity of a group and can explore the opportunities offered by an organization.

Moreover, research studies repeatedly show this connection: individuals with lower self-esteem are more likely to feel hostile, show a lack of respect for others, and attempt to retaliate against others to save face in a difficult situation.[15] Author and psychologist Dr. Milton Layden believes that a hostile response to others is a natural outcome of feelings of low self-esteem and inferiority. It occurs because the emotional system, like other systems of the body, is controlled by a "balancing mechanism." When a person feels a lack of respect toward himself or herself, or feelings of inferiority, the mechanism is knocked off balance and the person starts to feel hostile and anxious. These feelings then get translated into hostile actions.[16]

If a person is in a position of power, and has low self-esteem, it is improbable that subordinates or coworkers will be treated fairly. Workers with low self-esteem can also cause problems on several levels. They can affect the efficiency and productivity of a group because they tend to exercise less initiative, hesitate to accept responsibility or make decisions on their own, and may ask fewer question and take longer to learn procedures. They often have trouble relating well to others. Self-rejecting people generally have a pessimistic view of human nature and may always be on the lookout for an insult or "attack" from someone else, an attitude that can cause interpersonal conflicts. Also, their lack of self-confidence can be misinterpreted by coworkers as unfriendliness. They may require more supervision because they are afraid of making a mistake or appearing ignorant if they ask questions. Even when offered a chance to receive training or career development courses, they may feel they are being singled out as workers who need more instruction than other employees.

"HEY! C'MON, MAN! I'm
'arrogant, rude and smug'
because I got LOW
SELF–ESTEEM."
Reprinted by permission of
NEA, Inc.

Your Self-Esteem Influences Your Behavior

When you accept what others say about you during your early years, these comments are "programmed" into your subconscious mind. You form a mental picture of yourself, which influences your behavior. Your subconscious mind does not evaluate what is put into it; it merely acts on the information it receives — good or bad.

Most people do not realize that the subconscious mind represents a powerful creative capacity within their control. By controlling what goes into your subconscious mind, you can influence your self-esteem. This awareness can be used for positive or negative ends. For example, if you see yourself as a failure, you will use your creative capacity to find some way to fail. William Glasser, author of *Reality Therapy* and other books on human behavior, calls this the **failure syndrome**. No matter how hard you work for success, if your subconscious mind is saturated with thoughts and fears of failure, it will make your success impossible. On the other hand, if your subconscious has been intentionally or unintentionally programmed with positive thoughts to help you succeed, you will be able to overcome many

64

barriers, even those considered handicaps, such as age or a di
background.

The late Colonel Harland Sanders of Kentucky Fried Chi
(now KFC Corporation) began his franchise business at an age ь ..ıı most
people start collecting Social Security. He had been a moderately successful
businessman but had little to show for it beyond the belief that people
would buy his fried chicken prepared according to his secret recipe. All the
conventional wisdom of the business community was against him. They
told him he was too old; people wanted hamburgers, not chicken; his recipe
was too spicy; the franchise market was already flooded with fast-food
items; and he could never make it on his own.

But Colonel Sanders did not see himself settling down in a retirement
home and sitting on the sidelines for his remaining years. He was so confident of his own judgment that he took the risk and started his own business.
Within a few short years, his name was as familiar to consumers as the
McDonald's golden arches. Eventually, the colonel sold his franchise business for several million dollars.[17]

Maltz Discovers the Power of Self-Esteem

Although physical appearance, talents and abilities, background, and education all play a part in our success, *what we believe about ourselves* is the controlling factor that can override or undermine all the rest. This principle was
vividly demonstrated by the work of the noted plastic surgeon Dr. Maxwell
Maltz in his book, *Psycho-Cybernetics*. Throughout his twenty-five years of
practice, Maltz operated on soldiers wounded in war, accident victims, and
children with birth defects. Many of these individuals saw only their defects
and could not believe they would ever be successful in life. In many cases,
after he removed a scar or corrected some type of physical deformity, dramatic and sudden changes in personality resulted. Improving the person's
physical image seemed to create an entirely new individual.

Yet, curiously, not all patients responded this way. Dr. Maltz discovered
that, for some, corrective surgery did little to change their low self-esteem.
The deformity continued to exist in the patient's mind. Further, some people
came to see him who did not need plastic surgery at all. Their "deformity"
was in their mental pictures of themselves.

Maltz soon realized that if people could not reprogram their subconscious minds and change what they believed about themselves, plastic surgery would not help them. Once they understood how to use the creative
power of their subconscious minds, their physical appearance became less
important to them. The real change happened within; they began to believe
in themselves.[18]

THE POWER OF EXPECTATIONS

Your thoughts about yourself are often expressed in terms of expectations — how far you believe you can go and what you feel you can do. Many behavioral psychologists agree that people's expectations about themselves have a significant impact on their performance and how much risk they are willing to take. If you set out to learn a new skill and expect to master it, chances are you will succeed. If you secretly believe you will fail, that expectation is also likely to come true. Once you have acquired an idea about your abilities and your character, you will tend to live up — or down — to your expectations.

Your Own Expectations

People tend to behave in a way that supports their own ideas of how successful or incompetent they are. This somewhat mysterious power of expectations is often referred to as **self-fulfilling prophecy**. Your career successes and failures are directly related to the expectations you hold about your future.

In looking over applications for an M.B.A. program, an admissions director noticed that some students had answered questions about their future plans with phrases such as "I *am*..." or "I *can*..." Other students had written "I *hope* to..." or "I *might*...". The words used by the first group represented a statement of belief that they could achieve specific goals. Not surprisingly, their academic records and outside accomplishments showed that these students had set and reached high performance levels. The second group of students had lower expectations and less confidence in their ability to accomplish their goals.

The effect of self-fulfilling prophecies can be dramatic in terms of an employee's career aspirations and personal development. More than one manager has witnessed the phenomenon of capable, talented employees refusing promotions or being afraid to move out of the positions they have occupied for a time. On the other hand, managers have also seen average employees become motivated to succeed. These workers achieve far more than their personnel records or the opinions of their coworkers suggested they could accomplish.

Holding positive expectations about oneself can lead to positive results. Natalie wanted to become a field representative for a computer hardware company, but lacked self-confidence and the ability to mix easily with other people. She finally decided that she could learn to become more outgoing and self-assured, just as she had learned about the company's products. She enrolled in sales courses, practiced overcoming her shyness and reserve,

watched and imitated other people who had the skills she wanted to cultivate, and acted as if she were confident even when inwardly nervous. At
some point along the way, she began to *enjoy* talking with clients. She didn't
have to worry about what to say or how to introduce herself.

Not long afterward, a field representative position in the company became available, and Natalie applied. When she was offered the position a
week later, one of the interviewers commented on her "self-confidence and
ability to relate well with others." She was launched on her new career.

The Expectations of Others

Self-fulfilling prophecies reflect a connection between your own expectations for yourself and your resulting behavior. But people can also be greatly influenced by the expectations of others. The **Pygmalion effect** sometimes
causes people to become what others expect them to become.

This term was first used by Dr. Robert Rosenthal, a professor at Harvard University, and is based on a Greek legend about Pygmalion, the king
of Cyprus. In the legend, the king longs for an ideal wife. Since no mortal
woman meets his expectations, he fashions a statue of his ideal woman out
of ivory and eventually falls in love with his creation. His desire to make the
statue his wife is so intense that his belief brings it to life.

Zig Ziglar, author and motivational speaker, tells his own Pygmalion
story in his book, *See You at the Top*. Early in his career, Zig attended a sales
training session conducted by P. C. Merrill. When the training session was
over, Mr. Merrill took Zig aside and quietly told him, "You know, Zig, I've
been watching you for two and a half years, and I have never seen such a
waste. You have a lot of ability. You could be a great salesman and maybe
even one of the best in the nation. There is no doubt in my mind if you
really went to work and started believing in yourself, you could go all the
way to the top."[19]

Zig described himself as an "average" person as far as intelligence or
ability was concerned. He did not suddenly acquire a new set of skills that
day, nor did his I.Q. jump fifty points. Zig admired and respected Merrill.
When the man told him, "You can be a great salesman," Zig believed him
and started seeing himself as a top salesperson. He began to think, act, and
perform like one. Before the year was over, Zig ranked number two in a
company of over seven thousand sales personnel. By the next year, he was
one of the highest-paid managers in the country and later became the
youngest division supervisor in the nation. P. C. Merrill's image of Zig
helped him see himself as someone special who had something to offer others. Merrill was Ziglar's Pygmalion.

Organizations are beginning to realize the impact of management expectations on employee performance. Many companies are redesigning

their training programs to provide a supportive or enabling environment that fosters and encourages positive expectations in employees.

In one company, data processing trainees were regularly told that it would take them three weeks to master the program and that they would be able to program about two hundred cards per hour. Not surprisingly, employees met those expectations precisely. They learned the program in three weeks and could process only two hundred cards per hour. Then a new personnel director was hired, who scrapped the old training sessions, hired new trainees, and set up a program oriented toward increasing management expectations of employees. New recruits were told only that they could master the program quickly and were not given any limits on the number of cards per hour they could process. The new recruits learned the program in less than a week and by the end of the training session were programming five hundred cards per hour. Management realized the value of setting open expectations rather than limiting productivity by past performance.

Mentors

Mentors are people who have been where you want to go in your career and who are willing to act as your guide and friend. They take you under their wing and show you how to get to the next step in your career. They act as sponsors, teachers, devil's advocates, and coaches.

As sponsors, mentors will create opportunities for you to prove yourself. In an organization, this might mean they will ask you to help them on a project, analyze a problem, or make a presentation to higher levels of management. As teachers, mentors will present you with hypothetical situations and ask you, "What would you do?" An important part of the teaching responsibility is to explain both the written and unwritten rules of the organization. As devil's advocates, mentors challenge and confront you to give you practice in asserting your ideas and influencing others. Mentors can act as coaches, supporting your dreams, helping you find out what's important to you and what skills you have.

There are certain criteria you might want to consider as you select your mentor or mentors. Susan Nycum, senior partner in the international law firm of Baker & McKenzie, declares she has changed her mentors as often as she has changed bosses. The criteria by which she has chosen each mentor has depended upon his or her influence and perspective on her specific job. "I believe that the Lancelot who can ride through the world doing good, banishing evil, and coming out ahead exists only in Camelot. One simply must have the mentor or advisor to get through the underbrush of politics and rivalries and lack of information that block the road to advancement in most organizations."[20] In a book co-authored with Nancy Collins and Susan Gilbert, Nycum suggests certain criteria for selecting a mentor, some of which are paraphrased on the next page.

People who develop mentoring relationships are often happier with their careers, earn larger salaries, and follow a systematic career path.
Frank Siteman/The Picture Cube

1. Mentors must never be your boss, or someone in your chain of command. A mentor's career should not be affected by the advice he or she gives you or the work you do.

2. Mentors must be authorities in their field.

3. Mentors must be higher up on the professional ladder than you are.

4. Mentors must be influential.

5. Mentors must have a genuine interest in your personal growth and development so that they can recognize opportunities that will meet your potential.

6. Mentors must be willing to commit time and emotion to the mentoring relationship.

7. Mentors are not designed to be permanent, but usually last several years.[21]

Although mentors are not mandatory for success, they certainly help. Research indicates that business executives with a mentoring relationship earn larger salaries, engage in more formal education, and are more likely to follow a systematic career path. They are also happier with their careers and derive more satisfaction from their work.[22]

When 160 women listed in *Who's Who of American Women* were asked about their mentors' contributions to their careers, they responded with statements like the following:

Thought of me as a person first, a woman second.
Helped my orientation and assisted me in "learning the ropes."
Gave motivation and guidance.
Shared their philosophies with me.
Instilled determination and desire to excel.
Developed my long-term strategy.
Gave me access to powerful people.
Helped me to take risks.
Groomed me to be the boss.[23]

Mentoring is an important part of the Management Readiness Program (MRP), a six-month career development program established at Merrill Lynch & Co., Inc. One important goal of this program is to build bridges between high-level managers and employees. It helps participants learn about the firm's culture and career opportunities. Mentors at Merrill Lynch are department or higher-level managers who volunteer to serve as counselors or advisors to four individuals during a six-month period. They agree to meet with these persons once a month in either group or individual meetings.[24]

There will always be days when you feel nothing you do is right. Your mentor can help repair damaged self-esteem and encourage you to go on. With the power of another person's positive expectations reinforcing your own native abilities, it's hard to fail.

THINKING/LEARNING STARTERS

1. Do you believe you can alter your self-esteem once you have reached adulthood? If so, what actions can you take to raise your current level of self-esteem?
2. Do you agree with the statement "People tend to take you at the value you place on yourself; if you believe in your own potential abilities, so will others"? Explain your answer.

HOW TO BUILD YOUR SELF-ESTEEM

Now that you are aware of the power self-esteem has over your life, you can take the next step — examining the image you have of yourself and identifying what might need to be changed. You wouldn't think of trying to fix a machine until you attempted to understand something about how the machine was supposed to work. On the other hand, you don't need to understand the machine completely before you try to make improvements. The same applies to your self-esteem. Even though you may not be totally aware of your current level of esteem, you can begin making plans for improving it.

It isn't easy to meet yourself face to face. But bringing your present self-image out into the open is the first step in understanding who you are, what you can do, and where you are going.

Each day can mean another step toward higher self-esteem. The person you will be tomorrow has yet to be created. Most people continue to shape that future person in the image of the past, repeating the old limitations and negative patterns without realizing what they are doing. The development of a new level of self-esteem will not happen overnight, but it *can* happen. Such a change is the result of a slow evolution that begins with the desire to overcome low self-esteem.

Accept the Past, Change the Future

The first step toward higher self-esteem is to accept yourself as you are now. The past cannot be changed, but the future is determined by how you think and act. Various practices and theories have been developed to help people build high self-esteem. None of these approaches offers a quick, easy route for changing your picture of yourself. You developed your self-esteem over many years; it will take time to change it. But the results can be well worth the effort. Some of the basic principles common to all approaches are summarized here.

Identify and Accept Your Limitations   Part of creating a high level of self-esteem is learning to tolerate limitations in yourself and becoming more realistic about who you are and what you can and cannot do. Demanding perfection of yourself can make you less tolerant of others' faults as well as of your own. It can also place undue importance on failures and mistakes, robbing them of their potential to serve as learning experiences and to provide perspective.

Some women in business, such as Marcie Schorr Hirsch, director of career planning at Brandeis University, have decided they no longer want to live up to the "superwoman" image, juggling home, family, and career. They realize their time and energy are limited, and they are adjusting their schedules to accommodate those realities. She states: "I'm concerned about the quality of my existence. I'm willing to work hard; but I don't want to work so hard at everything that nothing gets done well, and I end up feeling like a failure."[25] Many men, also, are rejecting the super-achiever image.

If you often exhibit a behavior of which you are not proud, and want to change, hate the behavior but do not condemn yourself. Hating yourself tends to make the behavior worse. If you condemn yourself for being weak, for example, how can you muster the strength to change? However, if you become an "observer," and view the activity as separate from yourself, you leave your self-esteem intact while you work on changing the behavior. Acting as an observer and detaching yourself from negative thoughts and actions can help you break the habit of rating yourself according to some scale of perfection and can enable you to substitute more positive and helpful thoughts.

Visualize the Results You Want   The power to visualize is in a very real sense the power to create. We often visualize ourselves succeeding or failing in some enterprise without knowing that such mental pictures can actually affect our behavior. It is the *intentional* successful visualization that can slowly lead your self-esteem and your life in the direction you want it to go. Shakti Gawain, author of *Creative Visualization*, states that when we create something, we always create it first in the form of a thought:

> Imagination is the ability to create an idea or mental picture in your mind. In creative visualization you use your imagination to create a clear image of something you wish to manifest. Then you continue to focus on the idea or picture regularly, giving it positive energy until it becomes objective reality...in other words, until you actually achieve what you have been visualizing.[26]

Diane Von Furstenberg, noted fashion designer, has used mental imagery to produce positive changes in her life. She started her business in 1970 with the dining room table as her office and a small amount of money obtained by pawning her jewelry. Six years later her business was grossing over $60 million, and she was on the cover of *Newsweek* — a superstar at twenty-nine. Reflecting on her career, she says: "I believe nothing happens unless you can imagine it. I have to have images of where I want to go next." [27]

Former Olympic diving star Greg Louganis mentally rehearsed before each dive. He visualized the perfect performance in his imagination and then often executed the dive as perfectly as he imagined it. Salespeople often close the sale in advance. Most hosts plan the party in advance. When it comes time for the actual performance, the mentally rehearsed events have become habits.

Your concept of yourself is no exception. Visualize the behaviors you want to exhibit. When you consciously decide to improve your self-esteem, you are harnessing the mind's creative force to work for you. You are constructing an image of your ideal self and imagining all the qualities and skills you would like to have. Although it sounds like an exercise in fantasy, it is an accepted fact that mental practice has improved the performances of salespeople, executives, and others in the business community.[28]

Turn Your Goals into Positive Self-Talk   A person without goals is like a football team without a game plan. Can you imagine the Dallas Cowboys running onto the field, hoping that someone else will tell them what to do out there? By visualizing who you want to be, you have already begun your life's game plan. The secret to goal setting is very simple: establish clearly defined goals, write them down, and then dwell on them with words, mental pictures, and your emotions. Break down long-term goals into several attainable short-term goals. Don't set them out of sight, but rather just out of reach to pull you in the direction you want to go. Author Richard Grote recommends that at the beginning you set moderate goals for yourself. "Set reasonable objectives for each hour, each day, each week. Keeping long-term sights in mind is important, but don't put unnecessary obstacles in your way by setting objectives too high. People who don't reach those high goals many times feel like failures."[29] The feeling of success you will gain from achieving short-term goals will spur you on to set and attain even higher ones.

To help internalize these goals, it is helpful to create self-talk statements that describe the end result that will occur when you accomplish the goal. You talk to yourself every minute of the day. Through this self-talk, you are constantly in the process of conditioning yourself — negatively or positively, depending on the tone of your thoughts. Many people internalize negative self-talk, which produces negative behaviors. When you want to take control of your self-esteem, focus self-talk on your positive thoughts. Learn how to write **affirmations** for each of your goals. Affirmations are self-talk statements declaring your goals and the qualities you want to develop. When creating your personal and professional affirmations, be sure to follow these guidelines:

1. Begin each affirmation with a first-person pronoun, such as *I*, or *my*.

2. Use a present-tense verb, such as *am*, *have*, *feel*, *create*, *approve*, *do*, or *choose*.

3. Describe the end results you want to achieve. Be sure to phrase the statement *toward* where you want to go, not away from what you don't want. Say, "I am a slim, trim 120 pounds," as opposed to "I am losing 30 pounds." Table 3.1 offers several general affirmations that might help you improve your self-esteem.

Write affirmations for different facets of your personal and professional life. Put them on three-by-five-inch index cards and attach them to your bathroom mirror, refrigerator, car dashboard, desk blotter, and so on. Another technique for internalizing these thoughts rapidly is to record your affirmations on a blank cassette tape while quiet, one-beat-per-second music (largo) is playing in the background.[30] Play the tape repeatedly, especially when you are in a relaxed state, such as just before you fall asleep at

TABLE 3.1 Positive Self-Talk Affirmations

I look forward to new experiences confidently.

I do my own thinking and make my own decisions.

I am an employee who is able to be a strong team member.

I can sincerely recognize the accomplishments of others.

I am filled with a feeling of quiet calmness.

I am in control of my eating habits.

I am able to listen with full concentration to what is being said by the other person.

night. Your brain will accept the information without judgment. When these statements become part of your "memory bank," over time your behavior will follow accordingly. Your brain is like a computer. It will put out exactly what you put in. If you put positive self-talk in, positive behavior will result.

Make Decisions   Psychologists have found that children who were encouraged to make their own decisions early in their lives have higher self-esteem than those who were kept dependent on their parents for a longer period of time. Making decisions helps you develop confidence in your own judgment and enables you to explore options.

At age thirty, Mary Boone became one of the most successful art dealers in the United States. Her galleries are showplaces. But she can recall a time when her self-confidence was conspicuously lacking. "In a family of three girls," she states, "I was the oldest and homeliest." Her mother helped develop her artistic abilities, but Boone found she had more talent for organizing other students' shows than for her own painting.

After a few years as an assistant art dealer in New York, she made the decision to open a gallery of her own. "I had great ambivalence about making art a business. But I realized that [art] dealing had become important to me. Not knowing what you're going to do is like not knowing who you are," Boone says. "When I opened the gallery, I'd found my place in life."

The painters whose work she exhibits agree. As one commented, "In a business like this, clients are as much buying the vision of the dealer as they're buying the work. They look into her eyes and they think...'she really believes what she's saying.'" [31]

Take every opportunity you can to make decisions both in setting your goals and in devising ways to achieve them. Along with making decisions, be willing to accept the consequences of your actions, positive or negative. Organizations with supportive management personnel encourage decision making by employees at all levels in order to develop more employee initiative and self-management skills.

Updating job skills through adult education classes can help maintain high self-esteem.
© Frank D. Smith/Jeroboam, Inc.

Develop Expertise in Some Area   Developing "expert power" not only builds your self-esteem but increases the value of your contribution to the organization. Identify and cultivate a skill or talent you have, whether it is a knack for interviewing people, a facility with math, or good verbal skills. Alice Young, a resident partner in the law firm of Graham & James in New York, developed an expertise in her youth that she didn't know would be a major asset in her career. "I speak Japanese, Chinese, French, and English," she says. "I have a knowledge of Asian cultures that I developed before trade with the East opened up." She has been able to capitalize on her expertise to help American and Asian companies do business with one another and to smooth over many cultural differences that would otherwise make negotiations difficult or impossible. She advises others to "use what you know to benefit yourself and your company."[32]

Developing expertise may involve continuing your studies after completing your formal education. Some institutions offer professional courses to enable people to advance in their careers. For example, the Institute of Financial Education conducts courses for persons employed by financial institutions.

Your Organization Can Help

While each of us is ultimately responsible for the level of his or her self-esteem, we have the option of supporting or damaging the self-confidence and self-respect of everyone we work with, just as they have that option in their interactions with us. Organizations are beginning to include self-esteem modules in their employee and management training programs. R. J. Reynolds, Deere & Company, IBM, Shell Oil, and Calgon, to name just a few, realize the impact low self-esteem has on a worker's ability to learn and grow. These programs help employees at all levels understand how they can influence their own self-esteem as well as that of their coworkers. Participants are given the opportunity to look at and remove some of the self-limiting behaviors that create barriers to fully using their abilities. They are also encouraged to consider new areas of work and responsibility as well as to acquire new skills. William J. Rothwell, a special services officer in the Illinois Office of the General Auditor, has found that one of the main reasons people seek training is the desire to increase their self-esteem. He sees this as an opportunity for management to encourage workers to build their self-esteem. "We can emphasize to participants the strengths of training as a means of unlocking creativity and hidden potential."[33]

Research clearly shows that high-tech employees of the future will need more than training and good salaries to maintain their high self-esteem.[34] Today, many organizations are adopting long-range plans for investing in their people as well as their physical plants. They realize that employees with high self-esteem are more creative, more energetic, and more committed to both the work and the organization. While boosts to self-esteem may come from technical achievements, they must also come from other sources, such as increased opportunities for decision making and more personalized management-employee relationships.

Effective organizations are demonstrating to employees that their opinions and views matter and that their ideas are being implemented in significant ways. They are making sure that each person has a sense of belonging through warm, empathic relationships and open two-way communication that expresses feelings as well as facts. Organizations need to help employees feel they are accomplishing their own goals while helping the organization reach its goals as well. These steps will enable organizations to meet the self-esteem needs of their employees.

SUMMARY

Self-esteem is what you think and feel about yourself. It is the sum of your self-confidence and self-respect. If you have high self-esteem, you feel competent and worthy. If you have low self-esteem, you feel incompetent, unworthy, and insecure. Self-esteem includes your feeling of adequacy about the roles you play, your personality traits, physical appearance, skills, and abilities. High self-esteem is the foundation for a successful life and good human relations. Organizations are beginning to recognize the impact of employees' self-esteem on their ability to learn and to contribute to the organization's productivity.

People start acquiring and building their self-esteem from the day they are born. Parents, friends, associates, the media, and professional colleagues all influence the development of a person's self-esteem. Most of this process takes place in the subconscious mind; people do not objectively evaluate or censor the formative influences they take in. As a result, their self-esteem may represent an accurate reflection of their true abilities or a negative and distorted one.

High self-esteem is essential for success in an organization. Peoples' self-esteem is often expressed in terms of expectations — how much or how little they believe they can do. These expectations can become self-fulfilling prophecies. The power of other people's expectations is also very strong. They can result in a Pygmalion effect in which an individual lives up to the image another has of him or her. Mentors can strengthen a person's self-esteem by expressing belief in that individual's abilities and talents. They can act as sponsors, teachers, devil's advocates, and coaches. Managers in organizations can act as mentors to employees and provide a supportive or enabling environment for strengthening workers' self-esteem.

Building high self-esteem is important both personally and professionally. People who have high self-esteem tend to be future oriented; cope with problems creatively; handle their emotions; give and receive help; accept others as unique, talented individuals; exhibit self-confident behaviors.

Although there are many approaches to improving low self-esteem, such as writing positive self-talk affirmations, certain underlying principles are common to all. These principles include identifying and accepting personal limitations, visualizing positive results, setting goals, making decisions, and developing an expertise in one area. While everyone is ultimately responsible for the level of his or her self-esteem, each of us has the option of supporting or damaging the self-confidence and self-respect of anyone we work with. Several organizations are offering their employees training sessions on how to improve their own and coworkers' self-esteem.

KEY TERMS

self-esteem   Pygmalion effect
self-talk   mentor
failure syndrome   affirmations
self-fulfilling prophecy

REVIEW QUESTIONS

1. What is self-esteem? Why is the development of high self-esteem important in a person's life?

2. What influences help shape a person's self-esteem?

3. How do the expectations of yourself and others affect your self-esteem? Give examples from your own life.

4. What are some of the characteristics that people with high self-esteem exhibit?

5. Why are organizations concerned about employees' self-esteem? In what ways are they helping workers build high self-esteem?

6. List the basic guidelines for building high self-esteem. Which two do you feel are the most important? Why?

7. What role does the subconscious mind play in developing and changing a person's self-esteem?

8. How can visualization help change a person's behavior and self-esteem?

9. List the three elements necessary for the construction of positive self-talk statements. Give three examples of such statements.

10. Review Larry Wilson's Total Person Insight on page 59. Describe a mistake you have made and how it proved to be a growth experience for you.

██████████ ██ CASE 3.1

Slowing the Revolving Door

Kenn Ricci, president of a Cleveland air-charter operation called Corporate Wings, figured the high pilot turnover in his company was unavoidable. Deregulation of the airline industry in 1978 had opened possibilities for new and expanded routes by established carriers and for market entry by fledgling carriers. But to keep all those airplanes flying, the airlines needed more pilots, and most could pay them twice what Corporate Wings could. Like other air-charter organizations and the regional and commuter air companies, Ricci had built his business employing pilots who didn't mind relatively low pay and unpredictable schedules because they needed flight experience. That they would leave when they racked up enough flying time, he thought, was a foregone conclusion.

In fact, salary and schedules aren't the only considerations affecting pilots. Many corporate pilots weigh the higher salaries offered by airlines against the greater anonymity of working for a large company and decided to stay with the small-scale air charter. Others are attracted to small companies by the prospect of flying a wide variety of corporate-owned aircraft, some with well equipped, often advanced avionics. For flexible professionals who find satisfaction in performing both the flying and nonflying details of flight service — from greeting traveling executives to loading luggage — corporate air-charter employment can be rewarding.

Corporate Wings did well in the years from 1981 to 1985, but toward the end of 1986 Ricci began to realize he had underestimated the value of the one-to-one relationship between his pilots and his clients. The mounting rate of turnover meant new faces in the cockpit, and this so concerned two of the company's biggest clients they decided to go elsewhere for service. In five months Corporate Wings lost one-third of its business, and Ricci took a hard look at his employee policies. "We were programmed for turnover," he said.[1] To keep his clients, Ricci now needed to entice his pilots to stick with Corporate Wings.

Sources: Bruce G. Posner, "To Have and to Hold," *INC.*, October 1988, pp. 130–131; Eric Weiner, "Corporate Pilots; Are Airline Jobs All that They Are Cracked up to Be?" *Flying*, April 1986, pp. 59–62; Eric Weiner, "Boom Skies: As They Expand Their Markets, Airlines Are Snatching up Eager Pilots in Record Numbers," *Flying*, October 1986, pp. 69–71.

Questions

1. What did the interplay of expectations between pilots and management have to do with Ricci's problems? How could this situation have been avoided?
2. Beyond increasing salaries and modifying flying schedules, what could Ricci do to help retain his staff? What would be the benefits to the organization and the clients?
3. Could these improvements be carried over to the office and maintenance personnel as well? How?

■ CASE 3.2

Unmanagement at W. L. Gore & Associates

When Bill Gore founded his company, he "set out to recreate the sense of excited commitment, personal fulfillment, and self-direction" for his employees that he had in his own life. He organized a new system of management in which there were no titles, no orders, and no bosses. Everyone was expected to work effectively with everyone else. Associates, as all Gore employees are called, chose to work in an area of the company that they felt best matched their interests, skills, and abilities. They were urged to develop their potential to the fullest.

Gore found that the system worked well until the number of associates reached about two hundred. At that point, human relations and worker productivity began to suffer, and the group became less cooperative. Instead of

---

[1] Bruce G. Posner, "To Have and to Hold," *INC.*, October 1988, p. 130.

adding layers of management to the company to take care of the problem, Gore opened another plant. As the number of associates dropped to one hundred and fifty, morale lifted and the workers felt part of the team again. Each time the number of associates exceeded two hundred, Gore opened another plant. He has opened a total of twenty-seven plants, with plans for more if the need arises.

How is the system working? Sales have neared $125 million, and the company is profitable. Customers admit they have "seen at Gore remarkable examples of people coming out of nowhere and excelling." For the employees, the atmosphere is hard to describe; it's "a feeling, a state of mind."[1] And if that means a sense of excitement and personal growth, that, as much as anything, is what Bill Gore set out to create.

Source: Lucien Rhodes, "The Un-Manager," *INC.*, August 1982, p. 38.

Questions

1. List some of the ways that employees at Gore are encouraged to develop and expand their self-esteem.
2. Bill Gore found that when the company grew too large, it had a negative effect on workers. Besides making employees feel more anonymous, why would size tend to affect workers negatively? What impact might it have on their self-esteem?
3. What would you say are Bill Gore's expectations about the people who come to work for him?

SUGGESTED READINGS

Branden, Nathaniel. *How To Raise Your Self-Esteem*. New York: Bantam Paperback Edition, 1988.
Dyer, Wayne W. *Your Erroneous Zones*. New York: Funk & Wagnalls, 1976.
Gray, James, Jr. *The Winning Image*. New York: AMACOM, 1982.
Maltz, Maxwell. *Psycho-Cybernetics*. New York: Pocket Books, 1972.
Waitley, Denis. *The Seeds of Greatness*. Old Tappan, N.J.: Fleming H. Revell Company, 1983.

NOTES

1. Robert McGarvey, "The Confidence Factor," *Executive Female*, July/August 1988, p. 28.
2. William Watson Purkey, *Self-Concept and School Achievement* (Englewood Cliffs, N.J.: Prentice-Hall, 1970), pp. 14–17.

---

[1] Lucien Rhodes, "The Un-Manager," *INC.*, August 1982, p. 38.

3. "Task Force Feelgood," *Time*, February 23, 1987, p. 33.

4. Purkey, *Self-Concept and School Achievement*, pp. 14–17.

5. Judy Folkenberg, "Delinquency and Self-Dislike," *Psychology Today*, May 1985, p. 16.

6. A. H. Maslow, "A Theory of Human Motivation," in *Psychological Foundations of Organizational Behavior*, ed. Barry M. Staw (Santa Monica, Cal.: Goodyear Publishing, 1977), pp. 7–8.

7. Amy Bjork Harris and Thomas A. Harris, *Staying OK* (New York: Harper & Row, 1985), p. 24.

8. Sue Baugh, "Cool Path to the Top," *NABW Journal*, January/February 1982, pp. 28–30.

9. Margaret Henning and Ann Jardim, *The Managerial Woman* (New York: Anchor Books, 1977), pp. 106–107.

10. Denis Waitley, *The Double Win* (Old Tappan, N.J.: Fleming H. Revell Company, 1985), pp. 76–77.

11. *Current Biography Yearbook*, 1985, pp. 421–425.

12. Lee Iacocca with William Novak, *Iacocca* (New York: Bantam Books, 1984), p. 137.

13. Robert Conklin, *How to Get People to Do Things* (Chicago: Contemporary Books, 1979), p. 69.

14. "How to Gain Power and Support in the Organization," *Training/HRD*, January 1982, p. 13.

15. Judith Briles, *Woman to Woman: From Sabotage to Support* (Far Hills, N.J.: New Horizon Press, 1987), p. 77.

16. Milton Layden, "Whipping Your Worst Enemy on the Job: Hostility," *Nation's Business*, October 1978, pp. 87–90.

17. Zig Ziglar, *See You at the Top* (Gretna, La.: Pelican Publishing, 1975), p. 99.

18. Maxwell Maltz, *Psycho-Cybernetics* (New York: Pocket Books, 1972), pp. 6–7.

19. Ziglar, *See You at the Top*, p. 23.

20. Nancy W. Collins, Susan K. Gilbert, and Susan Nycum, *Women Leading: Making Tough Choices on the Fast Track* (Lexington, Mass.: The Stephen Greene Press, 1988), p. 43.

21. Ibid., p. 41.

22. Breda Murphy Bova and Rebecca R. Phillips, "Mentoring as a Learning Experience for Adults," *Journal of Teacher Education*, May/June 1984, p. 17.

23. Collins, Gilbert, and Nycum, *Women Leading*, p. 46.

24. Caela Farren, Janet Dreyfus Gray, and Beverly Kaye, "Mentoring: A Boon to Career Development," *Personnel*, November/December 1984, p. 22.

25. Anita Shreve, "Careers and the Lure of Motherhood," *New York Times Magazine*, November 21, 1982, pp. 38–43, 46–52, 56.

26. Shakti Gawain, *Creative Visualization* (San Rafael, Cal.: Whatever Publishing, 1978), p. 14.

27. Bob Colacello, "Diane Von Furstenberg: I Don't Believe in Fairy Tales," *Parade Magazine*, August 30, 1987, p. 5.

28. Albert Ellis and Robert A. Harper, *A New Guide to Rational Living* (North Hollywood, Cal.: Wilshire Book Company, 1975), pp. 210–215.

29. Richard Grote, "Make Sure Training Builds Self-Esteem and Peer Acceptance," *Training/HRD*, December 1981, p. 13.

30. Sheila Ostrander and Lynn Schroeder, *Superlearning* (New York: Dell Publishing, 1979), pp. 87–109.
31. Maggie Pale, "Mary Boone: A Confident Vision," *Savvy*, July 1982, pp. 62–67.
32. Cheri Burns, "The Extra Edge," *Savvy*, December 1982, p. 42.
33. Grote, p. 13.
34. Pete Bradshaw and Sandra Shullman, "Managing High-Tech Employees Through Self-Esteem," *Infosystems*, March 1983, pp. 111–112.

Chapter 4

Identifying Your Motivations

CHAPTER PREVIEW

After studying this chapter, you will be able to

1. See the relationship between needs and motivation.

2. Identify the steps in the motivational cycle.

3. Describe Maslow's hierarchy of needs.

4. Describe Herzberg's motivation-maintenance model.

5. Compare and contrast Herzberg's and Maslow's theories of motivation.

6. Summarize McGregor's Theory X and Theory Y of human behavior.

7. Summarize Ouchi's Theory Z.

8. Describe some important internal and external motivators in the workplace.

hen Dr. Norman Vincent Peale talks about motivation, he frequently mentions Mary Crowe. As a youngster, she was one of eight children living in poverty. There was seldom enough food on the family table, and everywhere that Mary Crowe turned, she was confronted by the symbols of poverty. As Dr. Peale notes, "The Great Depression had the country by the throat." Despite these depressing surroundings, she was not an unhappy girl. In her mind she pictured an attractive college campus with green lawns and ivy-covered buildings. She also visualized herself receiving a diploma on graduation day. Years later, her dreams turned to reality when she entered college.

Once in college she began thinking about a career. She decided to become an insurance salesperson. She visualized herself as a successful salesperson helping buyers whose lives would be more secure because of the insurance. After graduation, she applied for a job at one of the largest insurance agencies in the city. The man in charge of hiring turned her down. In those days there were almost no women selling insurance, and he wasn't about to take a chance with Crowe. She went away, but returned the next day and again requested a job. Again she was turned down. She returned several times and was finally given a job. She soon became the number one salesperson for the company and later became a member of the Million Dollar Round Table—the exclusive group of insurance agents who sell more than one million dollars' worth of insurance in a single year. From early childhood, she was motivated by the desire to achieve her goals.*

Learning what motivates you can be an essential part of knowing yourself, of finding out what is important to you. The information on motivation and needs presented in this chapter will provide some useful insights into your own needs. If you know what you want out of a job, you are in a better position to plan your career. The material in this chapter will also contribute to your knowledge of human relations. Knowing what motivates others is basic to establishing and maintaining effective relations with them.[1] This chapter also examines management's responsibility in motivating workers. Although you may not be planning to become a supervisor or manager at this time, it will be helpful to understand how management approaches the problem of employee motivation.

THE COMPLEX NATURE OF MOTIVATION

Human beings are motivated by many different kinds of needs. People have basic needs for food, clothing, and shelter, but they also need acceptance,

---

* Norman Vincent Peale, "Imagine Your Way to Success," *National Association for Professional Saleswomen*, October 1983. Used by permission of the author.

> **TOTAL PERSON INSIGHT**
>
> ❝ What motivates people? No question about human behavior is more frequently asked or more perplexing to answer. Yet knowing what motivates another person is basic to establishing and maintaining effective relations with others. ❞
>
> D. R. Spitzer

recognition, and self-esteem. Each individual will experience these needs in different ways and to varying degrees. For some, basic needs may be most important, whereas for others, the need to be accepted may be strongest. To make matters more complicated, people will be motivated by different needs at different times in their lives. Adults, like children and adolescents, continue to develop and change in significant ways throughout life. Patterns of adult development have been described in such popular books as *Passages* and *Pathfinders* written by Gail Sheehy and *Seasons of a Man's Life* by Daniel Levinson. No one approach to motivation will work for everyone or for the same person all the time.

Motivation Defined

Motivation can be defined as the reason why people do the things they do.[2] In a work setting, motivation is what makes people *want* to work. Employees and managers alike need to understand what strengthens or weakens their motivation on the job in order to fulfill both organizational and personal goals. Although some managers still subscribe to the theory that fear is the best motivator, modern management's thinking now leans toward a more positive approach. Over the long run, people will work harder to gain recognition or job satisfaction than they will to avoid negative consequences such as having their job terminated or being disciplined in some way. In addition, there has been a shift in the traditional work ethic. As we noted earlier in this text, many of today's better-educated and better-informed workers possess a heightened sense of their rights and are more likely to demand responsive and equitable treatment from the organization. They want to be treated as valued persons, and they display less tolerance for an authoritarian style of management. Although some managers may dismiss these workers as "prima donnas," failure to take their needs seriously can result in motivation-related problems such as poor morale, high turnover, and low productivity.

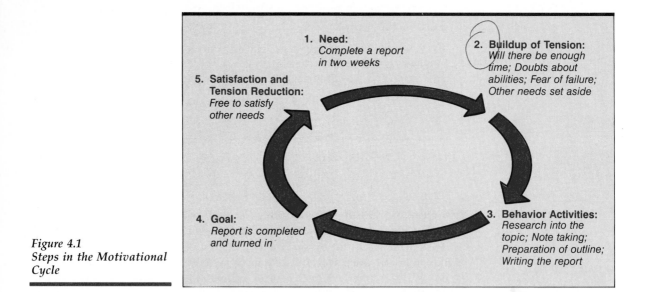

Figure 4.1
Steps in the Motivational Cycle

The Motivational Cycle

The **motivational cycle** describes how individuals go about satisfying a felt need. If your need is strong enough, such as acute hunger or thirst, you will be unable to concentrate on anything else until that need has been taken care of. Mahatma Gandhi reportedly said, "Not even God can talk to a hungry man." *Not true – Spirit more sensitive to the Holy Spirit*

There are five steps in the motivational cycle (see Figure 4.1). A sufficiently strong need creates tension, which in turn makes a person take action to satisfy the need. Once the goal has been achieved, there is a sense of satisfaction and reduction in tension. For example, suppose you have a report due in two weeks, one that others are counting on to help them make a crucial decision. The tension builds, and your activities become focused on completing the report—your highest-felt need at the time. You may work evenings and weekends, turning down invitations to go out with friends. After several days of hard work, you achieve your goal: the report is finished. You experience an enormous sense of relief from the tension that has kept you at the job. Now you are free to relax and satisfy your other needs.

The motivational cycle begins only when you feel a need is important to you. For instance, your boss may decide to institute a cost-control program in your department, whereas you feel the company should spend *more*

money on your area. Chances are you will not be highly motivated to follow the boss's cost-control guidelines very carefully. There is no felt need on your part to cut down on expenditures. Similarly, some students may enter college because their parents feel higher education is important. But if the students aren't motivated by the same need, they will have a hard time completing the required course work. People are most strongly motivated by those needs they *feel within themselves*.

Priority of Needs Determines Motivation

What happens when you have more than one need operating at the same time? How do you choose between them, or is there some process within you that does the selecting? What impact does culture have on people's needs?

Generally, even though you may feel more than one need at a time, one of those drives will be stronger than the rest, and you will be motivated to satisfy it first. If you are extremely hungry and thirsty, you will probably first satisfy your thirst and then eat. Someone who collects old phonograph recordings may forgo buying a pair of new shoes or some other practical item if the person comes across a rare recording that will complete the collection.

Cultural conditioning also affects what people perceive as needs. In Japan, for example, more business firms are committed to lifetime employment for their workers than in the United States.[3] This management philosophy, in part, satisfies the worker's need for job security.

In the United States, a great deal of emphasis is placed on a good education, a sound family base, a job that pays well, and some type of group affiliation, such as a church or social group. Most people will seek to fulfill these needs during their lifetime. The typical American is also influenced by advertising and marketing campaigns that tell them they "need" a power mower, a new high-performance car, or the latest kitchen appliance. Given this influence, it is not difficult to see how essential needs and more artificial needs can become confused.

If you are uncertain about your own needs, you may find it difficult to determine what truly motivates you. You may be unhappy with your job and feel that the solution is an increase in salary. But with each pay raise, you find your dissatisfaction remains. Your real need may be for more responsibility, greater recognition of your work, or more authority to do the job as you see fit. Managers who can discover employees' true needs are more likely to motivate their workers effectively than those who cannot.

The work of various psychologists and social scientists has added greatly to the knowledge of what motivates people and how motivation works.

The basic problem, as many leaders admit, is knowing how to apply that knowledge in the workplace.

THINKING/LEARNING STARTERS

1. Look over Figure 4.1 and apply the motivational cycle to your own experience. Choose an example from work or school, and fill in the steps:
   Need *what is more important to each individual*
   Buildup of tension *thinking about getting job done in a time frame*
   Behavior activities
   Goal
   Satisfaction and tension reduction *Completion of task*
2. What needs have been competing for your attention lately? List them; then rank them in their order of importance, with number one representing your top priority. Is the priority clear, or do some needs seem equally important?

MASLOW'S HIERARCHY OF NEEDS

Abraham Maslow, a noted psychologist, found that people tend to satisfy their needs in a particular order — a theory he called the "hierarchy of needs."[4] Maslow's theory rests on two assumptions: (1) people have a number of needs that require some measure of satisfaction, and only unsatisfied needs motivate behavior; and (2) the needs of people are arranged in a hierarchy of prepotency, which means that as each lower-level need is satisfied, the need at the next level demands attention.[5] Basically, human beings are motivated to satisfy physiological needs first (food, clothing, shelter), then the need for safety and security, and then social and esteem needs. Finally, they seek to realize their potential, what Maslow called "self-actualization." Maslow's theory is illustrated in Figure 4.2. It is not difficult to see how this theory can be applied to motivation on the job.

Physiological Needs

The needs for food, clothing, sleep, and shelter, or **physiological needs**, were described by Maslow as survival or lower-order needs. In most work environments, these basic needs rarely dominate because they are reasonably well satisfied. During the Great Depression, however, many people worked solely to ensure their own and their families' survival. In most cases, they were not concerned with the type of work they did or whether they liked it.

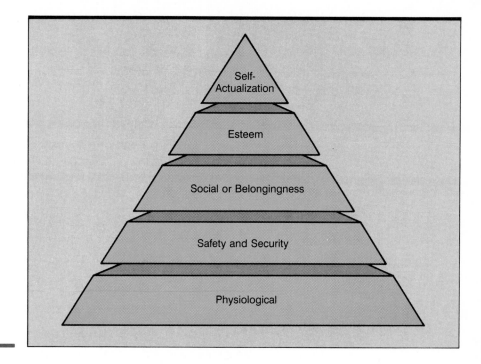

Figure 4.2
Maslow's Hierarchy of Needs

Safety and Security Needs

People's desire for some sort of order and predictability in the world is reflected in **safety and security needs**. In general, people tend to look for security in the known and familiar and avoid what they don't know or understand. They like to know that they won't lose their jobs, that they can provide for their families, and that they will have enough money and resources to take care of themselves in sickness or old age. During the recession in the early 1980s, massive layoffs put employees in a state of limbo. Even those not laid off wondered from day to day if they would have a job the next week. In the late 1980s it was the heavy volume of mergers, buyouts, and business closings due to the movement of production facilities to other countries that created a feeling of insecurity among many workers. Even the oldest and largest of organizations were not immune to the economic volatility that spread across America. This insecurity often affected productivity and strained human relations at home and at work.

Organizations recognize the need for security by offering employees pensions, profit sharing, stock option plans, and insurance plans. Workers are not simply earning a paycheck but protecting themselves against injury and laying aside money for retirement. Several American companies have made a major effort to avoid layoffs. Job security is given a very high

Unemployment forces many people to focus on basic motivational needs such as food, shelter, and safety.
© Gilles Peress/Magnum Photos, Inc.

priority at such companies as Hallmark Cards Inc., Johnson Wax, Federal Express Corp., and Worthington Industries.

Safety needs usually focus on protection from physical harm. On the job, this means a guarantee of safe working conditions. Unions or employee groups can make sure employers maintain safety standards and reduce the risk of accidents or injuries resulting from environmental hazards. Congress established the Occupational Safety and Health Act (OSHA) to help reduce deaths and injuries on the job.

Safety needs are also satisfied in other ways outside work. Advertisements for additional life or medical insurance, smoke detectors or burglar alarms, or guaranteed savings programs all appeal to people's need for safety and security.

Social or Belongingness Needs

Whereas the first two types of needs deal with aspects of physical survival, **social** or **belongingness needs** deal with emotional and mental well-being. Ron Parks, manager of manufacturing operations and human resources at the Dana Corp. plant in Columbia, South Carolina, can use his computer to contact any of his fifty-one employees. With a few keystrokes he can send a message to the video-display terminals at their work stations. However, he does not rely on this modern technology for all of his communication with the workers. Every Monday morning he goes to the plant with the plant manager to meet with the workers over coffee. These informal meetings not only improve communication, but also meet the social needs of many workers.[6]

Research has shown that fulfillment of people's needs for affection, a sense of belonging, and identification with a group are as important to their health as are food and safety.

Although social needs are felt throughout childhood, they may become more intense during adolescence, when the need to belong to a group becomes more important than family ties or what parents think. As adults, the need for belonging may take the form of joining various organizations — professional associations, church groups, amateur sports teams, or social clubs. Special uniforms or membership privileges reflect the desire to feel part of a group in which individuals share the same interests, values, and goals.

Many people's social needs are also satisfied on the job. People form attachments with coworkers and may join the company sports teams, take part in company picnics or outings, and get together after work. A growing number of business firms are sponsoring softball teams made up of their employees. Employers who are eager to see teamwork develop at the plant or office often pay for all or part of the bill for jerseys, equipment and post-game refreshments. David Abramis, an organizational psychologist at California State University at Long Beach, says, "People who play company-sponsored softball tend to think of work as being more fun."[7] In many cases, friendships developed at work may function like a "second family."

One of the basic motivational needs of most people is a sense of belonging.
Nancy Bates / The Picture Cube

This is not surprising when you consider that many employees spend more time with people on the job than they do with their own family members.

Many people are more highly motivated when they work as members of a team. Managers have found that when employees have a strong sense of being a part of the team, they are likely to be more productive and experience greater satisfaction than when they do not.

Esteem Needs

As discussed in Chapter 3, self-esteem is a term that describes how you feel about yourself. Self-esteem influences work behaviors and attitudes in two fundamental ways. First, employees bring to their work settings different levels of self-esteem, which in turn influence how they act, feel, and think while on the job. Second, individuals need to feel good about themselves; thus, much of what workers do and believe serves to enhance, preserve, or restore their self-esteem.[8]

Esteem needs relate to one's self-respect and to the recognition and respect one receives from others. Arthur Witkin, chief psychologist for the Personnel Sciences Center, believes that: "Perhaps the single most important thing is to be aware of a worker's need for self-esteem. Everyone needs to feel good about himself; if he doesn't, he'll not only turn in a poor job performance, he'll keep others from doing their best."[9]

Esteem needs can be satisfied in many ways. You may set your sights on winning the top-salesperson-of-the-year award, work to build a reputation as a highly skilled and reliable employee, or volunteer to chair a committee for the annual charity drive. Often, managers miss opportunities to reinforce the self-esteem of their workers. For most people, a word of appreciation or praise is a strong motivator. One employee stated, "It's such a simple thing, but hearing the boss say I did a great job makes me feel that all the work I put into a project was worth it. I go away wanting to work even harder on the next one." The power of praise and other reinforcement strategies will be discussed in Chapter 7.

Self-Actualization Needs

The four needs just described motivate people by their *absence*, that is, when people feel a lack of food, security, social relationships, or esteem. **Self-actualization needs**, on the other hand, represent the need for growth and motivate people by their *presence*. Self-actualization is fulfilling one's potential or realizing one's fullest capacities as a human being.

Maslow used *self-actualization* in a very specialized sense to describe a rarely attained state of human achievement. Because of the uniqueness of each person, the form or content of self-actualization is a very individual thing.[10] Most of us will probably not reach self-actualization in Maslow's sense of the term, but we do make steps toward it by seeking to expand ourselves through setting new goals and finding new means of expression. The achievement of one goal stimulates the search for new challenges. It is like being on a fascinating journey where the goal is not the end of the road but the journey itself.

Each person's journey toward self-actualization will be individual and unique. It may be difficult to satisfy this need on the job, since most jobs are limited in scope and have their duties fairly clearly defined. However, this is not to say that people haven't found ways to change their jobs, create new positions for themselves, or set new goals year after year. George Guzewicz took a $15,000 pay cut to leave Xerox Corporation, the company where he had worked for seventeen years, to enter a sales job.[11] (He had never sold a product or service before.) Feeling that his job at Xerox was not challenging enough, he went to work for Lambda Semiconductors. After only a few months in the new position, Mr. Guzewicz was achieving success and feeling a new sense of accomplishment. He was already setting his sights on another position within the company that would offer an even greater challenge.

The self-actualizing person may not only create his or her own job, but may have two or three careers in one lifetime. A retired elementary school teacher learned Braille at age sixty-five and taught blind children for fifteen years. In another case, a printer turned his carpentering skills into a side business and began manufacturing grandfather clocks. He kept at his "hobby" until well into his eighties.

Meeting employees' self-actualization needs on the job requires a combination of creativity, imagination, and a willingness to be flexible.

Maslow's Theory Reconsidered

Maslow based his concept of the hierarchy of needs on two observations. First, people will satisfy their needs systematically, starting with the most basic and moving up the ladder. Second, lower-order needs take precedence over higher-order needs.

In general, these observations hold true. But the theory should not be accepted too literally. Human beings are motivated at any one time by a complex array of needs and may satisfy several of them through one activity. One familiar example is the business lunch. Not only are you conducting business with a client, but you are also satisfying your need to eat and drink, to engage in social activities, and to feel important in your own eyes and, you hope, the eyes of your client.

People will sacrifice lower-order needs to satisfy higher-order needs if the drive is strong enough. When individuals take up a dangerous sport such as skydiving or mountain climbing, they are placing self-actualization needs over security or safety. A young lawyer may decide to open a storefront office to serve the poor rather than enter the security of an established law firm.

Despite these reservations, Maslow's contribution to the theory of motivation remains a landmark in the field. He pointed out that lower-order needs, when satisfied, no longer act as motivators. Usually, people do not keep eating after they are full; they wait until they are hungry again. Since higher-order needs are never completely satisfied—one goal leads to another—they will be the strongest motivators over the long run.

THINKING/LEARNING STARTERS

1. Reexamine the "needs priority list" you created for the Thinking/Learning Starter on page 86. Consider Maslow's basic concept: people will satisfy their needs systematically, moving from physiological needs, to safety and security needs, to social needs, to esteem needs, and finally to self-actualization. How do the priorities on your list compare with this hierarchy?
2. What opportunities do you have to satisfy more than one of your needs at a time? In what ways is it helpful to move quickly through your basic needs and focus on self-actualization?

HERZBERG'S MOTIVATION-MAINTENANCE MODEL

In the late 1950s, psychologist Frederick Herzberg proposed another theory of motivation called the hygiene theory, or the **motivation-maintenance model**.[12] The word *hygiene* is a medical term referring to factors that help maintain, but do not necessarily improve, health. According to Herzberg, two conditions or factors affect individual behavior on the job: maintenance and motivational factors.

Maintenance (Hygiene) Factors

These factors do not act as motivators; but if they are withdrawn, they create dissatisfaction and may result in lower productivity. At the least, the lack of maintenance factors will hurt employee morale. Herzberg's list of maintenance factors includes salaries and some fringe benefits, working conditions, social relationships, supervision, and organizational policies and administration. People take these factors for granted as part of the job.

Suppose, however, that the organization decides to cut costs by reducing the amount of medical or life insurance offered employees. Suddenly, fringe benefits become the focus of employee dissatisfaction. Once the coverage is reinstated, dissatisfaction disappears and workers return to a more neutral position. The medical plan does not motivate employees to be more productive, but the loss of it can cause workers to look for employment within another organization that provides the necessary coverage.

Maintenance factors, then, represent the *basic benefits and rights people consider essential to any job.*

Motivational Factors

These factors motivate employees when they are *present*; but according to Herzberg, their *absence* does not necessarily cause dissatisfaction. The relationship between satisfaction/dissatisfaction and motivational/maintenance factors is illustrated in Figure 4.3.

Herzberg's list of motivational factors parallels, to some degree, Maslow's higher-order needs. The list includes responsibility, recognition, achievement, the job itself, and opportunities for advancement. When these factors are present, they tend to motivate employees to achieve higher production levels, to feel more committed to their jobs, and to find creative ways to accomplish both personal and organizational goals. Herzberg found that their absence does not necessarily mean that workers will be unhappy or dissatisfied.

Motivational factors are those *benefits above and beyond the basic elements of a job.* Employees like to feel they are getting something beyond a paycheck for the time and effort they put into their work. If their *motivational* needs are not met, they may begin to ask for more *maintenance* benefits—fringe benefits, higher pay, better physical surroundings, or more liberal policies regarding sick leave or vacation time. Although these factors may increase satisfaction momentarily, they will not motivate workers over the long run. Each new maintenance factor quickly becomes part of the normal job benefits. For example, a Christmas bonus may start out as a motivational factor, particularly if it is based on individual performance. But if it is awarded every year regardless of employee output, it ends up as merely another fringe benefit offered by the organization.

A Final Comment on Herzberg

Critics of Herzberg's theory have pointed out that he assumes that most, if not all, individuals are motivated only by higher-order needs. These critics believe that, in reality, this is not necessarily so. A complex, challenging, and independent job is motivating to those who would ordinarily seek out that type of position. However, other people may prefer more routine, predictable types of work and may be motivated more by the security of a regular paycheck than by the prospect of advancement.

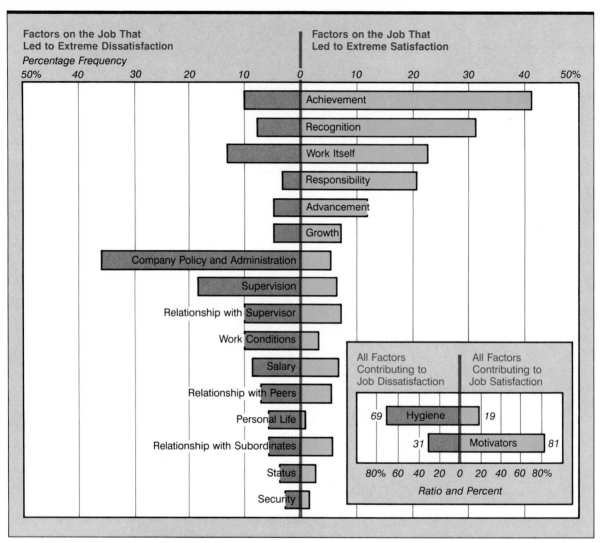

Figure 4.3
Relationship Between Satisfaction/Dissatisfaction and Motivational/Maintenance Factors
Source: Frederick Herzberg, *Harvard Business Review*

Perhaps the motivation-maintenance model can best be understood if you remember that the *employee's* perception of what is a motivating or maintenance factor is far more important than a *manager's* perception of it. A pay raise may strongly motivate an employee just out of college, but may

TABLE 4.1   Comparison of the Herzberg and Maslow Theorie

	Herzberg	Maslow
Motivational Factors	Work itself Achievement Responsibility	Self-actualization needs
	Recognition Advancement Status	Esteem needs
Maintenance (Hygiene) Factors	Interpersonal relations Supervision-technical	Social or belongingness needs
	Company policy and administration	Safety and security needs
	Job security Working conditions Salary Personal life	Physiological needs

simply be a routine part of the job for someone who has been in the work force for many years. Likewise, managers who believe that a more liberal vacation policy will motivate all their workers to be more productive may be in for a big disappointment.

Comparing Herzberg and Maslow

Overall, the theories of Herzberg and Maslow largely support each other. As shown in Table 4.1 , satisfiers or motivators relate to Maslow's higher-order needs, and dissatisfiers or maintenance factors correspond to lower-order needs.

However, the theories differ in one important respect. Maslow believes that an appeal to *any* level of need can act as a motivator. For example, someone saving to buy a house will be attracted to a high-salaried job, even if the work itself is not appealing. If the person takes on more financial obligations, such as starting a family, salary will continue to be a motivating factor. Herzberg, on the other hand, contends that only appeals to higher-level needs are truly motivational.

Both Maslow and Herzberg agree that higher-order needs are more motivating in the long run. The sense of personal satisfaction in one's work, an opportunity to learn new skills, and the feeling of being important seem to be lifelong motivating factors. On the other hand, salary, fringe benefits, and the like are at best short-term motivators.

THINKING/LEARNING STARTERS

1. What conditions or experiences at work have greatly increased your feelings of job satisfaction? What conditions or experiences at work have greatly increased your feelings of job dissatisfaction?
2. List the factors you have identified in question #1. Which would Herzberg most likely label motivational? maintenance?
3. How have feelings of job satisfaction affected your job performance?

McGREGOR'S THEORY X AND THEORY Y

In most organizations, day-to-day operations are significantly influenced by the relationship between workers and management. Douglas McGregor, management consultant and author, accepted the concept of a needs hierarchy, but he felt that management had failed to do so.[13] In his influential book, *The Human Side of Enterprise*, he outlined a set of assumptions that he said influenced the thinking of most managers. He divided these assumptions into two categories: Theory X and Theory Y.

Theory X: A Pessimistic View

Theory X represents a pessimistic view of human nature. According to this theory, people do not really want to work — they have to be pushed, closely supervised, and threatened with some type of punishment. Since they have little or no ambition, workers prefer to avoid responsibility and will seek security as their major goal.

Theory X reflects the "carrot and stick" philosophy, combining punishment and rewards to motivate employees. This approach has two major drawbacks. First, managers who accept Theory X as valid tend to use the stick more than the carrot. "If I ever fall behind in my quota," one worker said, "you can bet I hear about it. But if I break my back to get a job done, not a word." The general belief of management under this theory is that workers are paid to do a good job; management's function is to supervise the work and correct employees if they go off course.

Second, the carrot and stick image itself creates a negative attitude toward workers. The supervisor or manager who views others as lazy, incompetent, reluctant to accept responsibility, and interested only in a paycheck will often treat subordinates with distrust, suspicion, and little respect, and will practice a form of supervision wherein fault finding, blaming, and reprimands are frequent.[14]

Theory Y: An Optimistic View

Theory Y reflects an optimistic view of human behavior. According to this theory, work is as natural to people as play or rest. People's attitudes toward work depend on their previous job experiences and the conditions surrounding the work itself. If employees are able to understand and relate to an organization's goals, they will tend to be somewhat self-directed and will not need to be threatened or coerced into working. When given the proper encouragement, people will seek responsibility rather than avoid it; and they will often exercise considerable imagination and creativity in carrying out their responsibilities.

Managers who accept Theory Y as valid are likely to try to understand what motivates their subordinates, and in turn become better motivated themselves. They are fulfilling their own need for self-expression and achievement as managers by discovering the needs of their employees. A healthy, two-way relationship can create a work climate in which employees *want* to give more. A Theory Y manager will make a continuing effort to stress how important employees' efforts are to the organization as a whole.

Support for Theory Y

One of the strongest supporters of Theory Y is Jay Hall, a social psychologist whose ideas helped trigger a dramatic turnaround at Ford Motor Company during the 1980s. In his books *The Competence Process* and *The Competence Connection,* he drives home the point that within the great majority of workers there is a competence motive, that is, a need to demonstrate their competence.[15] He says that workers have a personal need to perform well and that management should provide a positive work environment in which this potential can blossom. Too often, he notes, we organize and manage as if workers were deficient.[16]

Bill Moog, president of Moog Inc., a company that manufactures electrohydraulic control products, is someone who takes an optimistic view of his employees. When you join this company located near Buffalo, New York, you receive an employee handbook that starts with the following statements: "Our philosophy at Moog is a simple one. We believe in the people who work for us. We believe work can be a more rewarding and satisfying experience for everyone in an atmosphere of mutual trust and confidence." This is a company without time clocks, a company that relies on each employee to report his or her performance. Moog does not have floor inspectors to check every product because employees are expected to check their own work.[17] Theory Y seems to be alive and well at Moog Inc.

OUCHI'S THEORY Z

Security Factor

UCLA management professor William Ouchi has spent years studying the major corporations in Japan. He formulated Theory Z to describe characteristics common to certain successful Japanese and American companies.[18] Organizations dedicated to this management style generally have a lifetime employment policy. Even when sales are down, employees know they will not be laid off and thus have good reason to feel that their own long-term fate is tied to the company's. Workers are likely to perform job tasks conscientiously and enthusiastically in order to achieve a perfect final product. There is open communication, both vertically and horizontally, with complete trust among groups and individuals, because all employees have the same goal: the good of the company. This sense of employees as a family, pulling together for the good of the organization, is the basis for the success of Theory Z. The Theory Z company satisfies lower-level motivational needs by being parental—looking after everyone's welfare.

Theory Z also assumes that the best management involves workers at all levels. In Theory Z organizations, employees gain a psychological sense of belonging because all decisions are made in groups. In Japan, these groups may be as large as sixty to eighty people. It takes time to make final decisions with this process; yet the advantage of this **collective compromise** is that once an agreement has been reached, no one in the group will try to sabotage it. Getting dozens of American executives to build a decision by collective compromise might tie an American company in knots. Yet Intel Corporation has encouraged a collective approach by dividing employees into project teams; Procter & Gamble uses partially self-governing work groups in some of its plants; and managers and employees at Hewlett-Packard have kept worker turnover down during economic slumps by agreeing that all employees—not just those at lower levels—have to give up some working hours and privileges.[19] Participating in decision making helps employees satisfy their higher-level motivational needs.

INTERNAL VERSUS EXTERNAL MOTIVATION

At the beginning of this chapter, we defined *motivation* as an internal drive to accomplish a particular goal. In a work setting, this definition may suggest that all motivation is the result of internal rewards that a person receives while performing the job. However, motivation at work can be triggered by rewards that occur apart form the job itself. These rewards are referred to as "external motivation." Motivation, then, is two-dimensional; it can be internal or external.

Internal Motivation

An **internal motivation** is an intrinsic reward that occurs when a duty or task is performed. If a nurse enjoys caring for a patient, the activity is in itself rewarding, and the nurse will be self-motivated. Frederick Herzberg said that motivation comes from an internal stimulus, resulting from job content, not job environment. He suggested that jobs be enriched in order to provide responsibility, opportunity for achievement, and individual growth. Herzberg used the term *vertical job loading* to describe attempts to enrich an employee's job and thereby trigger internal motivation.[20] Table 4.2 describes several principles of vertical job loading. Note that each principle increases the worker's personal contribution. Those who agree with Herzberg note that many of today's workers place a much higher value on intrinsic rewards such as achievement, personal growth, challenge, satisfaction, and quality of work life than on extrinsic factors such as pay and promotion.[21]

TABLE 4.2   Principles of Vertical Job Loading

Principle	Motivators Involved
Removing some controls while retaining accountability	Responsibility and personal achievement
Increasing the accountability of individuals for own work	Responsibility and recognition
Giving a person a complete natural unit of work (module, division, area, and so on)	Responsibility, achievement, and recognition
Granting additional authority to an employee in his or her activity; job freedom	Responsibility, achievement, and recognition
Making periodic reports directly available to the worker rather than to the supervisor	Internal recognition
Introducing new and more difficult tasks not previously handled	Growth and learning
Assigning individuals specific or specialized tasks, enabling them to become experts	Responsibility, growth, and advancement

Source: Frederick Herzberg, *The Managerial Choice: To Be Efficient and To Be Human* (Salt Lake City, Utah: Olympus Publishing, 1982), p. 131. Reprinted by permission of the author.

One way organizations are encouraging job enrichment is through **intrapreneurship**, or encouraging employees to pursue personal ideas as company projects by giving them the money, equipment, and time to do so. For instance, 3M Company permits employees to spend 15 percent of company time experimenting with their own ideas. This practice resulted in the development of Post-it Notes, the highly successful yellow pads with the gentle adhesive. Arthur Fry, the Post-it Notes creator, won "3M's Nobel Prize" and was promoted to senior scientist for his efforts. Hewlett-Packard's Charles House pursued an idea for an advanced picture tube despite a management order to kill the project. The tube was eventually used as a monitor in a space flight. House's persistence won him Hewlett-Packard's "Medal of Defiance" award.[22]

Many organizations are realizing that these "corporate tinkerers" can turn their hobbies into big business for their employers. Employees, in turn, see intrapreneurship as a way to inject excitement into otherwise dull jobs. Rosabeth Moss Kanter, an authority on organization change, states, "The idea that, yes, you can take action inside large companies—that you can run your own show—is very appealing."[23] The potential of being an intrapreneur may be a highly motivating factor for the workers of the future.

External Motivation

External motivation is initiated by another person and usually involves rewards or other forms of reinforcement. The reward or reinforcement is recognized as a motivational force because the worker will behave in ways that will ensure the receipt of the reinforcement. Typical external rewards in a work setting include money, feedback regarding performance, awards, and the like. Some organizations are using **incentives** to encourage workers to develop good work habits and to repeat behavior that is beneficial to themselves and the organization. The incentive may take the form of a cash award, bonus, certificate, or some type of prize. Another form of external motivation is the expectation of the supervisor or manager. When employees perceive that others expect them to succeed, they are likely to attempt to live up to that expectation.

A Balanced Approach

Most authorities on motivation agree that organizations should attempt to provide a mix of external rewards and internal satisfaction. External rewards are rarely enough to motivate people on an ongoing basis. Most employees need to obtain internal satisfaction from enriched jobs. Ideally, an organization will provide an appropriate number of external rewards while permitting employees to experience the personal satisfaction that comes from a challenging job.

THINKING/LEARNING STARTERS

1. In places where you have worked, would you say the managers believed in Theory X, Theory Y, or Theory Z? Give specific examples to support your answer.
2. Review the list of principles of vertical job loading in Table 4.2 . Have you, or has someone you know, had experience with one or more of these types of vertical job loading? If so, indicate which type(s), and in what (if any) ways this increased your/his/her motivation. If not, imagine expanding your job in one or more of these ways. Which would add the most satisfaction to your job? Why?

SUMMARY

Motivation is an internal drive to accomplish a particular goal. In a work setting, it can be defined as what makes people *want* to work.

People are motivated by different needs. The motivational cycle describes the steps an individual goes through in satisfying a felt need. In general, people tend to satisfy their needs in a particular order. According to Maslow's hierarchy of needs theory, physiological needs will come first, followed by safety and security needs, then social, esteem, and self-actualization needs. Maslow believed that although any need can be a motivator, only higher-order needs will motivate people over the long run.

Frederick Herzberg developed the motivation-maintenance model to describe individual motivational behavior. Herzberg found that maintenance factors do not motivate workers, but will cause dissatisfaction if they are withdrawn. Motivational factors, on the other hand, motivate workers when they are present; however, their absence will not necessarily create dissatisfaction. According to Herzberg, if there are few motivational factors in a job, maintenance factors will take on greater importance.

Managers must accomplish their goals through and with other people, and they are primarily responsible for motivating their subordinates. McGregor's Theory X and Theory Y reflect a pessimistic and optimistic view of human behavior, respectively. Theory X managers believe that employees do not really want to work, and can be motivated to do so only through close supervision and the threat of punishment. On the other hand, Theory Y managers will attempt to understand what truly motivates employees and will give them due respect and consideration.

William Ouchi formulated a third theory, Theory Z, which describes another management style. This style is based on a model within successful Japanese companies, and emphasizes treatment of employees like a family, lifetime employment, group decision making, and loyalty to the company.

Security

This management style has been found to satisfy both lower-level and higher-level needs.

Current research acknowledges that motivation is two-dimensional; it can be internal or external. Internal motivation is an intrinsic reward that a person feels when performing a job. A job that is enriched to provide added responsibility or opportunity for achievement will often trigger internal motivation. External motivation is initiated by another person and usually involves reward such as incentive pay, awards, and praise. Most authorities on motivation recommend that organizations attempt to provide their employees with a mix of external rewards and internal satisfaction.

KEY TERMS

motivation
motivational cycle
physiological needs
safety and security needs
social or belongingness needs
esteem needs
self-actualization needs
motivation-maintenance model
Theory X

Theory Y
Theory Z
collective compromise
internal motivation
vertical job loading
intrapreneurship
external motivation
incentives

REVIEW QUESTIONS

1. Based on what you have read in this chapter, how would you define motivation?

2. Why is the motivational cycle activated only by a felt need? List the steps in the cycle.

3. In what ways do Maslow's and Herzberg's theories differ? How are they similar?

4. Describe the needs present in Maslow's hierarchy. How do organizations attempt to meet these needs?

5. Explain the difference between a motivational and a maintenance factor.

6. Will both of these factors motivate workers? In what way?

7. Who is the best judge of what is and what is not a motivating factor for employees? Explain.

8. Describe McGregor's Theory X and Theory Y. What are the drawbacks of the carrot and stick approach?

9. What are some of the ways a Theory Y manager might motivate workers? What approach is a Theory Z manager likely to use?

10. What needs seem to be the strongest motivating factors over the long run? How can organizations meet these needs?

■ CASE 4.1

No Commissions Allowed

When Ceil Alperin took over the ladies' handbag department at R. H. Macy & Company's New York department store, she established several important goals for the department. One was to increase sales without increasing the number of salespeople or the way they were paid. Unlike some retail supervisors, Ms. Alperin was not in a position to use commissions to reward improved performance. All her employees were paid a straight wage without a commission, and all members of the staff were unionized. She also wanted to improve customer service and employee satisfaction.

This arrangement offered few motivational options, and this had a negative effect on employee attitudes. In other Macy's departments, customers were often shown a dressing room guarded by the dressing room "cop," who asked how many garments were included and gave them the appropriately colored tag. The original sales clerk rarely appeared for additional customer service. Many Macy's salespeople are painfully aware of the lack of personal committment to their job and customers. One employee commented, "There's a lot of talk about increasing customer service, but not much support from upper management."[1] Alperin knew she had to make some changes in order to improve the sales production in her department.

Her first step was to give all full-time employees their own counter area and their own line of merchandise. She also increased the responsibility of the sales staff for managing their own inventory and their own line of merchandise. Any salesperson who needed information or simply wished to offer the buying staff suggestions was encouraged to talk with the buyer of handbags. Previously, the sales staff had felt they were not supposed to talk to buyers.

Every week, Ms. Alperin brings the staff together for a meeting. At these meetings, she emphasizes the importance of customer service and reviews any changes in departmental policies and procedures. She also encourages employees to discuss problems and ask questions. These meetings provide Ms. Alperin with an opportunity to publicly recognize the accomplishments of employees.

Sources: Tom Peters, "The Store Is Where the Action Is," *U.S. News and World Report*, May 12, 1986, p. 58; Saul W. Gellerman, *Motivation and Productivity*, audio tape (San Diego, Cal.: University Associates).

Questions

1. What motivational needs did Ms. Alperin satisfy for her full-time employees?

---

[1] Tom Peters, "The Store Is Where the Action Is," U.S. News and World Report, May 12, 1986, p. 58.

X 2. Is Ms. Alperin a Theory X, Theory Y, or Theory Z manager?

3. Ms. Alperin achieved significant productivity gains because of a positive change in employees' attitudes. What motivational strategies did she use to achieve this success?

████ CASE 4.2

Publix's Remarkable Esprit

Daniel Yankelovich, respected industrial pollster and social analyst, explains: "Publix Super Markets Inc., is a remarkable operation. The people who work there are the most highly motivated people I have ever seen in a large organization. I admit I have seen people as highly motivated in a very small family organization. But . . . Publix is now a very large organization, and to see people with that quality of motivation is really outstanding."[1]

How can a corporation with 276 supermarkets and 51,000 employees generate this kind of motivation in its employees? Publix employees attribute it to maintenance of a small-company style and employee ownership. Employees often talk about their company as a family. A recent company magazine showed pictures of the twenty-six sets of twins who work for Publix. Throughout the year, Publix employees participate in the company sport, golf. Company founder George Jenkins built a par-three, nine-hole golf course next door to the company's Lakeland, Florida, warehouse so that employees could play a quick round whenever possible. Many supervisors take Wednesdays off to play golf and work on Saturdays. At Christmas everyone receives a bonus equal to about two weeks' salary. Each year 10 percent of the corporate profits are dedicated to the profit-sharing plan shared by all employees with over one thousand hours of work time.

The major incentive for Publix employees, however, is their option to purchase Publix stock. This stock is their personal property whether they stay with the company, retire, or resign. The Jenkins family can hold no more than 20 percent of the available stock; employees hold the rest. As a result, many long-time Publix employees have retired with a considerable sum of money. "It is not uncommon for people around here to retire with a half-million dollars," said Ben Brown, director of meat operations.[2]

The base salaries are $6.50 to $7.00 per hour, basically the equivalent of those at other supermarket chains. Absolutely everybody starts at the bottom—bagging groceries, working in the warehouse, or sweeping floors. After struggling for an advanced education and looking for the perfect job that compensates them for all their hard work, prospective employees in general are not very impressed with "entry-level positions." But Publix employees

---

[1] Robert Levering, *A Great Place to Work* (New York: Random House, 1988, p. 33.

[2] Robert Levering, Milton Moskowitz, and Michael Katz, *The 100 Best Companies to Work for in America* (New York: New American Library, 1985), p. 293.

have recognized the value of building their career with an organization that provides this motivational environment.

Sources: Robert Levering, *A Great Place to Work* (New York: Random House, 1988, pp. 33–39; Robert Levering, Milton Moskowitz, and Michael Katz, *The 100 Best Companies to Work for in America* (New York: New American Library, 1985), pp. 291–294; Robert Bork, Jr., "Call Him Old Fashioned," *Forbes*, August 26, 1985, p. 66.

Questions

1. How would you respond to a new job that offered $6.50 an hour and started in the warehouse loading trucks? Would this motivate you and fit into your picture of yourself? Why or why not?

2. What motivating factors are present at Publix that generate comments from employees such as: "I plan to be here until I retire," "They will have to drag me out of here," and "It's so much fun to be part of this organization"?

3. What motivating factors would you be seeking from an entry-level job?

SUGGESTED READINGS

Hall, Jay. *The Competence Connection*. The Woodlands, Tex.: Woodstead Press, 1988.

Herzberg, Frederick. *The Managerial Choice: To Be Efficient and To Be Human*. Salt Lake City, Utah: Olympus Publishing, 1982.

Herzberg, Frederick, Bernard Mausner, and Barbara Bloch Synderman. *The Motivation To Work*. New York: Wiley, 1959.

Levering, Robert. *A Great Place To Work*. New York: Random House, 1988.

McGregor, Douglas. *The Human Side of Enterprise*. New York: McGraw-Hill, 1960.

Maslow, Abraham H. *Motivation and Personality*. New York: Harper & Row, 1954.

Maslow, Abraham H. *The Farther Reaches of Human Nature*. New York: Viking Press, 1971.

Pinchot, Gifford, III. *Intrapreneurship*. New York: Harper & Row, 1985.

NOTES

1. D. R. Spitzer, "30 Ways to Motivate Employees to Perform Better," *Training/ HRD*, March 1980, p. 51.

2. Michael J. O'Connor and Sandra J. Merwin, *The Mysteries of Motivation* (Minneapolis: Performax Systems International, Inc., 1988), p. 1.

3. "Eastern and Western Management: Different Worlds," *Training and Development Journal*, August 1982, p. 11.

4. A. H. Maslow, *Motivation and Personality* (New York: Harper & Row, 1954).

5. H. C. Kazanas, *Effective Work Competencies for Vocational Education* (Columbus, Ohio: National Center for Research in Vocational Education, 1978), p. 12.

6. Stephen A. Stromp, "The Art of Corporate Communicating," *U.S. Air*, January 1989, p. 34.

7. James Cox, "Business Playing Softball," *USA Today*, July 8, 1988, p. B-1.

8. Joel Brockner, *Self-Esteem at Work* (Lexington, Mass.: Lexington Book, 1988), p. xi.

9. "How Bosses Get People to Work Harder," *U.S. News and World Report*, January 29, 1979, p. 63.
10. "Maslow's Term and Themes," *Training*, March 1977, p. 48.
11. "Eight Who Switched to Selling—Thanks to Hard Times," *Sales and Marketing Management*, September 13, 1982.
12. Frederick Herzberg, Bernard Mausner, and Barbara Bloch Snyderman, *The Motivation to Work* (New York: Wiley, 1959).
13. David J. Rachman and Michael H. Mescon, *Business Today*, 4th ed. (New York: Random House, 1985), p. 235.
14. John Nirenberg, "Constraints to Effective Motivation," *Supervisory Management*, November 1982, p. 27.
15. Jay Hall, *The Competence Connection* (The Woodlands, Tex.: Woodstead Press, 1988), p. 36.
16. Jay Hall, *The Competence Process* (The Woodlands, Tex.: Teleometrics International, 1980), p. 9.
17. Robert Levering, Milton Moskowitz, and Michael Katz, *The 100 Best Companies to Work for in America* (New York: New American Library, 1985), p. 231.
18. William G. Ouchi, *Theory Z: How American Business Can Meet the Japanese Challenge* (Reading, Mass.: Addison-Wesley, 1981).
19. Christopher Byron, "An Attractive Japanese Export: The XYZ's of Management Theory Challenge American Bosses," *Time*, March 2, 1983, p. 74.
20. Frederick Herzberg, *The Managerial Choice: To Be Efficient and To Be Human* (Salt Lake City, Utah: Olympus Publishing, 1982), p. 130.
21. Gary Schuman, "New Motivational Strategies to Pursue," *Management Solutions*, January 1987, p. 32.
22. Eric Berg, "Intrapreneurs: These Mavericks Shake Up Stodgy Firms," *Roanoke Times & World-News*, April 21, 1985, p. 32.
23. Ibid.

Chapter 5

Clarifying Personal and Organizational Values

CHAPTER PREVIEW

After studying this chapter, you will be able to

1. Explain the advantage of developing a strong sense of character.

2. Understand how personal values are formed.

3. Understand internal value conflicts.

4. Identify potential value conflicts with others.

5. Discuss the advantages and disadvantages of developing a strong organizational value system.

6. Learn how to harmonize personal values with those of the organization.

7. Understand corporate ethics and white-collar crime.

After Donald Douglas completed his engineering education at the Naval Academy and the Massachusetts Institute of Technology, he taught for a time at MIT. He also founded his own firm, which eventually came to be McDonnell Douglas.

It was important to Douglas that his company build and maintain for its customers a strong reputation for honesty. One of his major goals was to persuade Eddie Rickenbacker, who was president of Eastern Airlines at the time, to grant him Eastern's contract for its first fleet of jets. Rickenbacker leveled with him: Douglas's DC-8 model had the same problem as the 707 made by Boeing, a competitor for Eastern's business. The noise suppression on both kinds of jet engines was too weak. Promise me a quieter engine than Boeing's, he told Douglas, and I'll consider you for the contract.

Douglas knew that making this sale to Eastern would be a pivotal event in his company's success. But after discussing the technical points with other engineers, he determined there was not yet a solution to the noise problem Rickenbacker described. Douglas found himself in a dilemma. In order to get the contract, he realized, he'd have to make a promise he knew he couldn't keep.

In the end Douglas chose the only viable path he saw. "In all honesty," he reported to Rickenbacker, "I do not think I can make good on such a promise."

"Neither do I," agreed Rickenbacker. "But I was anxious to see if you were still honest with me." The next words he spoke convinced Douglas that truthfulness was his most reliable sales strategy. "You have a contract for $165 million," Rickenbacker said. "Now go and see what you can do about making those jet engines less noisy!"[1]

The decision Donald Douglas made to be honest with Mr. Rickenbacker was based on his personal values. Whether we are aware of it or not, values lie at the core of our personality and the culture of our organizations. On the basis of our value system, we determine what is important, which people to trust, what goals are worth pursuing, how we adapt to change, and what moral and ethical choices to make. Yet few people know consciously what their values are or what values guide the organization they work for. As a result, even though values represent the motivating force behind much of what is done, they remain a hidden, silent power.

In this chapter, we examine the importance of values, how they are formed, their influence, and the role they play in personal and organizational life.

THE STRENGTH OF CHARACTER

"I really like working with that guy! I can trust him." "She is the best supervisor I've ever had. I always know exactly where she stands. She has real character!" "When I'm in a conflict with someone, I know I can defeat them if they lack character. If they don't stand for something, they'll fall for anything." Statements like these sprinkle daily conversations in every organization. People by nature constantly make observations about other people's character and then base their own behaviors on the judgments they make.

What is character? One college graduate reflected, "I don't remember a course in high school or college called 'Character Building 101.' Where am I supposed to learn this skill that is at the root of human relations?" Good question!

Character applies to your personal standards of behavior. It encompasses your honor, integrity, veracity, constancy, and moral fiber.[2] It is based on your internal **values** and the resulting judgments about what is right and wrong. In Hamlet, Shakespeare wrote: "This above all—to thine own self be true. And it must follow, as the night the day, that thou canst not then be false to any man" (1.3.78–80). Being true to yourself is anything but easy if your coworkers' values and resulting attitudes and behaviors conflict with yours. The herd instinct is strong. To go against the tide is to risk rejection by your peers. As you develop a strong internal locus of control (meaning that your motivators are from an inner sense of right and wrong as opposed to external stimuli), you are able to make difficult decisions and still maintain your peers' friendship and respect. You also build strong self-respect and high self-esteem.

Where do we learn the set of values that determines our strength of character?

HOW PERSONAL VALUES ARE FORMED

We are not born with an internal set of values. We learn to measure the worth of things and ideas by observation and testing. Psychologists agree that individual values are formed early in life and are acquired from a variety of sources, as shown in Figure 5.1. Values are so deep-seated in our personality that they are never actually "seen." What we "see" is the way in which values manifest themselves through our attitudes, opinions, and behaviors.[3] For example, an individual may stay overtime to help a customer trace a lost order. We can see this behavior. The *attitude* displayed here is a willingness to help a customer solve a problem. The *value*, which serves as a foundation for this attitude, may be that of service to others or of loyalty to organizational policies.

Your values are more enduring than your attitudes. Although your attitudes toward various situations or people may change (see Chapter 2 for further understanding of attitude changes), values represent the deep preferences that motivate you. What really motivates you can only be discovered through careful examination and clarification of your personal value

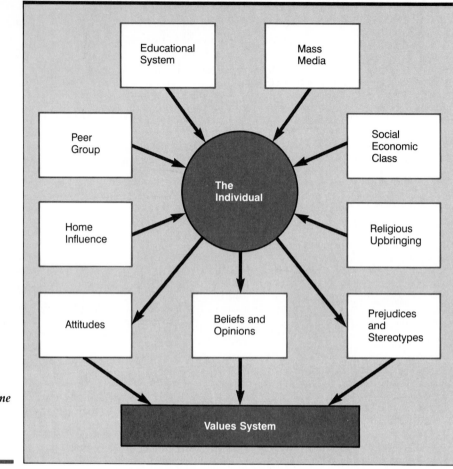

Figure 5.1
Influences That Determine
Your Value System
Source: Adapted from
Richard I. Evans: *Dialogue*
with Gordon Allport.

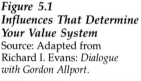

system. Once you clarify your values, you can pursue the career and select the organization that best fits your **value system.**

An understanding of values is equally important in understanding human behavior, since they so strongly influence people's actions. If people of different races, ethnic groups, religions, and backgrounds understand one another's value systems, they may be more appreciative and tolerant of differences in behavior. Similarly, work problems might be handled more effectively if management and labor have a better understanding of each other's values.

Environmental Influences

It has been said that values cannot be taught, but they are learned. Aristotle urged, "If you would understand virtue, observe the conduct of virtuous men." But where are these "virtuous men," the role models? Management consultant Charles Garfield, author of *Peak Performers, the New Heroes of American Business*, says: "The country has been hit hard by examples of shabby values. Where are our heroes? You look to business and you get the insider-trading scandals. You look to [our leaders] and you get Irangate. You look to religion and you get Jim and Tammy and Jimmy Swaggart. You look to sports and you get many examples of drug problems."[4]

Traditionally, values have been transmitted through the family, the church or synagogue, and the school. In certain sectors, one can observe the waning influence of these factors: many families are now single-parent, the influence of the church has decreased in what has become a very secular and legalistic society, and schools cannot reasonably be capable of instilling a sense of discipline, morality, and values that may not come from the family or the church.

Influence of the Family   A phenomenon of contemporary society is that there are many single-parent families. In this situation, where the resident

"Well, what did you expect to find on one of these new el-cheapo flights to Europe—our kind of people?"
Reprinted by permission of NEA, Inc.

parent may be overwhelmed with responsibility for career and family, may be bitter about his or her broken marriage, and may be struggling with his or her own values, the degree of stability necessary for the transmission of positive values may not be present.

Influence of Religion   Many people learn about positive and negative values through religious training. This may be through the accepted teachings of the church, religious literature such as the Koran and the Bible, or through individuals in the churches or synagogues who provide positive role models. Studies show, however, that religious observance is falling off. In a society which has become strongly secular, "wrong" or "right" may come to be identified by whether one is "caught in the act" or not, or by the letter of the law.   *New Age !*

Influence of the Schools   Many people believe that schools have been put in the position of providing training in values that students may not receive through their family or their church. In fact, in the 1970s, many schools included values clarification in their curricula. In response to objections to this from various factions of society, who feared that values would be "imposed" on children, these specific courses on values clarification were phased out of the curriculum. Teachers, reflecting their society, may or may not be good role models, and violence and drug abuse are not uncommon in many schools.

Influence of the Media   What, then, seems to be the strongest means of transmitting values to children? One must admit that training and learning through observation and repetition is often carried on by television and the loud and often amoral voices of mass entertainment. Of course, just as there are responsible parents and teachers, and effective religious influences, there are also positive media influences that teach basic values. "The Bill Cosby Show" has been recognized for its straightforward communication of strong moral values. "Sesame Street" has a positive influence on children's understanding of right and wrong behaviors. But most of mainstream television and entertainment deals with the things and people money can buy. The cover of a 1989 *TV Guide* stated that greed, ambition, and sex are the "in" things on television.[5] Even commercials send confusing messages. Isuzu ads involve a car salesman making outlandish statements about his cars while subtitles appear on the bottom of the screen disclaiming his comments. This leaves the viewer unsure of whom to believe. News reports are filled with coverage of negative behaviors and events because "bad news" events attract the attention of viewers.

   The reality is that you, as an adult, are the only one who can decide for yourself what it is *you* will value and who you will choose as a role model. This discriminating behavior is a great part of the maturing process. Morris Massey, noted psychologist, describes the most powerful process in establishing your values as **modeling**—basing your behavior on people *you* admire and embracing the qualities those people demonstrate. The heroes and heroines you discover in childhood and adolescence help you form a "dominant value direction" that complements your basic personality.[6] In organizations, mentors can serve as value models. They not only teach younger workers job skills, but they also transmit the values of the organization to their protégés.

Each generation is influenced by different events and different models (see Figure 5.2). A corporate manager of the 1950s, raised on "Father Knows Best," John Wayne, and President Eisenhower, and the manager of a food co-op in the 1990s, raised on "Miami Vice" and *Rambo*, will use some of the same organizing skills but for different purposes. Value differences account for much of the conflict between younger workers and older managers. More will be said about this issue later in this chapter.

The Valuing Process

There is no doubt that our value orientation has been influenced by our culture, our family, our peer group, our education, and countless other sources of which we may or may not be aware.[7] However, if we can understand the forces that have conditioned us, we are in a better position to consider alternatives. Sidney Simon, Leland Howe, and Howard Kirschenbaum suggest that we can learn a valuing process that can help us clarify and develop our values. In their book, *Values Clarification*, they recommend a valuing process that includes five dimensions.

Thinking We live in a confusing world where making choices about how to live our lives can be difficult. We are confronted by more choices than in previous generations, and we are surrounded by a bewildering array of alternatives.[8] The development of thinking skills is an important step in the process of developing clear values. As Simon, Howe, and Kirschenbaum noted, anything we can do to help people learn to think and to reason more effectively is useful in their value development.[9]

We need thinking skills to help us with the many issues of morality and ethics which surface every day in our lives. Of major importance is the development of "critical thinking" skills that help us distinguish fact from opinion, and supported from unsupported arguments. To develop critical thinking skills, many educators today are encouraging students to engage in higher-level thinking that involves analysis, synthesis, and evaluation.

In recent years many organizations have initiated programs designed to clarify the firms' values orientations. Some of these programs focus on the improvement of thinking and reasoning. At Chemical Bank, for example, about 250 vice presidents have taken part in two-day seminars on corporate values. Participants work through twelve case studies involving such issues as loan approvals, staff reductions, branch closings, and foreign loans.[10]

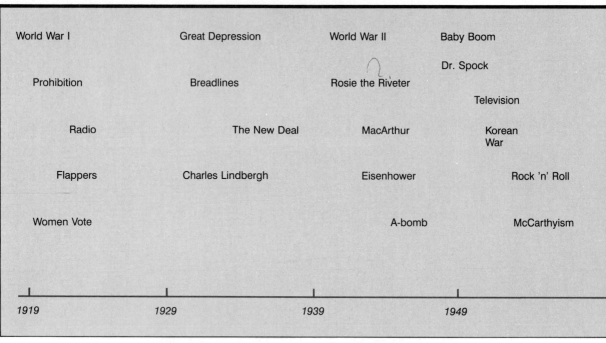

Figure 5.2
People and Events That Have Influenced the Formation of Values
Source: Adapted from Warren H. Schmidt and Barry Z. Posner, *Managerial Values and Expectations*

Case studies provide a good training method; choices (reflecting values) are made after the consequences of the alternatives offered are considered.

Feeling This dimension of the valuing process involves being "open to one's inner experience."[11] Chapter 1 introduced the concept of self-awareness, that is, gaining a better understanding of who you are and how your behavior influences other people. Increased levels of self-awareness help you become more fully aware of your attitudes toward others and help you determine your priorities in life. People who are "in touch" with their feelings, who understand what they prize and cherish, have taken an important step in the value development process.

Some of America's most profitable companies have created a climate in which employees can test their ideas and express their feelings at open meetings. At Ben and Jerry's Homemade Inc., staff meetings are held once a month. Production stops so that every employee can attend. Over coffee and doughnuts the employees exchange views on a wide range of issues. The open expression of feelings is never discouraged.[12]

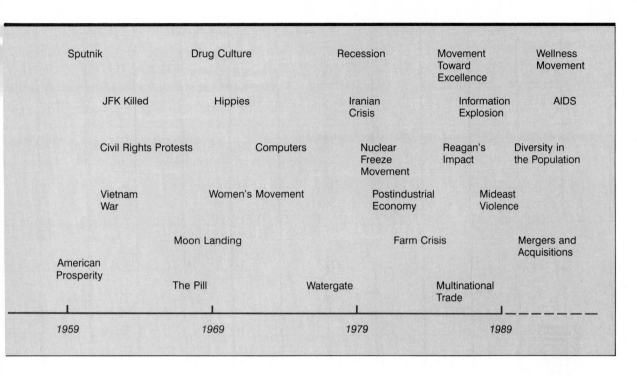

When people learn how to disclose distressful feelings such as anger, fear, or emotional hurt, they gain greater access to their inner experience, which is critical to value formation. Constructive self-disclosure can lead to a more open and supportive environment in the workplace.

3. *Communicating*   Values do not develop in a vacuum, but through an ongoing process of interaction with others. The ability to send and receive clear messages is, therefore, an important valuing skill.[13] This dimension, like other dimensions of the valuing process, contains several subprocesses, such as active listening; receiving clear messages filtered through emotions, body language, and the speaker's attitudes; and conflict resolution.

In Chapter 2 we noted that, after some careful soul searching, Stew Leonard adopted the "customer is always right" philosophy of doing business. He had to clarify his own views on this issue before he could communicate them to his employees. Once he determined that excellent customer service was the key to success in business, he had to build employee support for store policies and procedures that would result in a high level of customer

loyalty and repeat business. This required a great deal of person-to-person communication with his employees.

Choosing   Louis Rath, a well-known authority in values clarification, developed a step-by-step process—a values test—by which you can determine if you really value something. Rath states that values are the result of choices people make from several alternatives. These values must be freely selected, with no outside pressure.[14]

The valuing process, according to Rath, involves being well informed about alternatives and the consequences of various courses of action. One goal of the Chemical Bank seminars on corporate values is to let managers explore the consequences of alternative decisions.

Acting   Simon, Howe, and Kirschenbaum state that acting repeatedly upon our beliefs and acting consistently toward our goals increases the likelihood that our lives will have positive value to us.[15] Rath says that one way to test your values is to answer the question, Do I find that this value is persistent throughout my life?

One way to learn about the values held by another person is to observe that person's behavior. The Marriott Corporation is one of the most consistently successful service companies in America because the man at the top, J. W. Marriott, does not deviate from a series of basic beliefs about the proper way to operate a hotel. At nearly sixty years old, he still travels 200,000 miles a year in order to keep an eye on Marriott hotels and to keep in touch with his employees. Although his family worth is over $1 billion, he and his wife have lived in the same modest house for thirty-three years. His family and his church are the priorities in his life.[16] J. W. Marriott is a person who has incorporated a great deal of consistency in his life.

Terminal and Instrumental Values

Throughout your life your basic values may not change, but you may rearrange them in some sort of order or priority. Your priorities change as you mature and your needs and goals change. For example, early in your career, you may give education priority over earning money. After acquiring a full-time job, achieving material success and being accepted by coworkers may be more important.

Some values—such as security, family relationships, and spiritual growth—will continue to have high priority all through a person's life. Milton Rokeach calls these **terminal values**, representing goals you will strive to accomplish before you die. Other values will reflect the way you prefer to behave. Rokeach calls these **instrumental values**.[17] Each individual determines which of his or her values are instrumental and which are terminal. A list of some of these values is given in Table 5.1 .

People, Ideas, or Things?

Your interests, attitudes, and behavior often indicate whether your value system is oriented mainly toward people, ideas, or things. Someone who enjoys working with machinery, equipment, or other objects will have values that are oriented toward *things.* Other people may love to work with ideas and concepts, devising strategies or creating solutions to complex problems. They may be more interested in the theoretical than the practical

TABLE 5.1   Terminal and Instrumental Values

Terminal Values	Instrumental Values
Comfortable, prosperous, stimulating life	Ambitious and hard working
Sense of lasting contribution and accomplishment	Capable, competent, and effective
Equal opportunity for all	Cheerful, creative, courageous
Family security, loved ones taken care of	Independent, self-reliant, self-controlled
Freedom of choice and independence	Loving, affectionate
Enjoyable, leisurely life	Respectful, obedient, forgiving
Self-respect	Responsible and dependable
Social respect and admiration	Neat and tidy
	Polite and well-mannered

approach to problem solving. They are *idea* oriented. Still others are more comfortable working with people and find their greatest satisfaction in group activities, reflecting a value system that is *people* oriented.

You probably will not identify totally with any one category, but will tend to prefer one of these three value groupings. When people with different value orientations work together, conflicts can arise.

In the 1980s, American Telephone and Telegraph Company (AT&T) had to adjust to a more competitive, deregulated environment, which meant shifting from a somewhat passive sales and service approach to a more aggressive posture. One management faction, oriented toward products, wanted to make the switch quickly. Employees, they said, could be trained to sell services and equipment to the public in short seminars. But another faction, oriented more toward people, was concerned about the impact such a change would have on employees. They called in a consulting firm which found that an abrupt shift in company goals and values from "universal service" to "universal selling" would be a psychological shock to employees who had been oriented toward service. They recommended that the company introduce the new orientation as carefully and thoughtfully as they had instilled the previous one in workers. Since it took many years for the AT&T culture to develop, any attempt to make rapid changes in established policies and procedures might have negative consequences.

THINKING/LEARNING STARTERS

1. Identify those events and role models that have been influential in forming your value system. Are those of your childhood and adolescence still important to you?
2. Rank the terminal values listed in Table 5.1 in the order of importance to you. Do the same with the list of instrumental values. Review the priorities revealed by your rankings. Do your priorities reflect a value system oriented most strongly toward people, ideas, things, or a combination of these?

VALUE CONFLICTS

In the same way that common values tend to unite people, conflicting values can create divisions between them. One of the major causes of conflict within organizational settings is clashes between individuals' values. Dr. Don Beck, a leading proponent of value system analysis, points out that when it comes to values, people *are* different.

These differences pop out in offices, factories . . . anywhere and anytime people get together. . . . They prefer different jobs, work environments, learning systems, social relationships, and other expressions of their uniqueness.[18]

In fact, many observers suggest that organizations look for **value conflicts** when addressing the problem of declining productivity. The trouble may lie not so much in work schedules or production routines as in the mutual distrust and misunderstanding brought about by clashes in workers' and managers' value systems.

Internal Value Conflicts

Value conflicts within an individual usually force the person into choosing between strongly held values.

At 9:30 A.M. on a beautiful autumn day traffic was normal on Interstate 71 near Columbus, Ohio. Then a miracle happened that millions of people only dream about—the back door of an armored truck flew open and bags of money spilled out. Cars behind the truck hit the bags, splitting them open, and hundreds of thousands of dollars rained over the highway for more than a mile. When motorists realized that it was not maple leaves but $100 bills blowing about, they braked in the middle of the highway to help clean up. When the police arrived, two hundred people were swarming about, making off with whatever they could carry. A million dollars blew over Interstate 71 that day, and by late November only $100,000 was returned in answer to the authorities' pleas. Melvin Kiser, a telephone repairman, walked off with $57,000 that morning. Kiser kept the cash for a while. "It took me two hours to get a hold of myself," he said. He was among the first to turn his money in and later got a 10 percent reward. Many people have told Kiser that he was crazy to return the money.[19]

Eric was the director of training and development for a large corporation, a job he considered to be a step along the road to the position of administrator of office services. When he took over the job, he noticed that employees promoted to management positions from within the company were not given adequate management training and support. Eric felt a strong sense of responsibility to such people and proposed an in-house management development program. Upper management chose not to invest the time and money necessary for such a program. When Eric went to his mentor about this, the mentor told him to forget the training program proposal, since pursuing it further might jeopardize his promotions. Soon afterward, two employees talked with Eric about their desire to apply for supervisory positions. Eric knew that with proper training the two would probably succeed. Without it, they could fail. He found himself faced with a dilemma: should he press for the management development program and risk jeopardizing his career, or should he take his mentor's advice and drop his concern about management training, leaving the employees with supervisory aspirations to sink or swim? Eric's was a tough decision, but a typical predicament resulting from a conflict of internal values.

You may experience many kinds of value conflicts on the job. As a manager, you may be torn between loyalty to the workers and loyalty to upper management. As an employee you may find yourself in conflict between fulfilling family obligations and devoting the time and energy required to succeed at work. Whichever value proves to be the stronger over time is the one that will determine which choice you make. How you resolve these internal value conflicts will greatly affect your attitude toward yourself, your career, and the people close to you.

Value Conflicts with Others

Some of the most common interpersonal value conflicts arise between workers of different generations, races, cultures, ethnic backgrounds, or religions; between men and women; and between supervisors and workers. Older and younger employees may clash over different interpretations of the work ethic and the priorities of job and personal life.

> The profile of today's average worker is: A thirty-four-year-old baby boomer with two children and a working spouse who plans to work past retirement (and expects to because of the insecurities of the Social Security System), who does not belong to a union and would not consider joining one, who is willing to accept a certain amount of risk in exchange for the possibility of being rewarded for superior performance, who is increasingly likely to have some sort of flexible work schedule—or would prefer one. Increasingly, that "average worker" is a woman.[20]

A Public Agenda Foundation study determined that the top ten values the average worker expects to satisfy at work are as follows:

1. work with people who treat them with respect
2. have the opportunity to do interesting work
3. receive recognition for good work
4. have the chance to develop their skills
5. work for people who listen if they have ideas about how to do things better
6. think for themselves rather than just carry out instructions
7. have the opportunity to see the end results of their work
8. work for an efficient manager
9. perform a job that is not too easy
10. feel well informed about what is going on in the organization[21]

When this "new age" worker is placed in a position subordinate to a manager with the "puritan" work ethic who was raised to place high value on good salary, good benefits, and a spouse to take care of the kids and house, there is bound to be conflict. Put the "new ager" in a managerial role with the "puritan," and sparks will fly unless the manager and the employee learn to appreciate each other's priorities and perspective on work and life.

Value conflicts based on age, race, ethnic background, gender, or religious differences often provoke deep emotional reactions among workers. Unless such conflicts are handled skillfully, confrontation can make the situation worse, not better. The Fiber Industries subsidiary of Celanese Corp. in Charlotte, North Carolina, developed a ten-session training program to teach employees how to deal with such value conflicts.[22] The first session outlined the issues to be resolved, which ranged from interracial distrust to on-the-job discrimination experienced by women. In bringing up concerns, workers were encouraged to talk about the kind of workplace they wanted. This strategy focused their attention on improving the quality of life for everyone, not just for one group. The remaining sessions helped employees discover the common ground they shared and provided methods for solving their differences.

At the end of the workshop, employees felt they had forged a set of values that reflected more clearly their own expectations and needs. For example, managers were surprised to learn how strongly workers valued knowing more about the "whys" of business. All levels of employees were impressed by the commonality of their work values and their standards for personal relationships. Through the techniques and methods provided in the workshop, employees learned firsthand the value of using nonjudgmental attitudes, mutual respect, and understanding in handling value conflicts.

THINKING/LEARNING STARTERS

1. How have your personal values influenced your choice of a school or career? For which values did compatibility between yourself and the organization seem most important?
2. What value conflicts have you experienced within yourself? With others? What were the values involved? How did you resolve these conflicts?
3. Have you ever experienced a "generation gap" conflict with anyone? How did differing value systems influence the conflict? As you begin to understand value differences between generations, how can you offset such conflicts in the future?

DEVELOPMENT OF ORGANIZATIONAL VALUES

Like personal values, organizational values are forged over a number of years and are strongly influenced by key people in the organization as well as by events and conditions in the environment, as shown in Figure 5.3. For example, changes in the competitive or legal environment will cause changes within the organization as management responds to new conditions. Yet such responses do not take place haphazardly. Each organization has developed its own particular guidelines.

As noted in Chapter 1, every organization has a culture of its own, guided by a value system that acts as a standard for behavior, goal setting, and strategic decision making. Tom Peters and Robert Waterman, authors of *In Search of Excellence*, doubt that a company can be excellent without having clear values.[23]

A value system provides direction for the countless decisions made each day, at all levels of the organization. This is particularly valuable in today's turbulent, rapidly changing global economy. Choices or options that run counter to the organization's basic values are either rejected or simply not considered. The Dayton-Hudson Corp., a diversified retailing company,

Figure 5.3
Influences Affecting
Organizational Values

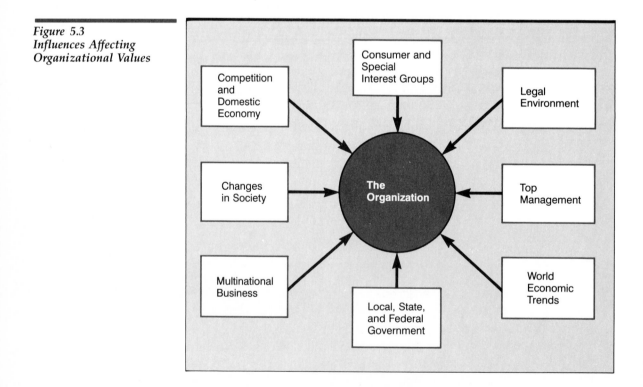

provides a good example of a corporation that has made a strong commitment to maintaining an organizational value system. The following information appears in their statement of philosophy:

> The policy of the corporation is to maintain a consistently high standard of business conduct, ethics and social responsibility. Individual employees are expected to demonstrate high levels of integrity and objectivity, unencumbered by conflicting interests in all decisions and actions affecting the corporation.[24]

Organizational values also have an impact on human relations within the organization. The value structure will indicate which matters will receive the most attention—public relations, finance, research and development, or sales. In the same way, the value structure will also influence whose input will be taken most seriously. If the value system determines what is most important and whose opinion is most important, it will also determine who will be the most respected—engineers, marketers, laborers, or financial advisers. This respect in turn plays an important role in determining who rises to the top of the organization. If research and development is the overriding value in the organization, then scientists, engineers, and technicians will tend to be promoted and occupy the top jobs. If service is an important value, field service and sales personnel will have the strongest support.

Procter & Gamble is a tightly disciplined organization dedicated to high performance. To achieve its high standards, P&G believes that the corporation's interests must be inseparable from those of its employees. The company carefully nurtures its employees, hiring at the entry level and promoting strictly from within. Throughout its history P&G has been a leader in employee benefits.

- Starting in 1885, in a move that stood traditional management strategy on its head, Procter & Gamble employees got Saturday afternoons off, and were paid for them.

- Two years later employees were able to join a P&G profit-sharing program, still the longest-running such program for American industrial workers.

- As early as 1915, P&G offered its employees comprehensive sickness, disability, and life insurance coverage. At that time only a handful of companies in the country were doing so.

- Production personnel at P&G have enjoyed an employment "guarantee" of at least forty-eight weeks of regular work per year since 1923. In return, workers must perform their jobs consistently well.

- P&G's current and retired employees together own approximately 20 percent of the company's stock, made available for purchase through a payroll-deduction program.

- In a 1980 survey, the U.S. Chamber of Commerce rated the quality of employee-benefits programs in 983 firms. P&G placed in the top 4 percent.[25]
- The company has liberal maternity and paternity leave policies.
- In 1987 the company celebrated its 150th year in business by asking employees to suggest a motto; over eight thousand responded, and the winner was "Excellence Through Commitment and Innovation."

Another strong value at P&G is the commitment to innovation and risk taking. Harley Procter, cousin to one of Procter & Gamble's founders, continually sought ways to reach consumers and increase sales. He was among the first to use display advertising, radio commercials, and an independent sales force. His innovative use of new technology and consumer trends kept the company at the top of its field. P&G is committed to the value of taking care of its employees, and its tremendously high sales volume and considerable product development are a direct result of the concomitant value placed on the importance of the consumer.

The Risks of Developing Strong Organizational Values

There are times when having a strong value system may be a problem as well as a source of organizational strength. It is important to be aware of some of the risks involved in building a strong set of values.

Obsolescence Changes in the environment may make an organization's value system obsolete. AT&T's early difficulties in moving from a service to a sales orientation is a case in point. Newer companies such as MCI Communications Corporation, GTE Sprint Communications Corp., and Telecom USA, have moved quickly to capture part of AT&T's market. Their value systems are already geared toward offering competitive consumer products, whereas AT&T has had to manage a change in values.

Resistance to Change New or expanding markets may challenge an organization's traditional values as it tries to change from one method of operation to another. Within recent years, Sears, Roebuck tried to become a merchandiser on the model of a department store such as Macy's. The new venture quickly faltered. Employees, trained to deliver value to middle-income consumers, found the change to a Macy's-style operation unfamiliar and difficult. The strategy, although potentially promising, had to be abandoned.

Inconsistency Management must adhere to the values it intends to promote. Executives cannot emphasize to employees the value of improving

Because of increased competition from K mart and Wal-Mart, Sears revamped its entire management and pricing structure to prepare for the 1990s.
Vic DeLucia/NYT Pictures

customer service and at the end of the year reward financial performance over customer service. By doing so they confuse employees and undermine the organizational value system.

One organization that has held consistently to its value system is McDonald's Corp. Throughout the world, from Australia to Europe to Japan, the consistent high standard of cleanliness, service, and quality assurance at every McDonald's restaurant is impressive.[26]

Values and the Manager

The values of management, particularly top executives, set the tone for the entire organization. The role of the manager is, among other things, to create an environment where good people make good decisions. A manager can most effectively encourage behavior that follows the organizational value system by providing a good example. When leaders adhere to organizational values, workers follow. In addition, managers must be flexible and sensitive enough to supervise people whose value systems and expectations differ from their own personal value systems. Yet the stereotype of the typical American manager has been that of a tough-minded pragmatist who makes decisions based on hard facts and who keeps personal feelings out of the decision-making process. Given a choice, so the stereotype goes, the manager would choose the organization over every other consideration.

This stereotype does not necessarily fit the managers of today. Managers of the post-Depression era were commonly driven by a strong work

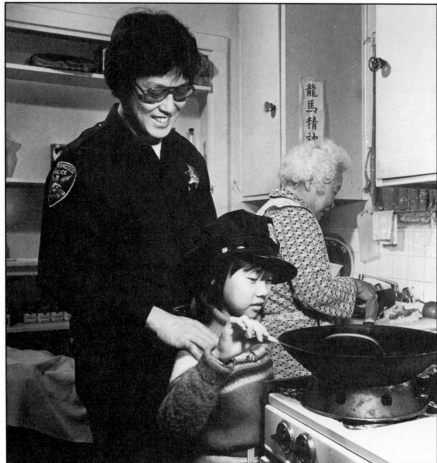

A personal value system often includes a balance between home and work environments. © Robert Holmgren/Jeroboam, Inc.

ethic and placed a premium on the security of their jobs and incomes. Today's better educated managers tend to place a high premium on work that allows for employee growth and development. Some of them reject their parents' aspirations of upward mobility and dedication to work in favor of a lifestyle that leaves them time to pursue leisure activities. When ranking items from a table of instrumental and terminal values developed by Milton Rokeach, they tend to list ambition below responsibility and honesty as an important attribute (see Table 5.2).[27]

For generations, organizations expected their managers to put their company priorities over family concerns. This is much less the case now. Lee Iacocca, for instance, refuses to work weekends. He believes it is important to spend time with his family, and he has been known to reprimand Chrysler executives who claim they have no time for a vacation.

TABLE 5.2   **Managers Rank Values and Attributes**

Values		Attributes	
Top Five	*Bottom Five*	*Top Five*	*Bottom Five*
Self-respect	Pleasure	Honesty	Obedience
Family security	World of beauty	Responsibility	Cleanliness
Freedom	Salvation	Capability	Cheerfulness
Accomplishment	Social recognition	Ambition	Politeness
Happiness	Equality	Independence	Helpfulness

Source: Rick Wartzman, "Nature or Nurture? Study Blames Ethical Lapses on Corporate Goals," *The Wall Street Journal*, October 9, 1987, p. 27. Reprinted by permission of *The Wall Street Journal*, © Dow Jones & Company, Inc., 1987. All Rights Reserved Worldwide.

Recently we have seen an apparent shift in the values on the part of women who rise to management positions. In one study, 60 percent of the women managers surveyed found greater satisfaction in their careers than in home life, compared with 37 percent of the males. The women surveyed were more willing than the men to relocate, to work longer hours, to accept job promotions, and to give up outside activities. They also seemed more confident that they would fulfill their life's professional and personal ambitions and were more likely to feel that their values were compatible with those of the organization.[28]

Like the shifts in personal values over the past decades, management values have also been influenced by changes in society. Table 5.3 shows some of the value shifts that have occurred in the past few years. The shifts in management values reflect the change in public awareness and concern about the environment, the impact of equal employment opportunity and antidiscrimination laws, the liberal movements of the 1960s and 1970s, and the growing trend toward interdependence and worldwide economic markets. American managers seem to realize that the entrepreneur works within a highly interdependent, complex environment.

THINKING/LEARNING STARTERS

1. What do you think are the most important values a manager should have? To what extent do you agree with the values and attributes chosen by managers, as listed in Table 5.2? To what extent do you agree with their ranking?
2. To which element of each pair do you give higher priority: home life and career; personal interests and organizational demands; concern for people and your own ambitions? Have there been shifts in these personal values in various periods of your life?

TABLE 5.3   Changing Management Values

Past Value	Current and Future Values
1. A business manager's sole responsibility: to optimize stockholder wealth; operational management dominant	1. Profit still dominant but modified by the belief that a business manager has other social responsibilities
2. Business performance measured solely by economic standards	2. Performance measured by economic and social standards
3. Emphasis on quantity of products	3. Emphasis on quality as well as quantity of products
4. Authoritarian management	4. Permissive/democratic management
5. People subordinate	5. People dominant
6. Financial accounting	6. Financial, human resources, and social accounting
7. Short-term intuitive planning	7. Long-range comprehensive, structured planning
8. Little concern for the social costs of production	8. Increasing concern for internalizing social costs of production
9. Centralized decision making	9. Decentralized and small-group decision making
10. Entrepreneurs who prosper by concentrating on exploiting opportunities they perceive in the environment	10. Entrepreneurs who are able to innovate but who also understand political, technical, social, human, and other forces influencing their organizations
11. Business standing aloof from government	11. Business-government cooperation and convergence in planning

Source: Adapted with permission of Macmillan Publishing Company from *Management Strategy and Policy,* 3/e by G. A. Steiner, J. B. Miner, and E. R. Gray. Copyright © 1986 by Macmillan Publishing Company.

HARMONIZING PERSONAL AND ORGANIZATIONAL VALUES

When individuals achieve management status, it is natural to assume their values are closely aligned with their organization's values. This harmony between personal and organizational values leads to success for the individuals as well as for the organization. It is also true that, in many highly successful firms, those employees below management status such as line workers, clerical personnel, and supervisors also share the basic values of the organization. These **shared values** are perhaps the strongest bond among workers in an organization.

Individuals who understand and clarify their own personal values are able to choose the career and organization that best suit their needs. For example, if you have a strong value orientation toward helping others, you might choose to work in a nonprofit service organization rather than a manufacturing plant. If you value self-development and your organization is committed to developing the skills and talents of its employees, you probably will feel that your personal values and those of the organization are in harmony. When this harmony exists, both the organization and the individual have a greater opportunity for success than if there is discord.

Barry Posner and J. Michael Munson of the University of Santa Clara (California) are convinced that value testing should be as much a part of matching employees to jobs as administering vocational interest tests. They say, "Knowing something about an individual's value system is essential in designing effective motivators . . . Employers must be sure that the rewards they offer are actually rewards."[29] They have found that subordinates with values similar to those of their manager often established better personal and working relationships than do those whose values differ from those of their superiors.

It is management's responsibility to enlighten employees about the organization's value system at the time of the job-entry interviews and to reinforce these corporate values through personal example, training sessions, group policies, and continual evaluation and feedback. When employees discover that they are able to express their personal values in the work they do, they are likely to feel more competent and fulfilled. Shared values are built by the employees' dual commitment to their individual values as well as by corporate interests and expectations.

Organizations that have employees with strongly shared values that harmonize with corporate values follow the Japanese style of management. In the Japanese system, the collective sense of responsibility for the work and success of the company serves as the foundation for the worker-management relations. This value expresses the belief that everything important happens as a result of teamwork or collective effort. This system puts little emphasis on rewarding individual effort or in singling out individuals for special recognition.[30] The same attitude is gaining momentum in American organizational culture in the form of self-management teams. In such organizations, employees come to think of themselves as "Motorolans," "IBMers," or "Pepsi-Cola People," not simply employees who happen to work for a particular organization.

In her book *The Change Masters*, Rosabeth Kanter warns, "Shared philosophy—family feelings—can't be stimulated or imposed artificially because top management wants to create a Japanese-style organization; it has to derive from the way work is done."[31] Such feelings must come from the employees' inner satisfaction that they are part of the organization's total success. Kanter identifies the typical organizational culture in America as overly centralized in terms of power, overly authoritarian, resistant to change, and extremely compartmentalized with respect to work units. As more companies examine the success of IBM, Procter & Gamble, Hewlett-Packard, Digital Equipment Corp., and Motorola, Inc., they are recognizing the power of shared values and focusing greater attention on the value system within their own corporate cultures.

CORPORATE VALUES AND ETHICS

It is in the area of corporate ethics that one can see clearly how the values of top management set the course for the organization. Ethics, as distinguished from values, is the study of right and wrong behavior, usually based on a moral or religious doctrine. However, many corporations are not asking "What's right or wrong," but only "Are we breaking the law?" Most managers working in this atmosphere believe that unethical behavior is largely dependent on the organizational climate—especially the actions of one's immediate boss. The issue of corporate ethics is receiving increasing attention from the public, various levels of government, and business itself.

A heavily publicized violation of business ethics involved the Ford Pinto, a car that tended to catch fire easily when it rolled over or was hit from the rear. Engineering documents proved Ford knew of the condition but decided it was cheaper to pay damages than fix it. Another example involved the Chrysler Corporation. When it was convicted and fined over $3 million for disconnecting odometers of "executive driven cars" and then selling them as "new," Chrysler president Lee Iacocca explained his position at a news conference and was commended for his approach to the problem. At one point he tried to spread the blame, saying that disengaging odometers used to be normal practice throughout the automotive industry. At another point, however, he admitted, "Did we screw up? You bet we did. We're human, and sometimes people do some pretty dumb things."[32] That seems to be the trend today. Actions are "dumb" and "stupid," but too few corporate leaders admit they are "wrong."

Ethical standards and corporate responsibilities are handled differently around the world. For many years Japan has had a custom that when a company does something that damages its community and its customers, even inadvertently, the chief executive officer takes personal responsibility and publicly apologizes, sometimes on his knees.

The Problem of Corporate Crime

James O'Toole, author of *Vanguard Management*, said: "No company has ever gotten into financial trouble because they adhered to ethical principles."[33] By the same token, however, many of America's largest corporations have gotten into serious trouble by ignoring ethical principles. In recent years the media have carried headlines concerning organizations involved in corporate crime.

> **Item:** Within one month of introducing its Clean Water Machine, Norelco Consumer Products Division knew its machines' filters were tainted with methylene chloride, a probable carcinogen. In 1988 a Federal Trade Commission judge ruled that the company deliberately sold 186,000 contaminated filters over a four-year period.[34]
>
> **Item:** The Hertz Corporation has admitted to overcharging their customers and insurers $13 million for repairs to damaged rental cars.[35]
>
> **Item:** Rockwell International Corp. has been indicted by a federal grand jury for defrauding the Air Force.[36]
>
> **Item:** The U.S. Chamber of Commerce estimates that white-collar crime robs organizations of up to $40 billion annually.[37]

These items represent only a small fraction of the corporate crime that goes on today. The majority of executives involved are rarely caught or brought to trial. What would you do if your organization asked you to do something you know is illegal or dishonest? This question led Henry Makow, a part-time professor at the University of Manitoba, Canada, to design a game called "A Question of Scruples." There are no right or wrong answers to this game and very few rules. The point of the game is the conversation sparked by questions such as "In the supermarket, you send a dozen packages tumbling into the aisle. No one sees you. Do you walk away?" One corporate executive commented, "After I played it [Scruples] with my attorney, I told him, 'I don't think I want to do business with you anymore.'"[38]

Corporate Ethics Gain Emphasis

Most people realize that unethical conduct is self-destructive and generates more unethical conduct. Therefore, entrepreneurs, corporations, and colleges are beginning to do something about it.

Alvin Burger, former owner of "Bugs" Burger Bug Killers, Inc., has founded The Society of Ethical Entrepreneurs (SEE). In order to join this group, an entrepreneur must subscribe to two basic tenets: "I and my company have an ongoing obligation to be fair, scrupulously honest, and ethical with my customers, suppliers, employees, and creditors"; and "I and my company have the obligation to give the highest possible quality goods or services to the customer and to unconditionally guarantee the foregoing."[39]

Alvin Burger founded the Society of Ethical Entrepreneurs to promote and recognize ethical behavior on the part of organizations.
Debra Lex

TOTAL PERSON INSIGHT

66 All organizations have a stake in the way their employees behave, and the way those actions may be interpreted by customers, government regulatory agencies and the courts, after the fact. Recent scandals in the defense and financial industries probably have done more to focus public consciousness on business ethics than any events since Watergate. 99

Chris Lee

Corporations are addressing the ethics issue. Boeing has line managers leading training sessions with CEO involvement. Its ethics committee reports directly to the board of directors, and employees have a toll-free number to report any ethical violation they observe. Johnson & Johnson has developed a "Credo" of corporate values and conducts companywide meetings to challenge the Credo's tenets as well as surveys to ascertain employees' compliance. Xerox has established an ombudsman that reports directly to the CEO identifying compliance with Xerox's new handbook, which includes policy statements emphasizing integrity, concern for people, and the organization's values and policies. Corporations are adopting codes of ethics, and hundreds of consultants are being hired to ensure "integrity" in corporate cultures.[40]

Many business executives see greater emphasis being placed on corporate values and ethics by top management. According to George Coombe, executive vice president and general counsel of the BankAmerica Corp., "The situation is very different today from what it was in the past. Most major corporations now have a law-compliance mechanism in effect, and more boards of directors are personally addressing this question than ever before."[41]

Harvard Business School now requires M.B.A. students to take a three-week course on business ethics. Stanford, Columbia, and Dartmouth are following the lead and are integrating ethics education into their management curricula. In 1987, Harvard Business School was given $23 million by John S. R. Shad, the former chairman of the Securities and Exchange Commission, to support ethics research. The Wharton School recently received a grant from the Exxon Corporation to incorporate more ethics into Wharton's curriculum. There is an obvious effort to defeat the problem before it exists by offering ethics training to the business people of the future.

Values and Ethics in
International Business

If the situation is complex on the domestic scene, values and ethical issues become even more complicated at the international level. The subject is too broad to treat in detail in this chapter, but we can provide an overview of some of the conflicts that exist in international business.

Foreign Corporate Ethics   Just as unethical business practices are carried on in some American businesses, there are foreign countries where bribery, under-the-table payments, kickbacks, and other practices considered illegal in the United States are part of everyday business. Many company managers in these foreign countries are underpaid and look to these additional "revenue" sources to supplement their incomes. It is also true that organized crime is affecting management and employees throughout the world. An American firm that wants to do business in these countries may find itself at a serious competitive disadvantage when it does not conform to the local value system.

Foreign Corporate Cultures   The nations of the world are becoming increasingly interdependent. It is ironic that Americans, who have been instrumental in making the world smaller, are often quite unprepared to deal effectively with persons from different cultures. Each culture has its own human relations "language" and customs that, when understood by foreigners, can enhance respect for other countries' value systems. This understanding can increase the chances of effective human relations. Here are some rules of protocol that exist in some representative countries.[42]

Japan   Trade between the United States and Japan has increased tremendously since the end of World War II. As Americans complete business transactions with the Japanese, they are identifying value differences. For instance, Japanese never say no in public. Furthermore, *naniwabushi*, getting on close personal terms with someone so that she or he will owe you a favor, is a commonly accepted business practice. In this environment, potentially awkward obligations could arise from accepting gifts from business acquaintances. In addition, the Japanese value system stresses teamwork, not individualism. Employees feel that they are part of a "family." In American organizations, people who stand out for their high achievements are rewarded. In Japan, they may be reprimanded.

France   In business matters, the French tend to be prompt about considering a decision, but like to examine all the details involved; therefore, decisions can be slow in coming. Once made, however, they are expressed candidly—whether the decision is in your favor or against you. The French operate within a highly bureaucratic culture. Their management styles tend to be impersonal and standardized, with rigid procedures and centralized hierarchies.

Italy   Shaking hands is the expected accompaniment to a verbal greeting with Italians in business situations. When addressing a university-educated Italian, certain titles should be used: *dottore* for liberal arts, *avvocato* for law, etc.

People's Republic of China   Contrary to the North American custom, Chinese people are likely to express esteem through physical affection with members of the same, rather than the opposite sex. The use of titles is very important to the Chinese: "Committee Member," "Factory Manager," "General," etc.

In joint ventures between nations, such as those in the automobile industry, it is important for all parties to recognize value differences and to spend time and effort building mutual respect and understanding.

The True "Transnational" Company   As more firms do business in other nations, they are realizing the importance of reflecting this international reality, not only on the balance sheet but also in the board room. Ciba-Geigy Corporation, a Swiss company, has put a foreign director on its executive board and conducts its meetings in English. Such practices can increase understanding of one another's value systems and help develop a more uniform code of ethics.

SUMMARY

A strong sense of character applies to your personal standards of behavior. It is based on your internal values and your judgment of what is right and wrong. Your values are the personal worth or importance you assign to an object or idea. People's values systems serve as the foundation for their attitudes, preferences, opinions, and behaviors.

Personal values are largely formed early in life and are influenced by parents, religious upbringing, schools, life experiences, the media, and changes in society's values. Howard Kirschenbaum suggests you can learn a valuing process to help clarify your values. This process includes five dimensions: thinking, feeling, communicating, choosing, and acting. Milton Rokeach has written that values can be categorized as terminal or instrumental. Most people's value systems are oriented toward ideas, people, or things.

Internal value conflicts involve choices between strongly held values. Value conflicts with others, often based on age, racial, religious, gender, or ethnic differences, require skilled intervention before they can be resolved.

Corporate values act as standards for behavior, goal setting, and strategic decision making. They also have an impact on human relations within the organization. They are strongly influenced by top management, which plays a significant role in setting the corporate climate by exemplifying and communicating it to others. By establishing strong corporate values, however, organizations may risk obsolescence, resistance to change, and inconsistencies between various departments.

The personal value systems of many modern managers are considerably different from those of previous generations. Changes in societal values have helped alter managers' values.

Shared values unify employees in an organization by providing guidelines for behavior and decisions and a feeling of belonging. Employees can choose the career and organization that best suits their needs by ensuring that their personal values are compatible with the values of the organization in which they work.

Corporate values and ethics on both the domestic and international levels are receiving increasing attention. As multinational organizations increase in number, the individuals involved will need to consciously examine their values and ethical standards in order to effectively deal with the differing value structures from each country. Top management, governments, and the public are holding organizations more accountable for their actions than in the past.

KEY TERMS

character
values
value system
value conflicts
shared values

modeling
terminal values
instrumental values
ethics

REVIEW QUESTIONS

1. How do values differ from attitudes, opinions, or behavior?

2. How are our values formed? How have the sources of our value systems changed in recent years?

3. Define terminal and instrumental values. How can clarifying these values help you in your choice of a career?

4. Explain the five dimensions of Sidney Simon, Leland Howe, and Howard Kirschenbaum's valuing process.

5. Explain some of the ways management values are changing. What factors seem to be influencing these changes?

6. What functions do values serve in an organization?

7. How do top management values affect the purpose and direction of an organization?

8. What are some of the most common types of value conflicts in organizations? Why do they often need skilled intervention to be resolved?

9. How can knowing something about employees' value systems help a manager?

10. How do seemingly accepted unethical business practices in foreign countries affect Americans' ability to compete for business contracts in those countries?

████ CASE 5.1

Whistle-Blowers: Fight or Flight?

In 1987 two ex-employees of Unisys Corporation, a NASA subcontractor that produces software programs for the space shuttle program, filed a $5.2 million lawsuit against their former company and Rockwell Shuttle Operations. Sylvia Robins and Ria Solomon charged that they had been harassed, demoted, and finally dismissed for pointing out safety violations and objecting to overcharges in shuttle work. Robins, a former section supervisor at Unisys, reported that the company had earlier ignored concerns she had voiced about security for shuttle-based Defense Department projects.

Shortly after the space shuttle *Challenger* exploded over the Atlantic Ocean in February 1986, the eight-member Rogers Commission was formed to investigate the reasons for the disaster. NASA's main contractor, Rockwell International, asked Robins to determine the quality of the system Unisys had developed to test the shuttle's back-up software. Robins reports that she did, in fact, discover a procedural flaw she insists resulted in invalid test results and danger to the flight crew, but her Unisys supervisors directed her not to inform Rockwell about it. Three months later, she says, she was demoted.

Robins subsequently went to work for Rockwell Shuttle Operations, a subsidiary of the larger Rockwell company. She discussed the problems she had encountered at Unisys, not only with her Rockwell supervisors, but with FBI officials and the Inspector General's Office at NASA as well. None-theless, she was shunned on the job and claims to have received three anon-ymous letters threatening her for being a "whistle-blower."

In its final, broadly critical report to NASA, the Rogers Commission cited evidence that caution and concern for safety in contracted work had often been eclipsed in favor of meeting schedules. Engineers who raised problems or complained about taking shortcuts that led, in their opinion, to hazardous or insecure conditions, had been severely punished.

Sources: "4 Say Problems in Space Shuttle Are Continuing," *The New York Times*, September 25, 1987, p. A14(L); "Unisys Ex-Aides Lost Jobs After Alleging Abuses, Lawsuit Says," *The Wall Street Journal*, September 25, 1987, p. 32(E); "Putting Schedule over Safety," *Time*, February 1, 1988, pp. 20–21.

Questions

1. What would you have done had you been in Robins's situation at Unisys when she discovered the procedural flaw? Keep in mind that this is *after* the Challenger explosion and during the preparation for the next shuttle flight.
2. How would a corporate policy of "schedule before safety" affect your behavior at work?
3. Is there any way to stay in an organization and initiate change? How?

▬▬▬▬▬▬▬▬▬▬ ▬ CASE 5.2

Managing Values

A great deal has been written about personal and organizational values in recent years. Marvin Chell, founder and chairman of Viking Engineering & Development, Inc., located in Fridley, Minnesota, thinks the main job of the top company official is to manage values.

> Boy, that becomes more and more apparent the larger you get. You see that the integrity of your company means everything. The world you operate in just isn't big, and the word travels fast.[1]

Chell is saying that in a small world word travels fast and your reputation can be ruined in a short period of time.

Fred Pryor, author of the *Pryor Report*, feels that lack of integrity has become a critical issue in the U.S. business community. He points out that

---

[1] "Managing Values," *INC.*, September 1987, p. 110.

some people lack a "moral" compass and have difficulty establishing ethical standards for themselves and others.

> The imaginary line a person draws and observes in personal and professional behavior may be his or her most valuable asset—or most devastating liability.
>   Knowing where that line lies when you deal with colleagues, employees, clients, customers—as well as with family and friends—is the most important thing you can possibly know about yourself.[2]

In a rapidly changing world, knowing where to draw that "imaginary line" will be more difficult. As noted by Doug Wallace, director of the Center for Ethics, Responsibilities and Values in St. Paul, "The rules for doing business are changing."[3]

Sources: "Managing Values," *INC.*, September 1987, p. 110; Fred Pryor, "Organizational Ethics: Know Them, Communicate Them and Stick to Them," *The Pryor Report*, September 1988, p. 3; Joel Dresang, "Companies Get Serious About Ethics," *USA Today*, December 9, 1986, pp. 1B, 2B.

Questions

1. What major changes have taken place in the business community over the past decade that make it more difficult for organizations to do the right thing? Prior to answering this question you may want to review the information on change presented in Chapter 1.

2. What steps can an organization take to encourage ethical behavior among employees at all levels?

SUGGESTED READINGS

Deal, Terrence E., and Allan A. Kennedy. *Corporate Cultures: The Rites and Rituals of Corporate Life.* Reading, Mass: Addison-Wesley, 1982.

Gellerman, Saul W. "Why Good Managers Make Bad Ethical Choices." *Harvard Business Review,* July/August, 1986.

Smith, Maury. *A Practical Guide to Value Clarification.* La Jolla, Cal.: University Associates, 1977.

Mark Stevens. *The Rise and Fall of E. F. Hutton.* New York: New American Library, 1989.

"What Ever Happened to Ethics?" *Time,* May 25, 1987, pp. 14–23+.

---

[2] Fred Pryor, "Organizational Ethics: Know Them, Communicate Them, and Stick to Them," *The Pryor Report,* September 1988, p. 3.

[3] Joel Dresang, "Companies Get Serious About Ethics," *USA Today,* December 9, 1986, p. 1.

NOTES

1. Spencer Johnson and Larry Wilson, *The One Minute Sales Person* (New York: Avon, 1986), p. 93.
2. "The Strength of Character," *The Royal Bank Letter* (The Royal Bank of Canada, 1988), Vol. 69, No. 3, May/June, p. 1.
3. Warren H. Schmidt and Barry Z. Posner, *Managerial Values and Expectations* (New York: AMACOM, 1982), pp. 12–14.
4. Charles Garfield, *Peak Performers, the New Heroes of American Business* (New York: Avon, 1987).
5. *TV Guide*, March 11–17, 1989.
6. Morris Massey, *The People Puzzle* (Reston, Va.: Reston Publishing, 1979).
7. Howard Kirschenbaum, *Advanced Value Clarification* (La Jolla, Cal.: University Associates, 1977), p. 44.
8. Sidney B. Simon, Leland W. Howe, and Howard Kirschenbaum, *Values Clarification* (New York: Hart Publishing Company, 1972), p. 15.
9. Ibid., p. 10.
10. "Businesses Are Signing Up for Ethics 101," *Business Week*, February 15, 1988, p. 57.
11. Howard Kirschenbaum and Sidney B. Simon, *Readings in Values Clarification* (Minneapolis: Winston Press, 1973), p. 102.
12. Erick Larson, "Forever Young," *INC.*, July 1988, p. 53.
13. Simon et al., *Values Clarification*, p. 11.
14. Louis Rath, Merrill Harmon, and Sidney Simon, *Values and Teaching* (Columbus, Ohio: Charles Merrill, 1976).
15. Simon et al., *Values Clarification*, p. 12.
16. "Rooms at the Inn," *Fortune*, January 2, 1989, p. 62.
17. Milton Rokeach, *The Nature of Human Values* (New York: The Free Press, 1973).
18. Don Beck, as quoted by Will Lorey, "Values System Analysis Theory," *Training/HRD*, January 1981, pp. 38–39.
19. "Million-Buck Windfall Just Too Tempting for Ohio Motorists," *Roanoke Times & World-News*, November 27, 1987, pp. A-1, A-4.
20. John Naisbitt and Patricia Aburdene, *Re-Inventing the Corporation* (New York: Warner Books, 1985), p. 95.
21. Ibid., pp. 99–100.
22. Charles M. Kelly, "Confrontation Insurance," *Training/HRD*, August 1981, pp. 91–94.
23. Thomas Peters and Robert Waterman, Jr., "Values: At the Heart of Corporate Excellence," *Roanoke Times & World-News*, May 29, 1983, pp. F-6, F-8.
24. Dayton-Hudson Corporation, *Statement of Philosophy*, Minneapolis, Minn., p. 10.
25. Robert Levering, Milton Moskowitz, and Michael Katz, *The 100 Best Companies to Work for in America* (New York: New American Library, 1984), p. 289.
26. Thomas J. Peters and Robert H. Waterman, *In Search of Excellence* (New York: Harper & Row, 1982), p. xix.
27. Benson Rosen and Thomas Jerdee, "Helping Young Managers Bridge the Generation Gap," *Training*, March 1985, pp. 43, 44.
28. Schmidt and Posner, *Managerial Values and Expectations*, pp. 27–28, 54–56.
29. "Value Studies Are a Clue to Organizational Behavior," *Training/HRD*, March 1981, p. 13.

30. William Ouchi, *Theory Z* (Reading, Mass.: Addison-Wesley, 1981), pp. 40–45.

31. Rosabeth Moss Kanter, *The Change Masters: Innovation for Productivity in the American Corporation* (New York: Simon & Schuster, 1982), p. 32.

32. "Chrysler Takes a Dumb Turn" (editorial), *Roanoke Times & World-News*, July 7, 1987, p. A-8.

33. "Values Added," *INC.*, January 1986, p. 31.

34. "Filter Case Shows Flaws of Regulator's Company," *Roanoke Times & World-News*, October 8, 1988, p. 2.

35. "Businesses Are Signing Up for Ethics 101," p. 56.

36. Ibid.

37. Rick Wartzman, "Nature or Nurture? Study Blames Ethical Lapses on Corporate Goals," *The Wall Street Journal*, October 9, 1987, p. 27.

38. Lisa Belkin, "Morality Becomes Party Game with a Question of Scruples," *Roanoke Times & World-News*, September 22, 1985, p. E-6.

39. Alvin L. Burger, "Breaking Away," *INC.*, April 1987, p. 125.

40. "Businesses Are Signing Up for Ethics 101," pp. 56–57.

41. "Corporate Crime: The Untold Story," *U.S. News and World Report*, September 6, 1982, pp. 25–29.

42. Adapted from Research Institute of America, "Do's and Don'ts for the Traveling Executive," *Personal Report*, October 5, 1985, p. 5.

Chapter 6
Learning To Achieve Emotional Control

CHAPTER PREVIEW

After studying this chapter, you will be able to

1. Explain why employers place a premium on emotional control.

2. Understand the conscious and subconscious influences on behavior.

3. Describe the principles of transactional analysis developed by Dr. Eric Berne.

4. Name the three distinct parts of the personality.

5. Achieve complementary transactions more frequently.

6. Make correct emotional decisions more frequently.

ow do you get customers to be faithful to you? A growing number of organizations in America are searching for an answer to this question. They have discovered that keeping customers happy is good business from an economic standpoint. Studies indicate that keeping a customer typically costs only one-fifth as much as obtaining a new one.[1]

The authors of *Service America* say that repeat business is an outgrowth of "service management." They describe service management as the process of managing the thousands of "moments of truth," those times when customers have contact with the organization and form their impressions. Although all contacts with an organization are important, the quality of the people contact creates the most lasting impression.[2] In an effort to help employees learn how to deal effectively with impatient or angry customers, many companies are investing in training programs that teach emotional control. Employees who receive this training are better able to deal effectively with angry customers and establish an emotion-free discussion of problems and issues.

EMOTIONAL CONTROL: AN INTRODUCTION

Much of the happiness we experience comes from the positive emotions that surface when someone recognizes our accomplishments or when we achieve something meaningful. The trust that builds within us when we work with supportive coworkers also produces positive feelings. Just spending time with friends or reading a good book can trigger the emotion of joy. By the same token, much of the unhappiness we experience in our lives comes from negative emotions such as envy, fear, hate, or worry. These are destructive emotions that often serve as barriers to good interpersonal relations. Displaying these emotions at work can damage not only relationships, but one's career as well. In an organizational setting, a premium is placed on a person's ability to control these negative emotions. We live in a society that tends to associate maturity with emotional control.

Destructive emotions can damage our psychological and physical well-being. They destroy peace of mind and often physical health.[3] Angry, cynical people are much more likely to suffer heart disease than people who are calm and trusting, according to recent research.[4] The starting point in achieving emotional control is to determine the source of emotional difficulties. Why do we sometimes display indifference rather than compassion? Why is it so easy to put down a friend or coworker, and so hard to recognize the person's accomplishments? Why do we sometimes worry about things that will never happen? To answer these and other questions regarding emotional control, it is necessary to study both conscious and subconscious influences on our behavior. We will give only a modest amount of attention to what goes on inside people and devote most of our attention to what goes on between people.

CONSCIOUS VERSUS SUBCONSCIOUS INFLUENCES

Your behavior is influenced by the conscious and subconscious parts of your mind. The **conscious mind** is the mental activity you are aware of and generally control. The ability to recall specific information about a letter typed last week is an example of the conscious part of the mind at work. So is recalling someone's phone number or address.

The **subconscious mind** is a storehouse of forgotten memories, desires, ideas, and frustrations, according to Dr. William C. Menninger, president of the famed Menninger Foundation.[5] He says that the subconscious mind can have a great influence on our behavior.

Although most people cannot remember many of the important things that happened to them during the first years of their lives, these incidents influence their behavior as adults. For many years, the nature of this influence was discussed in rather vague terms by psychologists and psychiatrists. Sigmund Freud is credited with discovering that different aspects of the subconscious mind influence people's daily thinking and behavior; but Freud and his followers had difficulty explaining the theory to laypeople.

A promising breakthrough in understanding the influence of the subconscious came several years ago with the development of the transactional analysis theory by Eric Berne. This theory of human behavior was explained in his best-selling books *Games People Play* and *What Do You Say After You Have Said Hello?* The practical applications of transactional analysis (TA) were further clarified in the books *I'm OK—You're OK*, written by Thomas Harris; *Staying OK*, by Amy Bjork Harris and Thomas Harris; and *Born to Win*, by Muriel James and Dorothy Jongeward.

TRANSACTIONAL ANALYSIS: AN INTRODUCTION

In very basic terms, **transactional analysis** is a theory of communication. Without relying on technical language or jargon, TA helps us better understand ourselves and others. It provides a positive tool for achieving emotional control on and off the job. TA also provides a means of understanding and changing an organization. Pan American World Airways has used TA to help customer-contact personnel handle difficult situations. United Telephone Co. of Texas used techniques drawn from transactional analysis in the context of a training program geared to help managers become more successful through teamwork. This training enabled managers to modify their personal reactions to behavior exhibited by others. TA helps people gain insight into their own emotional nature and that of others.

After years of study, Dr. Berne concluded that the brain acts like a two-track stereo tape recorder. One track records events, and the other records the feelings associated with those events. The tape recorder is on all the time from the day of birth.

Picture in your mind's eye a toddling three-year-old walking around his mother's sewing room. He picks up a pair of sharp scissors and begins walking toward the staircase. The mother spots the child and cries, "Tommy, drop those scissors! Do you want to kill yourself?" Tommy's tape recorder records both the event (walking with scissors) and the emotions (fear and guilt). Ten years later, Tommy is taking an art class and his teacher says, "Tommy, bring me a pair of scissors." As he begins to walk across the room, his mind is flooded by the feelings of fear and guilt attached to that earlier childhood event.

Today's experiences are filtered through the events and feelings of childhood, according to Amy Bjork Harris and Thomas A. Harris, authors of *Staying OK*.[7] If that early experience in the sewing room was traumatic, it may be relived later in life when Tommy is scolded for any reason. A scowling supervisor notices Tommy visiting with a fellow employee and shouts in a shrill voice, "If you don't get back to work, you may be looking for a new job!" The supervisor's tone and expression trigger the emotions associated with being scolded by his mother, and the familiar feelings of fear and guilt return.

Three Parts of Your Personality

People are often not aware of how their behavior looks to others. Sometimes people wonder why they behave the way they do, but more often they wonder why *others* act as they do. Dudley Bennett, author of *TA and the Manager*, says:

> To analyze behavior and its motivation, one must first understand that the basic component of behavior is an ego state. An *ego state* is a consistent combination of thought-feelings and related behavior.[8]

Eric Berne discovered, after many years of research, that everyone's personality is composed of three distinct ego states. He used three easily understood terms to describe these sources of behavior: Parent, Child, and Adult.

Parent Ego State   When people are acting, feeling, and thinking as they saw their parents behave, they are said to be in their **Parent ego state**. You acquire the Parent by recording in your brain the way your parents behaved. The name *Parent* was selected by Berne because most of the important tapes are produced when a young person observes and listens to his or her parents or older people who assume a parental role. The tapes inside you include all the do's and don'ts you heard as a child.

- "Don't cross the street if cars are coming."
- "Do clean off your plate."
- "Don't touch the knives. They are sharp and will cut you!"
- "Don't talk when Mommy's talking."

For the most part these messages entered your mind unedited. Although most of the messages were spoken for your safety and welfare, the mind was not mature enough to make this distinction. The verbal criticism and physical spanking were often perceived in a negative way. Most people have thousands of do's and don'ts recorded in their subconscious minds. The tapes recorded during those early years are still playing today and account for some of the "I'm not OK" feelings you may experience. On the other hand, you probably received many caresses, hugs, and kisses as a child that tended to offset some of the negative aspects of early childhood days.

The Parent has several useful functions. On the job you may be more safety conscious as a result of those early parental warnings. Your protective attitude toward others and your expression of sympathy can often be traced to early childhood experiences. If as an adult you have a strong desire to conserve resources (food, for example), your parents probably deserve part of the credit. A popular and wealthy country-western star with humble beginnings once said: "If you've been without, you learn to share, and to appreciate what you get. You never take it for granted. People sometimes say, 'It must be nice to be able to buy anything you want.' But I can hardly make myself spend $500 on a coat. And to this day, if I've cooked at home, I will not throw anything out, because I can still hear Mama saying, 'You threw that out with all of those children overseas starving to death?'"

In summary, the Parent ego state is two-dimensional, as shown in Figure 6.1. When you display a nurturing, caring attitude toward others, you are displaying what can be called the **Sympathetic Parent**. It is the Sympathetic Parent within you that makes it easy to express sincere praise and a caring attitude. The Sympathetic Parent is supportive and protective.

The other dimension of the Parent is referred to as the **Critical Parent**. When you are critical of others, opinionated, and judgmental, you are permitting your Critical Parent to surface. If instructions given on the job are accompanied by a stern look and a booming voice, the person giving these instructions is very likely receiving messages from his or her Critical Parent. It is the Critical Parent that causes you at times to be more faultfinding than helpful.

THINKING/LEARNING STARTER

Each of the statements below was made by the Sympathetic Parent (SP) or the Critical Parent (CP). In the space provided next to each statement, place the letters SP or CP, depending on which person you think made the statement.

1. _CP_ "Mary, like most young workers, does not take her work seriously."
2. _SP_ "Gordon, I was sorry to learn of your wife's accident."
3. _CP_ "I know why you can't find the payroll information. You pushed the data delete key."
4. _CP_ "Wendy, you know top management will not adopt your suggestion. It would violate store policy!"
5. _SP_ "Don't feel bad, Paul. Other technicians have had the same experience."

Child Ego State   As noted earlier, your mental tape recorder records events on one track and feelings associated with those events on another track. It records joy, happiness, and excitement associated with many childhood events. It also records terror, agony, and all the fearful emotions you have experienced as a child.[9]

The Child is the major source of your emotional responses in later years. Persons who display openness, spontaneity, and charm are drawing from their Child. They see nothing wrong with having fun and enjoying life. When a salesperson feels like jumping up and down after closing a big sale, it is the Child that is motivating this behavior. A person who grows up in a home where fun is encouraged and rewarded will find it easy to have fun in later life. Those who grow up in households characterized by negativism

Figure 6.1
Parent Ego State

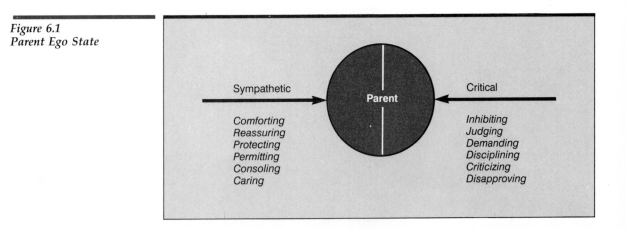

The affectionate and joyful aspects of our natural child can be a source of positive emotions in our adult years.
Bohdan Hrynewych/Stock, Boston

and conflict will often find it difficult to enjoy themselves in later years. These people recorded few "fun" tapes as children.

The **Child ego state** is also two-dimensional, as illustrated in Figure 6.2. Dr. Berne said the Child is exhibited by people in two forms: the Natural Child and the Adapted Child. The **Natural Child** is that part of us that acts as a child naturally would. It is affectionate, impulsive, joyful, and sensuous. Have you ever seen a middle-aged man skip happily along an ocean beach or a young housewife giggle at her birthday party? If so, you saw the Natural Child being expressed. Loud and spontaneous laughter provides yet another clue that the Natural Child is influencing behavior. The Natural

Figure 6.2
Child Ego State

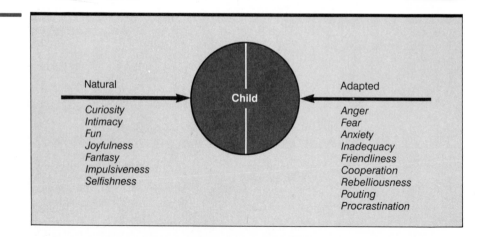

Child can also be rebellious, selfish, overly aggressive, and unwilling to consider the consequences of feelings and actions.

After birth a child begins to adapt to the demands of others. The behavior results in what Berne calls the **Adapted Child**. This part of the Child ego state is primarily influenced by parents. People frequently learn what others think they ought to do by being praised or punished. A smile or pat on the back from a parent communicates the idea of approval for doing what the parent thinks is right. The pride you feel today when somebody praises you for your good performance often comes from the Adapted Child. Similarly, the good feeling you get after you've done a job right (particularly if somebody notices or cares) is often a learned feeling.[10]

Children often learn how to get their own way during the first few years of life. The young child wants to go to bed when good and ready. When told to go to bed at 8:00 P.M., the youngster demonstrates unhappiness by moving very slowly. A child wants to eat a candy bar just prior to mealtime. The mother says no. The child responds by displaying a strong outburst of temper. If mother gives in, the child has learned one way to get what he or she wants.

Sometimes the Adapted Child resents complying with the demands of others and does so only grudgingly. The Adapted Child may also feel unsure about himself or herself and therefore procrastinate rather than meet deadlines established by others.

As is the case with the Parent ego state, there are pluses and minuses in the Child ego state. It is the Adapted Child that says "please" and "thank you." Taking turns, sharing, and being friendly are other behaviors learned early in life. However, the Adapted Child is often the troubled part of an individual's personality. If during early childhood you discovered that pouting helped you get your way or that a temper tantrum made a great impact on others, you may rely on these childlike behaviors later in life even though some other response is more appropriate.

Adult Ego State   When people are thinking and acting rationally, when they are gathering data and viewing circumstances with an objective point of view, they are said to be in the **Adult ego state**. Our Adult ego state is free from personal feelings and opinions. It functions like a computer, collecting and processing information from both the Child and the Parent.

TOTAL PERSON INSIGHT

❝ For most of us, the Adaptive Child has almost completely supplanted the Natural Child. Our feelings are stylized and ritualized, produced on demand for those who taught us to feel good or bad about what they valued. ❞

Dudley Bennett

> ### THINKING/LEARNING STARTER
>
> Many experts in the field of transactional analysis indicate that the positive aspects of our Natural Child (joy, trust, and affection) often become supplanted by the negative aspects of the Adapted Child (anger, impatience, and procrastination). In your own personal and work life, do you find yourself sometimes displaying the negative aspects of your Adapted Child?

Once this information is gathered, the Adult makes an objective decision. The Adult allows you to *think* about things before you make up your mind. Dorothy Jongeward and Philip Seyer describe the Adult ego state in this way:

> Whenever you are gathering information, reasoning things out, estimating probabilities, and so on, you are in your Adult ego state. While in this ego state you are cool and collected: you make decisions unemotionally. You just want the facts.[11]

Amy Bjork Harris and Thomas A. Harris note that body language and gestures provide clues to the Adult state.

> The Adult is not only a functional part of the personality, but also a state, observable by others in the present. A person in the Adult state appears thoughtful, rational, and in the here and now.[12]

The Adult starts to take form during the first year of life. You learn to choose from possible responses and to manipulate your surroundings. Adult data begin to accumulate as you find out for yourself how experience differs from the "taught concept" of life recorded by your Parent and the "felt concept" of life recorded by your Child.[13]

Without Adult self-awareness, you tend to be overly influenced by your Parent or Child. When the Adult is in control, you are more likely to think and act rationally.

In an organizational setting, the person who has the capacity to process data from their Parent and Child has the greatest potential for emotional control. A person who can handle these messages skillfully is apt to say and do the right thing. In any organizational situation, circumstances can trigger a response from your Child or Parent that may be inappropriate. When this happens, a relationship may be jeopardized. Consider the following conversation between Thomas Rand, sales representative for Telex Meter Company, and Harold Danville, purchasing agent for a firm that manufactures gas regulators:

Rand: Good morning. My name is Thomas Rand, and I represent the Telex Meter Company. We have a new product that may have application in your plant.

Danville: Several years ago, we did a great deal of business with your company, but stopped placing orders when your billing department sent us bills for merchandise we didn't purchase. We can't afford to do business with Telex!

Danville has just questioned the integrity of Telex Meter Company. As a representative of this firm, Rand might take the criticism personally. He might make the mistake of becoming defensive or displaying anger. These behaviors would probably ruin any chance of continuing his presentation. Instead, he answers with the following statement:

Rand: I must agree that several years ago we did have a short-term problem in our billing department. Due to an increasing volume of business, our staff was unable to handle billing in an orderly and efficient manner. Today we have a modern computerized operation that is virtually error free.

Danville: I'm glad to hear the problem has been taken care of. It was very frustrating to receive a bill for merchandise we didn't order.

Full development of the Adult is achieved in part by training yourself to employ self-control. When circumstances threaten to trigger an inappropriate response from the Parent or Child, you must use restraint and maintain the composure that defines you as a mature person.

There are times when even a mature Adult is unable to process data from the Parent or Child effectively. When you are under great stress, sick, tired, or extremely disappointed, the Child or Parent may operate as automatic responses. Tapes may replay spontaneously, and the damage is done before the Adult is able to make the right decision. In the stressful world of professional athletics, for example, we often see tempers flare.

Item: John McEnroe was suspended from playing tennis for two months and fined $17,500 for cursing and yelling at an umpire during the 1987 U.S. Open championships.[14]

Item: Indiana University coach Bobby Knight was fined $10,000 for pounding on the officials' table after being assessed a technical foul. The incident occurred during a regional basketball tournament.[15]

Item: Pete Rose, former manager of the Cincinnati Reds, was given a twenty-seven-day suspension and a $10,000 fine for shoving an umpire. The incident occurred during a game at Riverfront Stadium.[16]

Complementary, Crossed, and Ulterior Transactions

In the language of transactional analysis, each conversation between two people is called a *transaction*. Every social or work-related contact you have with another person involves a series of transactions between ego states. With practice, you can learn to analyze transactions in terms of which ego state (Parent, Adult, or Child) is speaking with which ego state of the other person. Transactions can be classified into three major categories: complementary, crossed, and ulterior.

Complementary Transactions James and Jongeward defined a **complementary transaction** as one that occurs when a message, sent from a specific ego state, gets the predicted or desired response from a specific ego state in the other person.[17] Let's assume that Randy goes to work Monday morning feeling very depressed. He is having financial problems and is worried about some overdue bills. He says to Harry, a fellow worker, "If things don't improve soon, I may have to find a job that pays more." Harry responds, "I know how you feel, Randy. It sure is hard to get by these days." Figure 6.3a illustrates the complementary nature of this transaction. In this example, Randy hoped to receive a response from Harry's Sympathetic Parent. He received the expected response, so communication will likely continue.

People sometimes bring their problems to work because they have no other outlet. They may seek sympathy from a fellow employee or supervisor because no one else will listen to them. A sensitive person will give an appropriate response.

Complementary transactions may also take place between the same ego states, as shown in Figure 6.3b. Consider this verbal exchange between Eric, a purchasing agent for a manufacturing firm, and Carl, a salesperson who visits his office. The weather is warm and sunny. Eric makes this statement: "Wow! Look at the weather outside. Let's take the afternoon off and play golf!" Carl responds enthusiastically: "Let's go, my clubs are in my car!" Here we have a complementary transaction between the Child ego state of each person.

Figure 6.3a (left)
Complementary
Transaction—Child to
Parent

Figure 6.3b (right)
Complementary
Transaction—Child to
Child

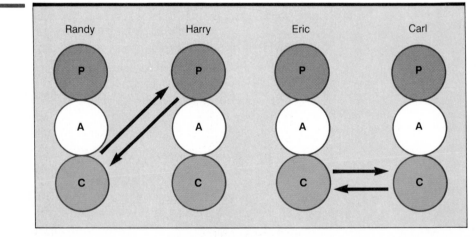

In TA language, each conversation between two people is called a transaction. In an ideal work setting, most transactions will be complementary.
© Laima Druskis/Jeroboam, Inc.

In an organizational setting, you would expect to observe many complementary transactions between Adult ego states. Mary, supervisor of data processing, approaches Peter, an employee in the department, and says, "How long will it take to get the data for the annual report?" Peter responds, "I can have it in one week." Figure 6.4 illustrates the Adult to Adult transaction.

Eric Berne said, "The first rule of communication is that communications will proceed smoothly as long as transactions are complementary."[18]

Figure 6.4
Complementary Transaction—Adult to Adult

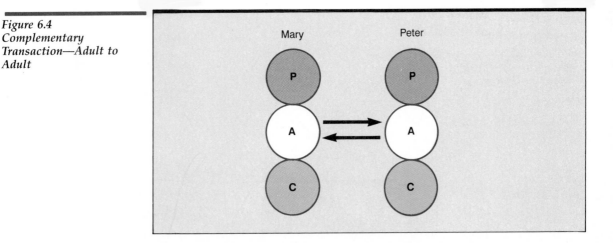

A complementary transaction gives a clear message to the other person and prompts a straightforward answer in return. In an organizational setting, complementary transactions are the most productive and result in fewer arguments and hurt feelings than other types of transactions.

Crossed Transactions   A **crossed transaction** occurs when the sender of the message does not get the response that he or she expected or hoped for from the other person. When this happens, communication and emotional control usually break down. A crossed transaction will create tension between two people. In an organizational setting, it is very important to avoid transactions that result in unnecessary tension or hostility.

To illustrate how crossed transactions develop, return to the conversation between Randy and Harry. Randy says, "If things don't improve soon, I may have to find a job that pays more." Instead of getting the hoped-for Sympathetic Parent response, Harry responds with a serious Adult comment: "It may not be possible for you to find another job. Things are pretty tight in the job market right now." You can see in Figure 6.5a how Harry's Adult response did not meet Randy's need for a sympathetic word.

In a typical crossed transaction, the second party is troubled or irritated by the message sent by the first and responds in a way that surprises and troubles the first party. The result is not effective communication but frustration that may cause the exchange to be terminated. William and Nancy walked up to a restaurant hostess and William said, "We would like a table for two." The hostess said, "The only available table is in the no-smoking section." William's Adult responded, "We'll wait until a table is available in the smoking section. We're not in any hurry." The hostess responded in an unfriendly (Critical Parent) manner, "Would you rather smoke than eat?" Figure 6.5b illustrates this crossed transaction, which damaged customer relations. In our highly competitive business environment, every customer must be treated with concern and respect. A cross transaction, even if it is not intentional, can result in a lost customer.

Figure 6.5a (left)
Crossed Transaction

Figure 6.5b (right)
Crossed Transactions Can
Alienate Customers

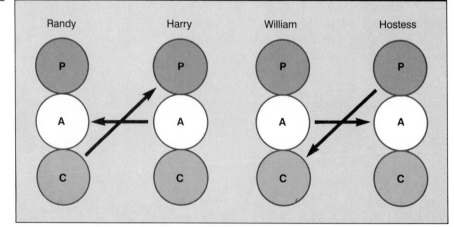

THINKING/LEARNING STARTER

Analyze the possible alternate responses below. Place the letters CT in the space
  if you feel the response will result in a complementary transaction, or XT if you
  feel the response will result in a crossed transaction.

1. *Situation A:* One employee says to another, "You sure took your time completing this project!"

    _CT_ "I know, I just can't seem to do these projects quickly."

    _XT_ "You should talk. Your production is always low."

2. *Situation B:* A secretary says to another employee, "My request for a raise was
  turned down."

    _XT_ "You think you have problems. Just listen to what happened to me."

    _CT_ "That's too bad. I know you must feel terrible."

3. *Situation C:* A customer says to a store employee, "Can I cash a check for
  $25?"

    _CT_ "I'm sorry, but we have a $20 limit" (spoken with understanding).

    _XT_ "Can't you read that sign on the wall? We have a $20 limit" (spoken with
  a critical tone).

Ulterior Transactions   An **ulterior transaction** occurs when the message
says one thing but has another meaning. The hidden message is sent dis-
guised as a socially acceptable communication. Ulterior transactions, like
crossed transactions, should be avoided because they create unnecessary
barriers to effective person-to-person communication. In this type of transaction, the second person does not know whether to respond to the hidden
meaning of the message (if it can be identified) or to the surface meaning of
the message. The result is very often an unproductive emotional reaction to
the situation.

Consider this verbal exchange between Ted, manager of the data processing section, and Sarah, his supervisor. Ted walks into Sarah's office with
a concerned expression on his face and says, "Sarah, most of my staff are
worn out trying to keep up with the schedule. Would it be possible to get
another computer operator assigned to the department? If not, I'm afraid
we'll have a rebellion on our hands." He appears to be making a polite request based on a serious problem, but he is also sending an ulterior message. He feels resentful because Sarah has been slow in responding to what
should have been an obvious problem, but he does not feel, in his position,
that it is appropriate for him to say so. As illustrated in Figure 6.6a, Ted's
spoken message seems to be coming from his Adult to Sarah's Adult, but
actually his Child is sending a message to Sarah's Parent.

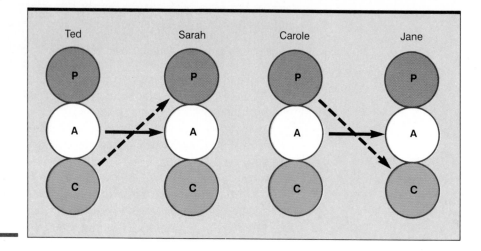

Figures 6.6a and 6.6b
Ulterior Transactions

Let's consider one more example. Jane walks into a staff meeting fifteen minutes late. Carole, her supervisor, points at her watch and says, "I'm glad you were able to make it." Carole has a look of anger on her face. The words appear to be coming from Carole's Adult, but the nonverbal messages (pointed index finger and frown) are coming from Carole's Critical Parent. Figure 6.6b illustrates this ulterior transaction.

Ulterior transactions waste time and often cause a breakdown in relationships. In the first example, Sarah may think, "What is Ted trying to tell me?" Effective human relations are sidetracked by vague ulterior transactions. It is best not to make people search for hidden meanings.

Identifying the Source of the Transaction

How can you identify Parent and Child responses? To pinpoint the source of the transaction, it will be necessary to consider both verbal and nonverbal aspects of the response. In some cases, nonverbal clues (facial expression, gestures, or tone of voice) may tell more than words about a person's real attitudes.

When someone speaks, listen closely to his or her tone of voice and pay attention to his or her facial expression and other body language clues. A harsh, judgmental tone of voice usually means the Critical Parent is speaking. An impulsive, informal tone probably means a person's Natural Child is talking. If the facial expression communicates disapproval, the source of the message is probably the Critical Parent. If the expression communicates

TABLE 6.1   Nonverbal Responses in Four Areas

	Parent Ego State	**Child Ego State**
Tone of voice	Critical, judgmental, demanding (Critical Parent)	Affectionate, impulsive, sensuous (Natural Child)
	Comforting, reassuring, protecting (Sympathetic Parent)	Self-centered, rebellious, whining (Adapted Child)
Facial expressions	Frowns, worried or disapproving looks (Critical Parent)	Excitement, surprise, wide-eyed looks (Natural Child)
	Concerned, supportive, warm (Sympathetic Parent)	Downcast eyes, quivering lips or chin, pouting (Adapted Child)
Body gestures	Pointing an accusing finger, hands on hips, or arms folded across chest (Critical Parent)	Spontaneous activity such as laughter, arms moving freely (Natural Child)
	Reaching for, hugging, holding, protecting and shielding from harm (Sympathetic Parent)	Wringing hands, hanging head, withdrawing into a corner (Adapted Child)
Postures	Puffed-up, very proper posture; back straight and shoulders pulled back (Critical Parent)	Jumping up and down, head cocked (Natural Child)
	Open arms protecting from a fall or hurt, arm around shoulder (Sympathetic Parent)	Slouching, burdened posture (Adapted Child)

excitement, the Natural Child is no doubt speaking. Table 6.1 categorizes nonverbal responses in four areas.

ACHIEVING GREATER EMOTIONAL CONTROL

William Crockett, a fellow of the NTL Institute, recognized that as human beings we live our lives in two distinct worlds—one of fact and certainty and one of emotions and ambiguity. The world of certainty is that part of our lives that deals with objects and our rational side; our world of ambiguity deals with people and our feeling, or emotional, side—our human world. Too often we try to handle our human world in the same way that we handle our factual world.[19] In organizational settings, for example, we

sometimes observe meetings that follow a very structured agenda. Discussion is limited to "facts," and the group leader discourages the sharing of "feelings." Once the agenda items have been dealt with, the meeting is promptly adjourned. In some situations, staff meetings will be more productive if the group leader provides a forum for discussion of both facts and feelings. The group leader can arrange the physical setting and time schedule of the meeting to encourage the disclosure of feelings.

Every occupation requires a certain amount of decision making. Some of these decisions are basic, such as how to organize the content of a memorandum. Other decisions are more complex, such as how much money to invest in advertising. In some cases, established policies act as guidelines to help you make the correct decision. Many of these decisions can be made in an emotion-free climate. When decisions deal with human issues and problems, however, emotions often enter the picture. With a knowledge and understanding of transactional analysis, you can make the correct emotional decision more frequently.

Emotional Maturity

It is a rare occupation that does not bring the worker into contact with other people. The typical receptionist, salesperson, nurse, bank teller, or account executive has contact with hundreds of people every week.

Every interpersonal encounter involves transactions between people's ego states. Making the correct response to each transaction requires taking charge of your emotions. **Emotional maturity** is one of the keys to a satisfying life both at home and at work. Crockett noted that our judgments and decisions are often polluted by our emotions.

> Our emotions may result from our unfulfilled needs for belonging, for feeling important, for recognition or for security. They may result from what seems to be unfair treatment by others. They may result from our fears, hopes and aspirations; or they may come from deeply hidden internal sources of which we are unaware.[20]

Emotional maturity develops as you achieve greater understanding of the emotions that affect your life. This involves becoming well acquainted with the five persons (Sympathetic Parent, Critical Parent, Adult, Natural Child, and Adapted Child) within. Emotional maturity also grows as you learn how to identify these five persons within others. To help you build a mental picture of the five persons, let's review the characteristics of each.

Sympathetic Parent   Figure 6.7 provides an illustration of the Sympathetic Parent. This is the type of person who will serve you hot chocolate and marshmallows on a cold day, or will sympathize when you make a mistake in programming and the computer prints all the payroll checks backwards. The Sympathetic Parent will offer comfort when you experience a deep disappointment or hurt. This person is supportive, protective, and caring.

Critical Parent   The Critical Parent, pictured in Figure 6.7, always seems to be around when you make a mistake and often makes a judgmental comment. The Critical Parent is apt to point a finger at you and say, "Always follow the rules." This person speaks with an "I know best" tone of voice most of the time and likes to voice slogans like "a penny saved is a penny earned." People often become defensive in the presence of the Critical Parent and feel like striking back.

Adult   The Adult shown in the figure represents the side of you that is not distracted by emotions. Cool and calculating, the Adult can be surrounded by an emotional storm and still make an objective decision most of the time. Your Adult is constantly processing data from the other four persons.

Figure 6.7
***The Five Persons Within
Us*** (clockwise, starting
top left and ending in the
center: *Sympathetic Parent,
Critical Parent, Adapted
Child, Natural Child, Adult*)

Natural Child   The Natural Child is the carefree, happy ego state within
you. It is the source of much of your curiosity, creativity, and intuition. The
Natural Child is the impulsive, spontaneous person who says, "What the
heck, let's have some fun!" Responses that come from the Natural Child are
often emotionally charged.

Adapted Child   The Adapted Child can become the most troublesome part
of your personality. If you are overcome by anger or depression when someone criticizes your work, the negative aspect of your Adapted Child is

influencing your behavior. An individual acting from the Adapted Child state may slam doors, sulk, or wait for someone to acknowledge that he or she is "right." The Adapted Child will not want to admit that he or she has made a mistake.

Pushing the Right Button: The Key to Emotional Control

As we saw earlier, your success in dealing with people depends on choosing the correct response to transactions initiated by others. You can't be right all the time, but you can reduce the number of wrong responses by developing emotional control.

It is helpful to visualize the five persons within you as buttons that appear on an **emotional switchboard**, illustrated in Figure 6.8. When you receive a transaction from another person, you push a button in response. Ideally, you will push the correct button, and a complementary transaction will occur. This happens when your mature Adult processes data from the

Figure 6.8
Emotional Switchboard

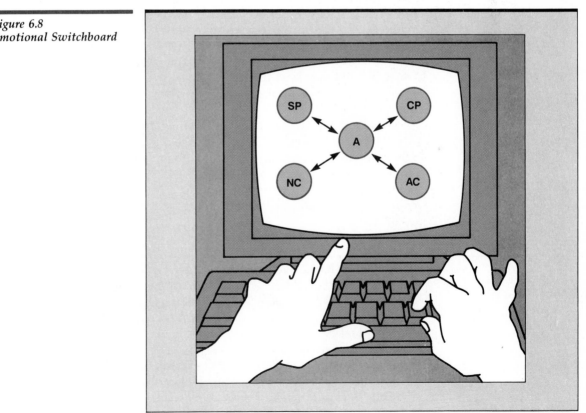

Parent and Child effectively. As noted earlier, you are less likely to push the correct button when you are ill, tired, under stress, or experiencing great disappointment.

Experiencing emotional control is knowing which button to push and when to push it. It requires a great deal of self-discipline, especially in jobs that involve large numbers of personal contacts every day. People who work in hotels, financial institutions, restaurants, hospitals, and busy retail stores face special challenges. The number of face-to-face and telephone contacts each day is surprisingly large.

The emotional switchboard is always with you. Throughout each day, you must make dozens of decisions about which button to push. Let's suppose that a customer enters the supermarket where you are employed and begins picking up items without a cart. After moving up and down several aisles, the person arrives at your checkout lane with an armload of groceries. A jar of apple jelly, tucked under one elbow, slips out, falls to the floor, and breaks. The customer's face turns bright red.

In this situation, you may receive messages from several of the persons within you. The Sympathetic Parent will tell your Adult that the customer needs a little compassion: "Don't lecture the customer—the person already feels bad enough." The Critical Parent will likely send your Adult a different message: "Make this person clean up the mess. Anyone who shops without a cart needs to be taught a lesson!" Of course, your Natural Child is going to find this situation very funny and tell your Adult to laugh! The Adapted Child may send the Adult still another message: "Oh, nuts. Now someone has to clean up this mess. Why do these accidents always happen in my work area?"

Consider another situation: It was late Friday afternoon and Stephanie was filing the last of several reports that had piled up in her in-basket. She wanted to return to a clean desk on Monday morning. Suddenly her boss, Sandy, ran into the office and said, "Please pull the Hatfield report and make a copy for me. It must go out in the 5:00 P.M. mail." Stephanie looked at the clock and said, "If I hurry I can get to the copy center before it closes at 4:30."

Stephanie arrived at the copy center at exactly 4:30 P.M. The copy center employee on duty said, "Sorry, we're closed. You'll have to come back on Monday." Stephanie felt both angry and frustrated. She knew her boss would be upset if she didn't return with a copy of the report. She also disliked working with people who watch the clock and refuse to do anything extra. Her first impulse was to push her Adapted Child button and say, "If you don't make a copy of this report for me I'll complain to your supervisor." She also considered pushing her Critical Parent button and saying, "If there is anything I can't stand it's a clock watcher. You should be ashamed of yourself!" Instead, she pushed her Sympathetic Parent button and said, "I'm sorry that I didn't get this report to you sooner. It is Friday afternoon, and I know you must be anxious to leave. But I sure would appreciate it if you would make an exception for me. My boss needs this report very badly." The look on her face communicated "I need your help." The operator took the report from her and began making a copy.

Stephanie pushed the right button (made the correct emotional decision) and avoided an argument with the operator. She also accomplished her objective by obtaining a copy of the report.

Emotional Control Can Be a Challenge

Every day at work you will have to make some difficult decisions. One option is to do only those things that feel good at the moment. In some cases, this will mean ignoring the feelings of customers, patients, fellow workers, and supervisors. Another option is to behave in a manner that is acceptable to those people around you. If you choose this option, you will have to make some sacrifices. Sometimes you must be warm and generous when the feelings inside say, "Be cold and selfish." You may have to avoid an argument when the feelings inside are insisting, "I'm right and the other person is wrong." In today's service economy, where teamwork and customer service are receiving great emphasis, emotional control is very important. Getting along with people requires pushing the right button.

SUMMARY

Throughout life your behavior is influenced by the conscious and the subconscious parts of your mind. The conscious part is the mental activity you are aware of and can control. The subconscious part of your mind has been described by William C. Menninger as a "storehouse of forgotten memories." It is mental activity that goes on without your knowledge.

Research conducted by Dr. Eric Berne can help you understand the influence of subconscious mental activity. He developed transactional analysis, a way of analyzing the transactions that take place when two people meet. Dr. Berne discovered that everyone's personality is composed of three distinct parts called ego states: Parent, Child, and Adult. People do not remain permanently fixed in any of these ego states but may fluctuate from one to another depending on the situation.

The contacts you have with people at work involve a series of transactions between ego states. With practice you can learn to analyze transactions and determine which of your ego states (Parent, Adult, or Child) is speaking and which ego state the other person is using.

Transactions between people can be classified into three major categories: complementary, crossed, and ulterior. A complementary transaction is one that occurs when a message, sent from a specific ego state, gets the predicted or desired response from a specific ego state in the other person. A crossed transaction occurs when the sender of the message does not get the response that was expected or desired. An ulterior transaction occurs when the message says one thing but has another meaning. Both crossed and ulterior transactions often cause breakdowns in communication. Making the correct response to each transaction requires considerable control over your emotions. Emotional maturity is an important key to success at work.

KEY TERMS

conscious mind
subconscious mind
transactional analysis
Parent ego state
Sympathetic Parent
Critical Parent
Child ego state
Natural Child

Adapted Child
Adult ego state
complementary transaction
crossed transaction
ulterior transaction
emotional maturity
emotional switchboard

REVIEW QUESTIONS

1. What is the difference between conscious and subconscious influences on your behavior?

2. How can an understanding of transactional analysis help improve human relations at work?

3. According to Eric Berne, everyone's personality is composed of three ego states: Parent, Child, and Adult. Provide a concise description of each.

4. Describe the two dimensions of the Parent ego state.

5. Describe the two dimensions of the Child ego state.

6. It has been said that our Adult ego state functions like a computer. Explain the meaning of this statement.

7. Certain mental and physical conditions can make it difficult for your Adult to function effectively. Explain.

8. What are the differences between complementary, ulterior, and crossed transactions? Give examples.

9. Describe the emotional switchboard that is always with us.

10. Review the Total Person Insight on page 149. Can you identify specific emotional responses in yourself that are stylized and ritualized, rather than natural? Who was it who taught you to feel good or bad about what they valued?

■ CASE 6.1

Crossed Transaction in an Emergency

Larry Boff filed a $300,000 damage claim against the city of Dallas, Texas after Fire Department ambulances arrived too late to save the life of his sixty-year-old stepmother. Boff had called the city's emergency line and requested an ambulance. The result was a heated exchange with nurse Billie Myrick, who was assigned to screen incoming calls. The screening had been built into the Fire Department ambulance system because there had been a lot of system abuse, with many people calling for ambulances in cases that were not truly emergencies. After this incident, the nurse was given counseling and received a two-day suspension with pay. A portion of the taped conversation between Boff and Myrick follows.

Myrick: And what is the problem there?
Boff: I don't know, if I knew I wouldn't be . . .
Myrick: Sir, would you answer my questions, please? What is the problem?
Boff: She's having difficulty in breathing.
Myrick: How old is this person?
Boff: She's sixty years old.
Myrick: Where is she now?
Boff: She is in the bedroom right now.
Myrick: Can I speak with her, please?
Boff: No, you can't. She seems like she's incoherent.
Myrick: Why is she incoherent?
Boff: How the hell do I know!
Myrick: Sir, don't curse me.
Boff: Well, I don't care. These stupid . . . questions you're asking. Give me someone who knows what they're doing. Why don't you send an ambulance out here?
Myrick: Sir, we only come out on life-threatening emergencies.
Boff: Well, this is a life-threatening emergency.

At this point, Boff had talked to a supervisor, and then Myrick had returned to the line. The heated exchange continued, but Myrick continued to refuse to send an ambulance unless she could talk with Mrs. Boff to confirm it was necessary. In the end, the Fire Department did dispatch an ambulance to Mr. Boff's home, but a short time later the woman died. Boff called Myrick again and the recorded transcript ends with these words: "She's dead now. Thank you, ma'am! Would you please send an ambulance? Would you please send an ambulance here?"

Sources: "Ambulance Call Delay for Dying Woman Brings $300,000 Claim," *The New York Times*, March 7, 1984, p. A-14; "Woman's Death Prompts Probe of Hotline Nurse," *USA Today*, March 7, 1984, p. 6.

Questions

1. What ego state is an emergency telephone operator likely to encounter when answering calls?

2. To avoid a crossed transaction, what button should Billie Myrick have pushed immediately after learning of the need for an ambulance?

3. Early in the phone conversation it appears that Mr. Boff is very angry. In response to a question about the problem, he says: "I don't know, if I knew I wouldn't be . . ." Would things have turned out differently if Mr. Boff had pushed his Adult button at this point?

4. Should persons who are involved in handling emergency phone calls be given the opportunity to study the principles of transactional analysis? Why or why not?

■■■■■■ ■ CASE 6.2

Breaking the Conference Budget

Helen Hall has been manager of the LaGrande Resort Hotel accounting department for three years. In this position, she supervises a staff of three clerks who handle daily transactions for hotel guests. As manager of the department, she must occasionally meet with guests who feel their bills are not accurate. In most cases, billing problems are handled routinely with no loss of customer good will. However, there are some exceptions.

This morning Glenn Howell, national sales manager for Rider Shoe Corporation, came to the office and requested clarification of his master billing charges. He felt his company had been overcharged for hotel services. Mr. Howell calmly explained his concern:

Glenn Howell: I must confess I don't understand all of the items on my bill. It is about nine hundred dollars more than I expected.

Helen Hall: Well, we seldom make an error, but let me review the charges.

Glenn Howell: Here is the bill. I don't understand why it includes so many individual room charges.

Helen Hall: My records indicate that seventy-three Rider Corporation employees stayed with us for three nights. It looks like a large number of your people used room service for food and beverages. Frankly, I don't think this bill is out of line. (Spoken with a hint of indifference.)

Glenn Howell: I did not authorize these individual purchases. My boss will be furious if I exceed the budget for this conference by nine hundred dollars.

Helen Hall: Mr. Howell, you arranged for seventy-three Rider Corporation employees to register at this hotel. At no time did you request that we restrict room service for these people. Do you expect our staff to refuse service to a registered guest? (Spoken with a hint of anger in her voice.)

Glenn Howell: Look, this is the first time I have been in charge of a national sales conference for our employees. I simply didn't realize that so many people would use room service.

Helen Hall: Next time I would suggest you discuss this matter with your employees prior to the beginning of the conference. (Spoken in a critical tone of voice.)

At the conclusion of the meeting, Mr. Howell walked out of the accounting office with a dejected look on his face. Miss Hall turned to a clerk seated nearby and said, "All sales managers are alike. When it comes to conference planning, they never pay any attention to the important details."

Questions

1. What ego state(s) did Helen Hall rely on during most of her conversation with Glenn Howell?

2. When handling customer complaints, what buttons should Helen Hall use most frequently?

3. If you were director of personnel training for the LaGrande Resort Hotel, what steps would you take to improve Miss Hall's customer relations skills?

SUGGESTED READINGS

Bennett, Dudley. *TA and the Manager*. New York: AMACOM, 1976.

Berne, Eric, M.D. *What Do You Say After You Say Hello?* New York: Bantam Books, 1984.

Harris, Amy Bjork, and Thomas A. Harris. *Staying OK*. New York: Harper & Row, 1985.

Harris, Thomas A. *I'm OK—You're OK*. New York: Harper & Row, 1969.

Hollar, Hunter R., and O. C. Brenner. "TA in the Office." *Supervisory Management*, January 1983, p. 14.

James, Muriel and John James. *The OK Boss*. Reading, Mass.: Addison-Wesley, 1975.

James, Muriel and Dorothy Jongeward. *Born to Win; Transactional Analysis with Gestalt Experiments*. Reading, Mass.: Addison-Wesley, 1971.

James, Muriel and Louis Savary. *A New Self*. Reading, Mass.: Addison-Wesley, 1977.

Jongeward, Dorothy, and Dru Scott. *Women as Winners*. Reading, Mass.: Addison-Wesley, 1982.

Jongeward, Dorothy, and Philip Seyer. *Choosing Success—Transactional Analysis on the Job*. New York: Wiley, 1978.

Meininger, Jut. *Success Through Transactional Analysis*. New York: Grosset & Dunlop, 1973.

Steiner, Claude. *Scripts People Live*. New York: Grove Press, 1974.

NOTES

1. Patricia Sellers, "Getting Customers to Love You," *Fortune*, March 13, 1989, p. 38.
2. Karl Albrecht and Ron Zemke, *Service America* (Homewood, Ill.: Dow Jones-Irwin, 1985), p. 8.
3. Allen R. Russon, *Personality Development for Business* (Cincinnati, Ohio: South-Western Publishing, 1973), p. 51.
4. "Anger, Not Anxiety, Leads to Early Death," *Roanoke Times & World-News*, January 17, 1989, p. A2.
5. William C. Menninger and Harry Levinson, *Human Understanding in Industry* (Chicago: Science Research Associates, 1956), p. 29.
6. "Working Together as a Team . . .," *Training and Development Journal*, June 1982, p. 8.
7. Amy Bjork Harris and Thomas A. Harris, *Staying OK* (New York: Harper & Row, 1985), p. 24.
8. Dudley Bennett, *TA and the Manager* (New York: American Management Association, 1976), p. 1.
9. Jut Meininger, *Success Through Transactional Analysis* (New York: Grosset & Dunlop, 1973), p. 20.
10. Dorothy Jongeward and Philip Seyer, *Choosing Success — Transactional Analysis on the Job* (New York: Wiley, 1978), p. 46.
11. Ibid., p. 11.
12. Harris and Harris, *Staying OK*, p. 18.
13. Thomas A. Harris, *I'm OK—You're OK* (New York: Harper & Row, 1969), p. 29.
14. "McEnroe Fined $17,500, Suspended for Tantrum," *Roanoke Times & World-News*, September 7, 1987, p. P–1.
15. "Bobby's Nightmares," *USA Today*, May 3, 1988, p. 2c.
16. "Rose Suspension Upheld," *Roanoke Times & World-News*, May 7, 1988, p. B–1.
17. Muriel James and Dorothy Jongeward, *Born to Win: Transactional Analysis with Gestalt Experiments* (Reading, Mass.: Addison-Wesley, 1971), p. 24.
18. Eric Berne, *Games People Play* (New York: Grove Press, 1964), p. 30.
19. William J. Crockett, "Our Two Worlds," *Training and Development Journal*, May 1982, p. 60.
20. Ibid., p. 61.

Chapter 7

The Power of Positive Reinforcement

CHAPTER PREVIEW

After studying this chapter, you will be able to

1. Create awareness of the strong need people have for positive reinforcement.

2. Understand how to use positive reinforcement to improve relationships and reward behavior.

3. List the various forms of positive reinforcement that are applicable in an organization.

4. Explain the use of incentives and awards by organizations.

5. Describe the major barriers to the use of positive reinforcement in an organizational setting.

o one in Racine, Wisconsin, was surprised when S. C. Johnson & Son, Inc. was listed in *The 100 Best Companies to Work for in America*. After all, this is a company that has never had a layoff and treats employees as family.[1] Contrary to the situation in most large corporations (those with annual sales of over $2 billion), management at Johnson is quite visible. Sam Preston, a recently retired executive vice president, is typical of the people who rise to executive positions in this company. Throughout his career he took the time to recognize positive acts by employees. When he observed an act of kindness or good performance, he would write a note to the person involved and sign it with the initials "DWD." It took a little time, but eventually the persons who received the notes figured out the "DWD" stood for "Damned Well Done."[2]

Written notes, verbal words of praise, a pat on the back, incentives, and awards represent common forms of positive reinforcement. This chapter discusses the impact of positive reinforcement on both individual and group behavior. The various types of positive reinforcement are examined in detail, and you will learn why so many people have difficulty giving positive feedback to others. A special section is devoted to awards and incentive programs currently used by a variety of organizations.

PERSONAL AND ORGANIZATIONAL GROWTH THROUGH POSITIVE REINFORCEMENT

Positive reinforcement (PR) is an important key to improved human relationships. Jack Taylor, author of *12 Basic Ideas About People*, notes that the most successful human relations spring from words and actions that evoke responses from the positive side of the emotional scale. People who understand the power of positive reinforcement and are able to employ positive reinforcement strategies are more likely to achieve success on and off the job.

According to psychologist Erik Erikson, recognition is key to the development of what he called ego identity. **Ego identity** is the individual's inner idea of himself or herself—who the individual is, what he or she stands for, and what he or she wants out of life.[3] The psychological ingredient of recognition contributes to the development of ego identity; it is as vital to the mind as a nutritious diet is to the body.

Positive reinforcement can also be an inexpensive way to increase organizational effectiveness. Dr. Bruce Baldwin, psychologist and consultant, believes that positive feedback is the most cost-effective way to help an organization run smoothly and improve productivity at all levels.[4] A major component of productivity is employee satisfaction. Employees who feel unappreciated will not perform to the best of their ability. In the absence of positive feedback, the organization assumes the posture of a negative entity to its employees because most information they receive emphasizes what is wrong rather than what is right. In such an organizational climate, employees become progressively demoralized and defensive because they feel their work is not appreciated.

Employee Reward Preferences

Several studies have pointed out that upper management and supervisors frequently do not understand employee reward preferences. Managers and supervisors often expect pay or monetary rewards, job security, and good working conditions to rank highest as reward preferences among employees. However, when employees are surveyed, a different picture develops. Professor Kenneth Kovach, professor of business administration at George Mason University, gave a list of ten morale-building factors to a group of supervisory personnel with instructions to rank them in order according to what they felt their employees wanted.[5] This same list was then given to their employees, who were instructed to rank the items according to their perspective. The results of this survey, shown in Table 7.1 , indicate that "full appreciation of work done" ranks very high among employees. When employee reward preferences are not in harmony with management's reward system, problems arise.

There is also evidence that positive reinforcement improves communication throughout an organization. Studies conducted by Dr. C. B. Stiegler and others found that positive feedback reduces stress within the working environment, which results in improved interpersonal communication:

TABLE 7.1   Ten Morale-Building Factors

What Managers Think Employees Want	What Employees Really Want
1. Good pay	1. Interesting work
2. Job security	2. Full appreciation of work done
3. Promotion and growth	3. Involvement
4. Good working conditions	4. Good pay
5. Interesting work	5. Job security
6. Tactful discipline	6. Promotion and growth
7. Loyalty to employees	7. Good working conditions
8. Full appreciation of work done	8. Loyalty to employees
9. Help with personal problems	9. Help with personal problems
10. Involvement	10. Tactful discipline

Source: Reprinted by permission from Kenneth Kovach, "Why Motivational Theories Don't Work," *S.A.M. Advanced Management Journal*, Spring 1980, p. 56. Society for Advancement of Management, Cincinnati, OH 45206.

Positive reinforcement (PR) involves "putting people at ease" in interpersonal communication. Whether one is speaking with, writing to, or listening to another person or persons, PR serves to put people at ease, thereby facilitating open communication. By reducing business pressures, PR results in a free flow of information, both vertically and horizontally, which in turn increases efficiency.[6]

OUR NEED FOR POSITIVE REINFORCEMENT

How strong is an individual's need to receive positive reinforcement from others? Psychologist William James believed that the craving to be appreciated is a basic principle of human nature. Mark Twain, the noted author, answered the question by saying he could live for three weeks on a compliment. He was willing to admit openly what most people feel inside. Many have a deep desire for personal recognition but almost never verbalize these thoughts. One exception is Tom Peters, author of *Thriving on Chaos*, who says: "I myself can never get enough of that wonderful stuff called positive reinforcement."[7]

Few people have the strength of ego to subsist upon self-esteem alone. Most are very dependent upon **positive feedback** from others. Kenneth Blanchard and Spencer Johnson, authors of *The One Minute Manager*, stress the importance of "catching the employee doing something right" and engaging in "one minute praisings."[8] Without this positive feedback employees suffer from a sense of incompleteness.

Support from Maslow

The hierarchy of needs developed by Abraham Maslow (see Chapter 4 for a discussion of this concept) provides additional support for the use of positive reinforcement in an organizational setting. In part, the need for security (a second-level need) is satisfied by positive feedback from an approving supervisor, manager, or fellow employee. You are apt to feel more secure when someone recognizes your accomplishments. A feeling of belonging (a third-level need) can be satisfied by actions that communicate "You are part of the team." One employee reported that he felt like a member of the corporate team when the manager of the firm said, "I want you to become more familiar with our business. Let's review this year's sales reports together."

Maslow stated that as each lower-level need is satisfied, the need at the next level demands attention. It would seem to be almost impossible to satisfy the esteem needs (fourth level) without positive feedback. One's level of self-esteem is usually not stable; it may diminish in a work environment where accomplishments receive little or no recognition.

THINKING/LEARNING STARTER

Recall a situation in your life when you accomplished something important, but no one seemed to notice. Try to remember the feelings that surfaced inside of you. Did you experience disappointment? Hurt? Anger? Feelings of inadequacy? Why do you now think your accomplishments were ignored?

Support from Skinner

The research of B. F. Skinner at Harvard University has contributed to our understanding of reinforcement as a factor influencing the behavior of people in a work setting. Skinner maintained that any living organism will tend to repeat a particular behavior if that behavior is accompanied or followed by a reinforcer.[9] A **reinforcer** is any stimulus that follows a response and increases the probability that the response will occur again.[10] Skinner also demonstrated that the timing of reinforcement has an important effect on behavior change. He discovered that if the delay between a response (behavior) and its reinforcement is too great, a change in behavior is less likely to take place.

Some organizations have discovered creative ways to apply Skinner's concepts. Faced with a growing problem of employee tardiness and absenteeism, one company decided to involve workers in a card game. When an employee arrived at work on time, he or she could choose a card from a deck of cards. At the end of each week, the employee with the best poker hand was given a reward. Over a sixteen-week period this method resulted in a 20 percent decrease in absenteeism.[11]

Negative reinforcement is another option available to supervisors and managers. If a supervisor emphasizes areas needing improvement during a performance review and ignores all accomplishments, the employee is being subjected to negative reinforcement. The supervisor who uses this tactic may take the position that negative feedback should be discontinued only after performance is outstanding in all areas. Tom Peters believes that positive reinforcement is much more beneficial than negative. However, he states that "negative reinforcement (criticism) is far and away the most common means by which American companies try to influence performance."[12]

unfortunately

Support from Berne

In the previous chapter, you learned the fundamentals of transactional analysis (TA). TA is a simplified explanation of how people communicate. Eric Berne's research also provided new evidence that most people have a strong need for recognition, or "strokes."

The word *stroking* is used to describe the various forms of recognition one person gives another. Strokes help satisfy the need to be appreciated. A **physical stroke** may be a pat on the back or a smile that communicates approval. **Verbal strokes** include words of praise and expressions of gratitude.

Eric Berne said that stroking is necessary for physical and mental health. He found that infants who were deprived of physical strokes (hugs, caresses, and kisses) began to lose their will to live. As people grow into adulthood, they are willing to substitute verbal stroking for physical stroking. Adults still need and want physical stroking, but they will settle for words of praise, incentives, awards, and other forms of recognition.

A stroke can be positive or negative. Positive strokes, called "warm fuzzies" in TA language, include such behaviors as listening with genuine attention, smiling, or simply saying "thank you" sincerely to a customer who has just made a purchase. Negative strokes, sometimes called "cold pricklies," produce "I'm not OK" feelings inside of people. A negative stroke may take the form of sarcasm, failure to remember the name of a regular customer, or making fun of another person's appearance.

Stroke Deficit:
A Common Condition

Claude Steiner, author of *TA Made Simple*, says that most people live in a state of **stroke deficit**. They survive on a less-than-ideal diet of strokes, like people who never have enough to eat.[13] Some individuals are so hungry for positive recognition they will ask for strokes. The following statements,

Most employees appreciate positive recognition. Recognition for work well done fulfills our basic need for positive strokes.
MacDonald Photography/The Picture Cube

made by an ad layout employee working for a large newspaper, may reveal the need for positive feedback:

- "Did you see my appliance ad on the sports page?"
- "I heard that the Reed's Department Store ad I prepared attracted a store full of people."
- "I've been thinking of entering some of my ads in the annual newspaper ad competition. Do you think my work is good enough?"

A person who is starved for recognition may say or do things that damage relationships with others. The individual who doesn't receive enough positive strokes may engage in exaggerated self-criticism. The newspaper employee described above might make these statements:

- "None of my ads look good. I think I'll quit this job."
- "The department manager must hate my work. He hasn't commented on any of my ads for weeks."

No one enjoys working around people who constantly fish for compliments or who spend a lot of time finding fault with themselves. Both of these behaviors may indicate the need for more positive reinforcement.

FORMS OF POSITIVE REINFORCEMENT

You have no doubt heard of employees who worked thirty or forty years for an organization but did not receive any significant form of recognition until retirement. The traditional gold watch, or some other token of appreciation, was given to the worker on his or her final day. Times have changed. Most progressive organizations recognize that positive reinforcement should be provided at various intervals throughout the employee's career. Continuity is one key to a successful program of positive reinforcement.

Variety is another important element of a successful positive reinforcement program. Everyone needs to become aware of the many different ways to give positive recognition to other people. Without variety, attempts to give recognition may seem mechanical and insincere. In this section, you will be introduced to a wide range of PR strategies.

Confirmation Behaviors

Evelyn Sieburg uses the term **confirmation** to name a whole series of behaviors that have a positive, or "therapeutic," effect upon the receiver.[14] In most cases, confirmation behaviors develop feelings of self-worth in the mind of the worker and may be reflected in increased productivity, less absenteeism, and greater interest in work.

To understand the wide range of possible confirmation behaviors that may exist in a work setting, let's follow a new worker throughout the first year on the job. Mary Harper graduated from a local community college where she completed a legal assistant program, and then obtained a position with a large law firm.

Upon arriving at work, she was greeted warmly, given a tour of the office complex, and introduced to the people with whom she would be working. A highlight of the tour was a stop at the president's office, where she met the founder of the firm. The president briefly reviewed the history of the firm and extended a warm welcome.

The orientation included a review of the firm's policies and procedures (explained in a handbook) and training that helped her learn how to use the firm's data retrieval system. As she demonstrated competence in using the equipment, the supervisor made comments such as "Well done . . . you're a quick learner" and "Good job . . . you're doing fine."

During the morning coffee break of her first day, she was surprised to see a notice on the bulletin board that said, "Please welcome Mary Harper to our office." This notice reminded other workers that a new person had joined the staff. The bulletin board announcement also made it easier for everyone to remember her name.

As the weeks passed, Mary Harper was given positive reinforcement on several occasions. She received positive feedback from fellow workers as well as her supervisor. When she had a problem, her supervisor proved to be a good listener. After six weeks, she was given a formal performance review by her supervisor. Another review followed six months later. These performance reviews helped her become aware of her strengths and of some areas that needed improvement. Because of the professional way her supervisor handled these reviews, Mary always came away with a desire to do better. At the end of the first year, Mary received a letter from the president of the firm (see Figure 7.1).

Would you enjoy working in this organizational setting? Chances are your answer is yes. A host of confirming behaviors gave Mary support during her first year on the job. These confirmations included the following:

Praise   Praise is one of the easiest and most powerful ways to make an employee feel important and needed. The person who receives the praise knows that his or her work is not being taken for granted. When handled correctly, praise can be an effective reinforcement strategy that ensures repetition of desired behaviors.

Courtesy   The poet Tennyson once said, "The greater the man, the greater the courtesy." When Mary Harper reported to work she was welcomed in a courteous manner and introduced to people throughout the office. Even the president of the firm was not too busy to greet her. Courtesy means being considerate of others in small ways, showing respect for what others revere, and treating everyone, regardless of position, with consideration. You display courtesy when you refuse a request gracefully and remain calm under pressure.

Active Listening   Everyone feels a sense of personal value when speaking with a good listener. Active listening can be a powerful reinforcer. **Active listening** is the process of sending back to the speaker what you as a listener think the speaker meant, in terms of both content and feelings.

Positive Written Communication   Most people respond positively to notes and letters that express appreciation. However, this form of positive reinforcement is used all too infrequently in organizations. Mary Harper will probably keep the letter written to her by the president and may show it to friends and relatives. A letter of appreciation can have considerable impact on employee morale and can improve interpersonal communication within the organization.

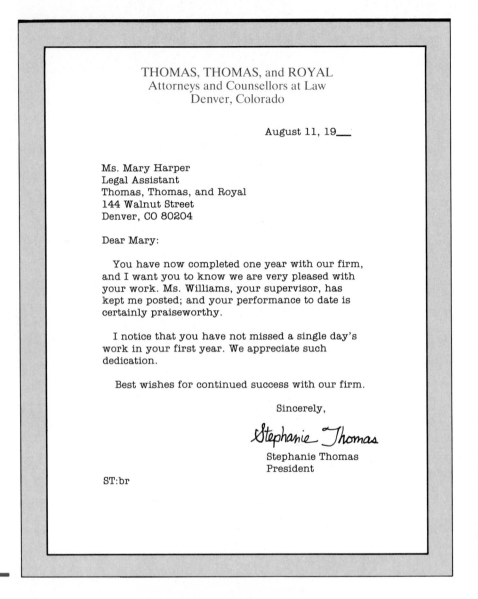

THOMAS, THOMAS, and ROYAL
Attorneys and Counsellors at Law
Denver, Colorado

August 11, 19___

Ms. Mary Harper
Legal Assistant
Thomas, Thomas, and Royal
144 Walnut Street
Denver, CO 80204

Dear Mary:

You have now completed one year with our firm, and I want you to know we are very pleased with your work. Ms. Williams, your supervisor, has kept me posted; and your performance to date is certainly praiseworthy.

I notice that you have not missed a single day's work in your first year. We appreciate such dedication.

Best wishes for continued success with our firm.

Sincerely,

Stephanie Thomas

Stephanie Thomas
President

ST:br

Figure 7.1
A Letter Can Give
Positive Reinforcement

Performance Review Mary Harper, like most other employees, wants to know if her work is satisfactory. Feedback from a respected supervisor during the **performance review**, especially positive feedback that has been earned, can be very rewarding. Donald Schuster, director of management development and training at World Color Press, Inc., uses the term **performance recognition** to describe an approach in which supervisors motivate employees with meaningful personal recognition.[15] He feels performance recognition should be the primary focus of the performance review because it results in more open communication between supervisor and subordinate.

THINKING/LEARNING STARTER

Chances are you owe somebody a thank-you note. Think about events of the past six months. Has someone given time and effort to assist you with a problem? Make a list of at least three people who deserve a thank-you note. Pick one, write that person a note of appreciation, and mail it today.

Positive Reinforcement: Everyone's Responsibility

Too often we think of positive reinforcement as the responsibility of supervisors and managers. This view is much too narrow. As shown in Figure 7.2, everyone in the organization has opportunities to recognize the accomplishments of others. Persons in supervisory and management positions can benefit from positive reinforcement initiated by subordinates. Recognizing the accomplishments of peers also provides positive motivation.

The authors of *How to Manage Your Boss* state that "subordinates too often wait until they have something negative to report before giving the boss feedback." Catching the boss doing something good and rewarding him or her is a far more effective way to change behavior than criticizing or complaining about it.[16]

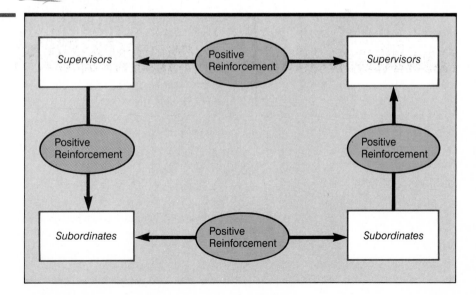

Figure 7.2
Everyone Is Responsible for Positive Reinforcement

TOTAL PERSON INSIGHT

❝ I think you must treat other people as you want to be treated. If you do that, you will get along better, earn their respect, and lessen the aggravations in your relationships. Emphasizing the positive aspects of a person and that person's work will get you much better results than harping on the negative. **❞**

Jan Hartman

AWARDS AND INCENTIVES

Every year U.S. companies spend about $10 billion for incentives and awards given to their employees. This money is spent on color TVs, vacation trips, rings, plaques, pins, certificates, cash bonuses, and a host of other items (see Table 7.2). One of the primary purposes of **awards** and **incentives** is to encourage desired employee behaviors. They are used to

1. reward behavior that helps reduce or prevent accidents.
2. reduce absenteeism.
3. reward years of service with an organization.
4. improve sales.
5. build morale.
6. improve quality control.

TABLE 7.2   Types of Achievement Awards Presented

Type of Award	Percentage of Companies*
Cash bonus	58%
Certificate or letter of recognition	38
Plaque or trophy	37
Vacation or cruise	11
Savings bond	10
Watch, pin, or other jewelry	8
Choice of gift items	5
Paid leave	1

* Percentages are based on 73 companies with achievement awards programs.
Nearly all employers responding to a survey conducted by The Bureau of National Affairs, Inc. reward employees for achievement, performance, suggestions, or length-of-service. The table above shows the types of awards given for employee achievement or performance.
Source: Reprinted by permission; Personnel Policies Forum Survey No. 145, *Employee Award Programs* (September 1987). Copyright 1987 by The Bureau of National Affairs, Inc.

NCR Corp. has a long-standing practice of giving awards to sales employees for superior performance. This is an historic photo of a National Cash Register Co. sales training class.
NCR Corporation

7. increase learning in training programs.
8. improve customer relations.

The use of awards and incentives is by no means a new phenomenon. John H. Patterson, founder and head of The National Cash Register Co. (now NCR Corporation) from 1884 to 1922, used a variety of incentive programs to motivate his sales force. Sales personnel earned merchandise or travel awards when their performance exceeded a fixed goal. Many of Patterson's ideas are still popular in the business world today.

One of the most widespread developments in recent years has been the introduction of innovative incentive plans that reward increased productivity, improved quality, lower operating costs, or some combination of these factors. The American Productivity and Quality Center reports that about 75 percent of all employers today use at least one type of nontraditional pay plan.[17] The source of motivation for adopting such a plan is often linked to increased competition. New levels of competition require that compensation be linked to performance. The most common incentive plans are briefly described here.

Gain sharing In a gain-sharing plan, managers and employees develop methods of improving productivity, improving quality, and cutting costs.

When a unit betters a predetermined performance objective, the resulting gains are divided according to a formula. This plan tends to encourage coordination and teamwork. One of the best examples of gain sharing is at the Firestone Tire & Rubber Co. plant at Wilson, North Carolina. Since the plan was initiated in 1977, the plant has had no layoffs and annual employee turnover is less than 0.5 percent.[18] Gain sharing is one of the fastest-growing incentive plans.

Profit sharing   In a profit-sharing system, employees receive a share of the company's profits, which may be paid in cash or put into a retirement fund. To be successful, participating employees must be able to influence profits. Profit sharing is a very popular incentive plan among employers because the company faces no risk. The company shares its profits only when it has enough funds to do so.

Production incentives   Under a production-incentives plan, employees receive payments based on how well they perform in relation to standards that have been established. In a factory setting the rewards are often based on piecework. For each acceptable piece they produce, workers receive a specific payment. One of the oldest and most successful production incentive plans can be found at Lincoln Electric Company, a ninety-four-year-old Cleveland, Ohio, manufacturer of welding machines and motors. Employees receive no base salary. Earnings are based on individual output and on bonuses from profits earned by the company. Lincoln Electric has been profitable every year since the incentive plan was initiated in 1934.[19]

Pay for knowledge   In a **pay-for-knowledge** system, workers are paid for the skills they master or the tasks they can perform. This plan is used by companies that want employees to be able to perform more than one job. By increasing the flexibility of the individual employees, the company may be able to operate with fewer workers. Although training costs may be higher, workers who can perform several jobs gain a broader perspective and thereby become more valuable to the company.

Special recognition awards   Employees can earn special recognition awards in the form of cash payments for contributions that management recognizes as above and beyond their normal duties.[20] For example, an employee may receive an award for outstanding customer service. Mercedes-Benz of North America, Inc. was concerned that its dealers' mechanics were forgetting what they had learned in company-sponsored training programs. To solve this problem, they developed a post-training program that connected incentives to retention and application of newly acquired information. Once each month for the first three months following service schools, mechanics received a ten-question review test. Merchandise prize points were awarded to those who answered the questions correctly.[21]

Suggestion systems Under this plan, a monetary reward is given to employees who suggest ways to improve company operations. The amount of the award is usually based on the estimated value of resulting increases in efficiency or cost cutting. Figure 7.3 shows a suggestion form used by Deere & Company.

To encourage the development of new technologies and products, 3M Company gives Golden Step awards each year to teams that have developed

Figure 7.3
Typical Suggestion Form
Source: Deere & Company;
Moline, Illinois

JOHN DEERE COMPONENT WORKS
SUGGESTION FORM

"THANKS FOR YOUR SUGGESTION"

SUGGESTION NO. DO NOT WRITE HERE.				DATE FILL IN THIS BOX.		DATE REC. DO NOT WRITE IN THIS BOX.	

EMPLOYEE NO.	SALARIED DEPT.	SHOP DEPT.	SHIFT	JOB CLASSIFICATION	LAST	NAME FIRST	INITIAL

ARE YOU WILLING TO DISCUSS YOUR IDEA WITH AN EVALUATOR?
☐ NO ☐ YES ☐ IN PRIVATE ONLY

DO YOU OBJECT TO PUBLICITY IF AN AWARD IS PAID?
☐ NO ☐ YES

YOUR SIGNATURE AND DATE

Please read the Suggestion Plan rules which are printed on the back of this form.

In submitting this suggestion I agree to all provisions of the Suggestion Plan rules and procedures as shown on the back of this form.

This form must be signed by all parties.

Describe your suggestion fully. If necessary, use another sheet of paper and attach it to this form. Enclose a sketch if possible. The Suggestion Administrator or your supervisor will be glad to help you with any problems you may have in filling out this form.

PART NO.	OPER. NO.	MACH. NO.	L.G.	DEPT.	FIXT., FORM OR TOOL NO.

PRESENT METHOD OR CONDITION

SUGGESTED IMPROVEMENT

3M Chairman and CEO Allen F. Jacobson presents the 1989 Golden Step award to the leader of the winning team.
3M

new business for the company. To be eligible for this award, the new product must generate at least $2 million in annual sales and show promise of more growth. These treasured awards have helped develop an "entrepreneurial" culture at 3M.[22]

Awards and incentives can serve as the backbone of suggestion systems. To draw more ideas from employees, many companies are using merchandise awards in addition to, or in place of, the traditional cash award. Cost-saving ideas, and ideas for new product development, can make a major contribution to a company's profitability.

Although the popularity of award and incentive programs is growing, the movement is not without its critics. One concern is that incentives treat the symptom, not the problem. For example, a firm may use trading stamps or cash incentives to reduce absenteeism. However, the problem may actually have its roots in poor working conditions or poor supervision. In this example, the incentive program may reduce absenteeism but fail to cure the real problem.

Some critics also say that incentive programs often reinforce the wrong behavior. The salesperson who is set on winning a trip to England may sell a customer a product he or she does not really need. In this case, the incentive has reinforced an undesirable behavior. In addition, an incentive program that rewards employees for increased productivity, but ignores quality, may backfire.

Another concern expressed by critics is that the effect of an incentive program may be temporary. They say the positive feelings that accompany winning the TV set or trophy are often short-lived.

Although these criticisms are valid in some cases, it is possible to design incentive programs that will have long-range benefits for both the organization and the individual employee. A well-designed program can help an organization achieve a variety of goals such as reduced expenses, improved product quality, improved customer service, and increased sales.

Planning the Incentive Program

The key to successful incentive programs is careful planning and implementation. The challenge to management is to develop a plan that motivates the right kinds of behavior. Any confusion about which behavior is to be rewarded can create serious problems. Programs must also be administered fairly, or some eligible employees may not participate or will participate with little enthusiasm. The following guidelines should be observed when designing and implementing an incentive program.

1. *Start with a well-defined purpose.* Companies with established incentive plans that are not related to specific goals almost always encounter problems.[23]

2. *Spell out requirements carefully before the program begins and make rules easy to understand.* A written description of the incentive program should be given to every employee who is eligible. It's often a good idea to introduce new programs at meetings or conferences so that employees will have an opportunity to raise questions and discuss items that are not clear. At the conclusion of the meeting, employees should be able to explain how the new program works and what they need to do to earn the incentive.

3. *Provide meaningful rewards.* If the rewards are not significant or if there are not enough of them, little interest in the program will develop. If achieving the award is too difficult, some employees may not even try. If rewards are too easily attained, participants will not be motivated to do their best.

4. *Administer the award program fairly.* Once the policies and procedures have been established, employees must be confident that they will be adhered to. Incentives should be given only when results are achieved, and withheld when goals are not met.

Charles Alden, former manager of Special Projects at 3M's Audio/Video Products Division, states that incentive programs should stimulate motivation. Every element of the program should be judged in light of two questions. First, does the incentive program offer real potential for greater self-realization, or is it just another obligation? Second, will it result in increased social recognition and greater confidence in personal worth for the achievers?[24]

Although most programs are designed within the organization, some companies are turning to consulting firms that specialize in recognition, award, and incentive-motivation program design. The E. F. MacDonald Co. of Dayton, Ohio; Josten's, Inc. of Minneapolis, Minnesota; and O. C. Tanner Co. of Salt Lake City, Utah, represent three such firms.

REMOVING BARRIERS TO POSITIVE REINFORCEMENT

The material in this chapter is based upon two indisputable facts about human nature. First, people want to know how well they are doing and if their work is satisfactory; second, they appreciate recognition for a job well done. Performance feedback and positive reinforcement can satisfy these important human needs. People often say they prefer negative feedback to no feedback at all. "Don't leave me in the dark" is a common plea (spoken or unspoken) of the American worker. You will remember from Chapter 2 that behaviors resulting in satisfying consequences for the individual are more likely to be repeated. Positive reinforcement is one way to ensure that desirable behavior is repeated.

Yet, if all these things are true, why isn't PR used more frequently? If it is such a good way to improve human relations and motivate people to achieve higher levels of performance, why are so few people willing to give recognition to others? Some of the most common barriers will be discussed in this section.

Preoccupation with Self

One of the major obstacles to providing positive reinforcement is preoccupation with oneself. The term **narcissism** is often used to describe this human condition. Narcissism is a Freudian term based upon the mythical youth who wore himself out trying to kiss his own reflection in a pool of water.

Some social critics feel that the tendency to become preoccupied with oneself became more prevalent during the 1970s. One writer labeled this period the "me decade." Many of the books published during this period communicated the theme "Look out for Number One!" Here are a few examples:

1. *The Art of Selfishness* by David Seabury
2. *Winning Through Intimidation* by Robert Ringer

3. *Winning with Deception and Bluff* by Sydney Schweitzer
4. *Power! How to Get It, How to Use It* by Michael Korda
5. *Pulling Your Own Strings* by Wayne Dyer

There is certainly nothing wrong with taking charge of your life and making more of your own decisions. Nor should you apologize for pursuing your own goals as long as you don't walk over other people in the process. However, you need to avoid the kind of self-centeredness that prevents you from recognizing the accomplishments of others.

Sydney Harris, in his book *Winners and Losers*, makes some interesting comments about behaviors that contribute to our success or failure in life. Here are just a few concise comments from his book:

A *winner* is sensitive to the atmosphere around him; a *loser* is sensitive only to his own feelings.

A *loser* feels cheated if he gives more than he gets; a *winner* feels that he is simply building up credit for the future.

A *winner* acts the same toward those who can be helpful and those who can be of no help; a *loser* fawns on the powerful and snubs the weak.

A *winner*, in the end, gives more than he takes; a *loser* dies clinging to the illusion that "winning" means taking more than you give.[25]

Misconceptions About Positive Reinforcement

Positive reinforcement is not used by some people simply because they have misconceptions about this human relations strategy. One misconception is that people will respond to positive feedback by demanding tangible evidence of appreciation. "Tell people they are doing a good job and they will ask for a raise" seems to be the attitude of some managers. Actually, just the opposite response will surface more often than not. In the absence of intangible rewards (such as praise), workers may demand greater tangible rewards.

A few managers seem to feel they will lose some of their power or control if they praise workers. Yet if managers rely on power alone to get the job done, any success they might achieve will no doubt be short-lived. A final misconception is the belief that "employees are hired to do a job, and they don't deserve any rewards beyond the paycheck." One part of this statement is correct. Employees are hired to do a job. However, it is the manager's responsibility to let them know if the job is being performed correctly. If they are doing a good job, why not reinforce that behavior with a little praise? The manager who operates from the viewpoint "We never bother anyone around here if they are doing their job" has fallen into a trap. Essentially, this person is saying, "My people are not going to get any recognition unless they fail to do their jobs."[26]

The "Too Busy" Syndrome

When you are under a great deal of pressure to get the job done and work is piling up on your desk, it's easy to postpone sending a congratulatory note or phoning someone simply for the purpose of saying thank you. Dr. Bruce Baldwin, practicing psychologist and consultant, describes the problem this way:

> There is not enough positive feedback given these days. With intense life-styles and countless pressures on men and women at work and in the home, positive feedback may sometimes completely disappear. In many organizations and in just as many homes, an emotionally destructive pattern emerges. No one says a thing about what is positive or done well.[27]

Managers often complain that they don't have time to assess the strengths of their people, let alone plan and deliver some type of recognition. The key to solving this problem is planning. Managers need to set aside time for this important area. A consciously planned PR program will ensure that recognition for work well done is not overlooked. One approach might be to set aside a few minutes each day to work on performance feedback and positive reinforcement activities, such as the letter in Figure 7.4. In other circumstances, immediate, on-the-spot commendation of a behavior is more appropriate. In *The One Minute Manager*, the authors point out that positive feedback need not take long. They suggest the simple plan outlined in Table 7.3 .

TABLE 7.3   One Minute Praisings

The one-minute praising works well, say authors Kenneth Blanchard and Spencer Johnson, when you

1. tell people *up front* that you are going to let them know how they are doing.
2. praise people immediately.
3. tell them what they did right—be specific.
4. tell them how good you feel about what they did right, and how it helps the organization and others who work there.
5. stop for a moment of silence to let them *feel* how good you feel.
6. encourage them to do more of the same.
7. shake hands or touch people in a way that makes it clear that you support their success in the organization.

Source: "One Minute Praisings" excerpted from p. 101 of *The One Minute Manager* by Kenneth Blanchard, Ph.D and Spencer Johnson, M.D. Copyright © 1981, 1982 by the Blanchard Family Partnership and Candle Communications Corporation. By permission of William Morrow and Company Inc.

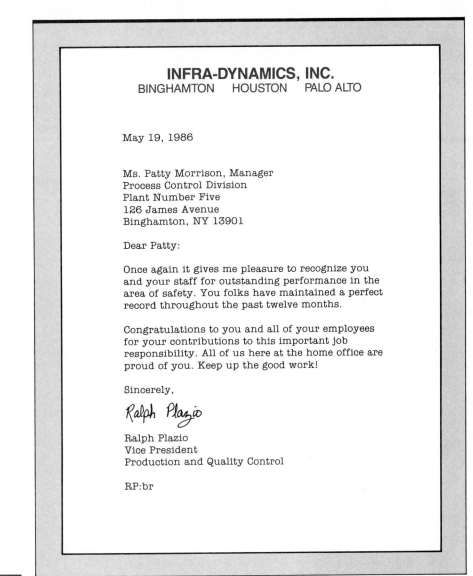

INFRA-DYNAMICS, INC.
BINGHAMTON   HOUSTON   PALO ALTO

May 19, 1986

Ms. Patty Morrison, Manager
Process Control Division
Plant Number Five
126 James Avenue
Binghamton, NY 13901

Dear Patty:

Once again it gives me pleasure to recognize you
and your staff for outstanding performance in the
area of safety. You folks have maintained a perfect
record throughout the past twelve months.

Congratulations to you and all of your employees
for your contributions to this important job
responsibility. All of us here at the home office are
proud of you. Keep up the good work!

Sincerely,

Ralph Plazio

Ralph Plazio
Vice President
Production and Quality Control

RP:br

Figure 7.4
A Thank You or
Congratulatory Letter
Reinforces Desirable
Behavior

Failing to Identify Commendable Actions

There are numerous opportunities to recognize the people you work with. However, it is possible to get in a rut and end up saying "thanks" automatically, without really noticing what employees do. By exercising just a little creativity, you can discover many actions that deserve to be commended.

Assume you are the manager of a large auto dealership. One of the key people within your organization is the service manager. This person schedules work to be performed on customers' cars, handles customer complaints, supervises the mechanics, and performs a host of other duties. If you want to give your service manager performance feedback and positive recognition, what types of behavior can you praise? Table 7.4 lists some examples.

The approach to positive reinforcement, of course, should be tailored to the requirements of the job. Positive reinforcement strategies designed for a sales staff may not work in a machine shop. Workers in the machine shop might be rewarded for performing preventive maintenance or spotting potential machine problems and calling maintenance to have equipment repaired.

Everyone needs to become more aware of the many behaviors that deserve positive recognition. It's easy to add variety to your positive reinforcement activities.

Not Knowing What to Say or Do

You can also show appreciation for work well done in a great variety of ways. It's a good idea to avoid saying or doing the same thing over and over

---

TABLE 7.4   Job Performance Behavior to Be Reinforced

1. *Performance Related to Interpersonal Relations*
   a. Empathy for customer needs and problems
   b. Ability to handle customer complaints effectively
   c. Ability to keep all employees well informed
   d. Cooperation with supervisory personnel in other departments
   e. Ability to maintain a sense of humor
   f. Recognition of the accomplishments of employees
   g. Effective supervision of employees

2. *Personal Characteristics*
   a. Honesty in dealings with people throughout the organization
   b. Punctuality
   c. Does not violate policies and procedures
   d. Maintains emotional stability
   e. Maintains a neat appearance
   f. Uses good judgment
   g. Alert to new ways to do the job better

3. *Management Skills*
   a. Avoids waste in the use of supplies and materials
   b. Maintains accurate records
   c. Spends time on short- and long-range planning
   d. Takes steps to prevent accidents
   e. Delegates authority and responsibility
   f. Maintains quality control standards

again. There are many words and phrases that communicate approval. Here are several examples of different expressions you can use to show appreciation.

- "Good thinking!"
- "I'm pleased."
- "You are improving."
- "This is the best yet!"
- "Excellent idea."
- "Good answer."
- "Thank you."
- "Great!"
- "Please continue."
- "Keep up the good work."

Of course, you can express appreciation without using verbal communication. There are many nonverbal expressions of approval.

- Eye contact
- Nodding agreement
- Laughing happily
- Pat on the back
- Moving closer to someone
- Clapping hands
- Signaling okay
- Smiling
- Thumbs up
- Firm handshake
- Placing a hand on someone's shoulder

And finally, you can give recognition to others through some type of action. Here are some activities that show approval.

- Ask an employee for advice.
- Ask an employee to demonstrate the correct performance or procedure.
- Ask an employee to serve as chairperson of a committee.
- Compliment the work of another person.
- Display an employee's work.
- Recognize the work of an employee at a staff meeting.
- Ask an employee to explain a complex procedure.

Lack of Appropriate Role Models

Most employees tend to look to organizational leaders for clues regarding what is acceptable behavior. The leaders provide a role model for everyone else. If the store manager in your neighborhood supermarket is aloof, seems indifferent to the needs of employees and customers, and generally displays a negative attitude, the store's supervisors are apt to imitate this behavior. After all, if the boss behaves this way, it must be right. Pretty soon the grocery clerks, baggers, and cashiers—who look to the supervisors for guidance—get the message: Customer relations is not important. Getting along with coworkers isn't important. Providing positive reinforcement for one another is not important.

The people at the top are always in the spotlight. Their actions are constantly being watched by the people they supervise, and their attitudes are contagious. James Balkcom, CEO of Techsonic Industries Inc., understands the importance of positive reinforcement and the need for positive role models. During one period of high sales demand his work force was working fifteen-hour workdays and six-day workweeks. Concerned about fatigue among his 250 employees, and the time they were spending away from their families, he decided to give them a special reward. He closed the plant, gave the employees a four-day weekend, and gave each of them a crisp $100 bill.[28]

Other factors support a program of positive reinforcement. This human relations strategy flourishes in a supportive environment. Within the organization, there should be respect for each person regardless of job title, duties performed, or earnings. The prevailing climate within the organization should also be positive. People must feel good about the organization, its leadership, and other employees. Positive reinforcement comes naturally in a positive work environment. On the other hand, positive reinforcement will almost never flourish in a negative work environment.

SUMMARY

People usually feel good when their accomplishments are recognized, and conversely become upset when work well done is ignored. Positive reinforcement, when used correctly to reward accomplishments, is a powerful motivator. Everyone needs to receive personal recognition and to feel important.

Although many studies indicate that positive reinforcement is an important employee reward preference, often ranked higher than monetary rewards and job security, many people seem unable or unwilling to reward a job well done. Confirmation behaviors need to be used in organizational settings more often. Praise, simple courtesy, being a good listener, written thank-you notes, and incentives and awards represent some of the ways people can reinforce another's behavior.

Preoccupation with self is a major obstacle to providing reinforcement to others. Self-centered persons are more apt to overlook the accomplishments of other people. Another obstacle is the view that "employees are hired to do a job, and they don't deserve any rewards beyond the paycheck." Some managers say a busy schedule does not allow time to give recognition to others. These and other barriers tend to minimize the use of positive reinforcement.

KEY TERMS

positive reinforcement (PR)
ego identity
reinforcer
physical stroke
verbal stroke
stroke deficit
confirmation
active listening
performance review

awards
incentives
gain sharing
profit sharing
production incentives
pay for knowledge
special recognition awards
suggestion system
narcissism

REVIEW QUESTIONS

1. What evidence is there to support the contention that positive reinforcement is a major employee reward preference?

2. What is the difference between a positive stroke and a negative stroke?

3. What are some behaviors a person might display that would indicate the presence of a stroke deficit?

4. How can one's identity and self-worth be influenced by confirmation behaviors?

5. In a typical organizational setting, what are some confirmation behaviors that might have a positive or "therapeutic" effect on an employee?

6. What are some of the major arguments for and against the use of incentives and awards?

7. List and describe the most common incentive programs used by organizations today.

8. What are some common misconceptions about positive reinforcement?

9. What are some employee behaviors that might be recognized by a supervisor or manager? List at least five different performance-related behaviors.

10. Review the Total Person Insight on page 180. Do you agree with the views of Jan Hartman?

■ CASE 7.1

Seeking Suggestions

A growing number of organizations are turning to their employees for suggestions for improving efficiency and cutting costs. One example is Marion Laboratories, Inc., which is headquartered in Kansas City. This company has a generous suggestion-award program that rewards good ideas with company stock. Each year the company distributes about ten thousand shares of stock to employees who have proposed the best suggestions.

At Eastman Kodak Co., employees can receive cash awards for introducing money-saving ideas. One employee felt cameras should be loaded with batteries, film, and flash bulbs just prior to filling dealers' orders. As a result, customers are now provided with the freshest possible batteries and film. In addition, the company realized tremendous cost savings since less storage space is required and investment in batteries and flash bulbs is delayed. The employee won a $50,000 award for the idea.

Small companies can also benefit from employee suggestions. The officers at Resource Information Management Systems, Inc., a developer of software for health administrators, host twice-monthly lunches during which workers are encouraged to share suggestions. Five employees are invited to each lunch. One officer noted: "It makes employees feel important, and we get invaluable feedback."

Sources: Robert Levering, *A Great Place to Work* (New York: Random House, 1988), p. 40; "How to Encourage Suggestive Behavior," *INC.*, October 1988, p. 112; "Incentive 'Carrots': Make Them Large and Plentiful," *Training*, February 1981, p. 8.

Questions

1. Some companies have experimented with employee suggestion programs and have had great success. Other companies, however, say they receive very few ideas from employees. What are some of the factors that seem to contribute to a successful employee suggestion program?

2. Should public-sector organizations, such as hospitals, schools, and bus companies, solicit suggestions from their employees?

3. Some companies are seeking suggestions from their customers. Do you support this practice? Explain your answer.

■■■■■■■ ■ CASE 7.2

Mary Kay Is Having a Party

Mary Kay Ash started Mary Kay Cosmetics, Inc. in 1963, as much to give women a chance to "be somebody" as for any other reason. Two decades later the firm had a sales force of almost 200,000 (of which 99 percent were women), working under 4,000 regional sales directors. The firm markets its products directly to consumers at "parties" in which a sales representative meets with up to five potential customers. The representative, called a beauty consultant, teaches potential customers how to use and care for their skin with Mary Kay products and then takes orders for the products.

A part-time beauty consultant can earn upwards of $50 in commissions at a sales party, and full-time employees of the company earn over $25,000 per year. But money isn't all they earn. Top salespeople are rewarded with diamond rings, mink coats, vacations, shopping sprees, and pink Cadillacs. Consultants also work for a Mary Kay "ladder of success" pin, whose rungs are filled with sapphires or diamonds as succeeding sales goals are met. Everyone connected with the firm can recognize a top salesperson from her pin. And these gifts are usually presented in a hall packed with applauding salespeople and sales directors.

Each regional sales director holds regular two-hour Monday night meetings for prospective and experienced consultants. The director leads the meeting but also stands as a model for the others; she has risen in the organization as a result of her success as a consultant. The meeting itself is structured to build and maintain motivation, teach new sales skills, and reward performance. The first hour is devoted mainly to an orientation for prospective consultants, while experienced hands exchange selling ideas or receive advanced training in a separate area.

Recruits and veterans get together for the second hour. Soon after it begins, the director describes and praises the sales accomplishments of various consultants who are at the meeting. The group stands, applauds perhaps, sings, and offers congratulations to those who did well. In a way, everyone at the meeting experiences their accomplishments. Then the group sets it sales goals, which are reinforced and encouraged by the director. Individual consultants may also voice their personal selling goals. If a consultant has not met such a publicly stated goal, there is no negative feedback. Instead, other experienced consultants offer suggestions on how to reach that objective.

Sources: Douglas M. Brooks and Kathy Bristow, "Monday Night Motivation at Mary Kay Cosmetics," *Mirrors of Excellence* (monograph), Robert Houston, ed., 1986, pp. 45–48; "Mary Kay Cosmetics: Looking beyond direct sales to keep the party going," *Business Week*, March 28, 1983, p. 130; Rebecca Fannin, "The Beauty of Being Mary Kay," *Marketing & Media Decisions*, December 1982, pp. 59–61, 150, 151.

Questions

1. Which forms of positive reinforcement are practiced in the Mary Kay organization, and by whom?
2. Would the approach used by Mary Kay Cosmetics work in other marketing-oriented firms?

SUGGESTED READINGS

Baldwin, Bruce A. "Complimentary Guidelines." *Pace*, August 1988, pp. 17–21.

Baldwin, Bruce A. "Positive Feedback as Incredible Information." *Pace*, May/June 1982, pp. 11–13.

Blanchard, Kenneth, and Spencer Johnson. *The One Minute Manager*. New York: Morrow, 1982.

Elmers, Robert C., George W. Blomgren, and Edward Gubman. "How Awards and Incentives Can Help Speed Learning." *Training/HRD*, July 1979, pp. 83–86ff.

"Employee Recognition: A Key to Motivation." *Personnel Journal*, February 1981, pp. 103–107.

King, Dennis. "Rewarding Can Be Rewarding." *Supervisory Management*, January 1985, pp. 32–33.

Nordstrom, Rodney R., and R. Vance Hall. "The Platinum Rule." *Training and Development Journal*, September 1986, pp. 57–58.

Perry, Nancy J. "Here Come Richer, Riskier Pay Plans." *Fortune*, December 19, 1988, pp. 50–58.

Renken, Henry J. "An Employee-Incentive Program Can Be the Answer to Increased Productivity." *S.A.M. Advanced Management Journal*, Spring 1984, pp. 8–12.

Strang, T. Scott, "Positive Reinforcement: How Often and How Much." *Supervisory Management*, January 1985, pp. 7–9.

Tylczak, Lynn, "The Concept of Value Management." *Pace*, July 1985, pp. 51–53.

NOTES

1. Robert Levering, Milton Moskowitz, and Michael Katz, *The 100 Best Companies to Work for in America* (New York: New American Library, 1985), pp. 173–177.
2. Tom Peters, "Letter to the Editor," *INC.*, April 1988, p. 80–81.
3. "The Power of Recognition," *The Royal Bank Letter*, published by the Royal Bank of Canada, Vol. 66, No. 5, 1985, p. 1.
4. Bruce A. Baldwin, "Positive Feedback as Incredible Information," *Pace*, May/June 1982, p. 13.
5. Kenneth Kovach, "Why Motivational Theories Don't Work," *S.A.M. Advanced Management Journal*, Spring 1980, p. 46.
6. C. B. Stiegler, "Know Others—Make Your Communication Work with Positive Reinforcement," *Management World*, May 1976, p. 10.
7. Peters, p. 81.
8. Kenneth Blanchard and Spencer Johnson, *The One Minute Manager* (New York: Morrow, 1982), p. 43.
9. Harry L. Miller, *Teaching and Learning in Adult Education* (London: Macmillan, 1964), pp. 34–36.
10. Sandra Scarr and James Vander Zanden, *Understanding Psychology*, 5th ed. (New York: Random House, 1987), p. 565.
11. "Poker for Pokies," *Women in Business*, November/December 1988, p. 6.
12. Peters, p. 80.
13. Claude Steiner, *TA Made Simple* (San Francisco: Transactional Pubs, 1973), p. 6.
14. Evelyn Sieburg, "Confirming and Disconfirming Organizational Communication," in *Communication in Organizations*, ed. James L. Owen, Paul A. Page, and Gordon I. Zimmerman (St. Paul, Minn.: West, 1976), p. 130.
15. Donald V. Schuster, "Performance Recognition: The Power of Positive Feedback," *Training*, January 1985, p. 72.
16. Christopher Hegarty with Philip Goldberg, *How to Manage Your Boss* (New York: Rawson, Wade, 1980), p. 125.
17. Nancy J. Perry, "Here Come Richer, Riskier Pay Plans," *Fortune*, December 19, 1988, pp. 50–58.
18. Ibid, p. 54.

19. Bruce G. Posner, "Right From the Start," *INC.*, August 1988, pp. 95–96.
20. Bruce G. Posner, "A Company of Salespeople," *INC.*, June 1988, p. 124.
21. "E. F. MacDonald Links Motivation and Incentives," *Training/HRD*, April 1981, p. 62.
22. Dave Beal, "Golden Steps Point to Strength in 3M's Culture," *St. Paul Pioneer Dispatch*, April 19, 1987, p. B1.
23. Perry, pp. 51–52.
24. Charles L. Alden, "Incentives Can Unlock Self-Motivation," *Sales and Marketing Management*, March 6, 1981, p. 92.
25. Sydney J. Harris, *Winners and Losers* (Niles, Ill.: Argus Communications, 1968), pp. 53, 61, 105, 117.
26. Thomas J. Von der Smase and Herbert E. Brown, "Authentic Motivation: How Psychological Touching Works," *Supervisory Management*, February 1979, p. 20.
27. Bruce A. Baldwin, "Complimentary Guidelines," *Pace*, August 1988, p. 19.
28. "Give 'em A Break," *INC.*, October 1986, p. 127.

Chapter 8

Developing Positive First Impressions

CHAPTER PREVIEW

After studying this chapter, you will be able to

1. Explain the importance of a positive first impression in an organizational setting.

2. Discuss the factors that contribute to creating a favorable first impression.

3. Distinguish between assumptions and facts.

4. Define *image* and describe the factors that form the image you project to others.

5. List the three things that influence your choice of clothing for work.

6. Understand how manners affect first impressions.

everal years ago James Gray, Jr., author of *The Winning Image*, created a college course that was designed to help people refine and enhance their personal image. The course was offered at The American University in Washington, D.C., and attracted people who wanted to learn more about the art and science of image projection. To emphasize the importance of his subject, Gray noted that "image is the way others see you, and it often determines how they treat you."[1]

Gray has joined the ranks of a growing number of image consultants who work with individuals and organizations. Today, the *Directory of Personal Image Consultants* includes almost three hundred names. An image consultant is someone who helps ensure that all elements of the visible person—speech, dress, body language, and manners—match the inner talents and aspirations of that person. Each year several million dollars are spent on image consulting in the United States.[2]

Lyn Pfaelzer is typical of the new wave of image consultants. This former teacher instructs men and women on how to develop what she describes as "visual communication skills." She has discovered that many people do not feel confident about the image they project and want advice.[3] People feel more secure when they look their best and are dressed appropriately for their job.

As organizations experience increased competition for clients, patients, and customers, awareness of the importance of public contact is increasing.[4] They are giving new attention to the old adage "First impressions are lasting impressions." Research indicates that initial impressions do indeed tend to linger. Therefore, a positive first impression can set the stage for a lasting relationship. A negative first impression can serve as a barrier to building good personal and customer relations. A major goal of this chapter is to discuss important factors that contribute to an effective first impression.

THE PRIMACY EFFECT

The tendency to form impressions quickly at the time of an initial meeting illustrates what social psychologists call a **primacy effect** in the way people perceive one another. The general principle is that first impressions establish the mental framework within which a person is viewed, and later evidence is either ignored or reinterpreted to coincide with this framework.[5]

Martha Kelly met a middle-aged man at an outdoor cookout. He was wearing cutoff blue jeans and an old pair of worn-out sneakers. He had had several drinks and tended to interrupt people and monopolize any conversation. Throughout the afternoon, people avoided him whenever possible. About two weeks later, Martha stopped at a drug store to get a prescription filled. To her surprise, the pharmacist was the same man she had met at the cookout, only now he was dressed in a neatly tailored white jacket, blue shirt, and pin-striped tie. Although he projected a very professional image in dealing with his customers, Martha left the store and went to another pharmacy to get her prescription filled. The positive impression communicated on this day was not strong enough to overcome her first, negative impression.

THE FIRST FEW MINUTES

When two people meet, their potential for building a relationship can be affected by many factors. Within a few moments, one person or the other may feel threatened, offended, or bored. Leonard and Natalie Zunin, coauthors of *Contact—The First Four Minutes*, describe what they call the **four-minute barrier.**[6] In this short period of time, human relationships will be established, reconfirmed (in the case of two former acquaintances meeting), or denied. It is during the first few minutes of interaction with others that people's attention spans are at their greatest and powers of retention at their highest.

Why four minutes? According to the Zunins, this is the average time, determined by careful observation, during which two people in a social situation make up their minds to continue the encounter or to separate. They say the four-minute concept applies to both casual meetings and ongoing contacts, such as husbands and wives meeting at the end of a day.

The way you are treated depends largely on the way you present yourself—the way you look, the way you speak, the way you behave.[7] Although human contact is a challenge, you can learn to control the first impressions you make on others. The key is to become fully aware of the impression you communicate to other people.

THINKING/LEARNING STARTERS

To test the practical application of the Zunins's theory in a real-life setting, examine it in the context of your past experiences. Review the questions below and then answer each with yes or no.

1. Have you ever gone for a job interview and known instinctively within minutes that you would or would not be hired?
2. Have you ever met a salesperson who immediately communicated to you the impression that he or she could be trusted and was interested in your welfare?
3. Have you ever entered a restaurant and developed an immediate dislike for the waiter or waitress after a few opening comments?
4. Have you ever entered a business firm and experienced an immediate feeling of being welcome after the receptionist spoke only a few words?

First Impressions in a Work Setting

In a work setting, the four-minute period in which a relationship is established or denied is often reduced to seconds. The U.S. Postal Service is concerned about perceptions created during this brief period of time. In selected regions of the nation, postal workers have completed the Dale Carnegie human relations course.[8] The examples below serve to illustrate the effect that immediate first impressions can have in a variety of work situations.

Item: Paula rushed into a restaurant for a quick lunch—she had to get back to her office for a 1:30 P.M. appointment. The restaurant was not crowded, so she knew she would not have to wait for a table. At the entrance of the main dining area was a sign reading "Please Wait to Be Seated." A few feet away, the hostess was discussing a popular movie with one of the waitresses. The hostess made eye contact with Paula, but continued to visit with the waitress. About twenty more seconds passed, and Paula began to feel anxiety build inside her. She tried to get the hostess's attention, but the hostess did not respond. After another ten seconds had passed, Paula walked out of the restaurant.

Item: Terry had completed his business in Des Moines, Iowa, and decided to rent a car for a trip to Omaha, Nebraska. He dialed the number of a popular rental car agency and was greeted by "May I help you?" spoken in a very indifferent tone of voice. Terry said that he wanted to rent a compact car and drive it to Omaha. The agency employee replied irritably, "You can't rent a compact car for out-of-town trips. These cars can only be used for local travel. You'll have to rent a full-sized car." Terry felt as though the employee didn't want his business and was criticizing him for not knowing the company's rental policy. He told the employee he would call another rental agency. The entire conversation lasted only thirty-seven seconds.

Item: Sandy and Mike entered the showroom of a Mercedes-Benz dealer. They noticed two salespeople seated at desks near the entrance. One salesperson was dressed in a well-tailored gray suit and white shirt, with a blue tie highlighted by subtle stripes. The other salesperson was wearing a dark green suit, yellow shirt, and a patterned brown tie. The suit, made of polyester fabric, had long ago lost its shape. The salesperson wearing the dark green suit walked over to Sandy and Mike and asked, "May I be of assistance?" Mike said, "We're just looking today." After a few moments, they left the showroom. On the way to their car, Sandy said, "I can't believe someone selling a $40,000 automobile would dress like that." "I agree," Mike said.

In each of these examples, the negative first impression was created in less than sixty seconds. The anxiety level of the restaurant customer in-

> **TOTAL PERSON INSIGHT**
>
> 66 If people aren't quickly attracted to you or don't like what they see and hear in those first two to four minutes, chances are they won't pay attention to all those words you believe are demonstrating your knowledge and authority. They will find your client guilty, seek another doctor, buy another product, vote for your opponent or hire someone else. 99
>
> Janet G. Elsea

creased because she was forced to wait while two employees talked about a personal matter. The rental car employee antagonized a potential customer by using a tone of voice that was offensive. And the car salesperson apparently was not aware that people will make judgments about others that are based solely on appearance. Unfortunately, these employees are probably not fully aware of the impression they communicate to customers.

Assumptions Versus Facts

The impression you form of another person during the initial contact is made up of both assumptions and facts. Most people tend to rely more heavily on **assumptions** during an initial meeting. As the Zunins state, people live in an assumptive world.

> When you meet a stranger, and sometimes with friends, much of the information you get is based on assumption. You form positive or negative feelings or impressions but you must realize that only superficial facts can be gathered in four minutes. Depending on assumptions is a one-way ticket to big surprises and perhaps disappointments.[9]

Cultural conditioning, especially during the early years, leads you to form impressions of some people even before you meet them. People often stereotype entire groups. Here are a few of the common stereotypes that still persist in our society:

- "Old people are grouchy."
- "Italians are highly emotional."
- "Football players are dumb."
- "Chess players are all intellectual giants."
- "Executive women are all aggressive."

These are just a few of the assumptions that some people perceive as facts. With the passing of time some assumptions tend to lose support as factual information surfaces. Fewer people today support the idea that all married couples should have children than was the case a generation ago, and women are no longer viewed as unacceptable candidates for executive positions. However, people rarely reach the point in life where they are completely free of assumptions. In fact, the *briefer* the encounter with a new acquaintance, the greater the chance that misinformation will enter into your perception of the other person.

THE IMAGE YOU PROJECT

Image is a term used to describe how other people feel about you. In every business or social setting your behaviors communicate a mental picture that others observe and remember. This picture determines how they react to you. Your image depends on more than exterior qualities such as dress and grooming. In the words of James Gray, ". . . image is more than just a veneer."[10] He observes:

> Image is a tool for communicating and for revealing your inherent qualities, your competence, abilities and leadership. It is a reflection of qualities that others associate with you, a reflection that bears long-lasting influence in your bid for success. Image is not a tool for manipulation. Nor is it a false front. It cannot substitute for substance.[11]

In many respects, the image you project is very much like a picture puzzle, as illustrated in Figure 8.1. It is formed by a variety of factors, in-

The image you project at work contributes to your job success.
Kindra Clineff/The Picture Cube

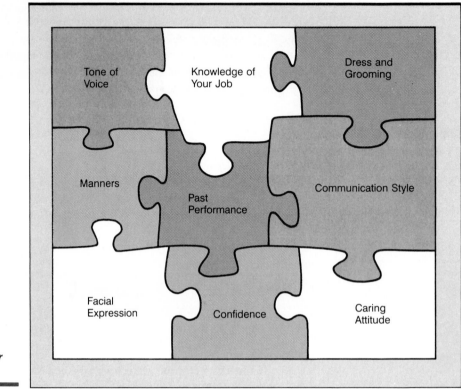

Figure 8.1
Factors That Form Your Image

cluding manners, communication style, clothing, hair style, facial expression, tone of voice, and the way you treat other people. Although a wide variety of things contribute to the impression you create in the minds of others, each is under your control.

Why be concerned about your image? Because many studies indicate that the image you project can be as important to job success as your skills. Put another way, your ability to get a job and advance to positions of greater responsibility will often depend upon the impression you communicate to others.

Surface Language

As noted earlier, we form opinions about other people based on both facts and assumptions. Unfortunately, assumptions often carry a great deal of weight. Many of the assumptions you develop regarding other people are based upon what the Zunins describe as "surface language." **Surface language** is defined as a pattern of immediate impressions conveyed by appearance. The clothing you wear, your hair style, the fragrances you use, and the jewelry you display all combine to make a statement about you to others.

According to many writers familiar with image formation, clothing is particularly important. John T. Molloy, author of *Dress for Success* and *The Woman's Dress for Success Book,* was one of the first to acknowledge publicly the link between professional accomplishments and wardrobe. According to his research, what you wear immediately establishes your credibility and likability.[12] Egon Von Furstenberg, author of *The Power Look* says that discrimination on the basis of appearance is a fact of life in the business world.[13]

One of the strongest statements made about the importance of clothing in image formation comes from William Thourlby, author of *You Are What You Wear—The Key to Business Success.* He says that when you step into a room, people who have never met you before begin making decisions about you solely on the basis of your appearance. These decisions relate to

- your trustworthiness.
- your level of sophistication.
- your social heritage.
- your moral character.
- your level of success.[14]

Thourlby points out that clothing and appearance are among the most important criteria we use to judge people. In addition, he notes that people judge your appearance long before they judge your talents. You should therefore take your wardrobe seriously. Physical attractiveness, a strong determinant of first impressions, can be enhanced by your choice of clothing.

THINKING/LEARNING STARTER

Do you recall a coworker or supervisor in a business setting whose surface language impressed you—either positively or negatively? What specific elements (dress, communication style, etc.) were evident in this person's surface language? What type of image do you think he or she was trying to project?

Selecting Your Career Apparel

Large numbers of people employed in the business community wear uniforms. Some employees, such as the Hertz rental car sales representatives, wear a uniform that was especially designed for their particular job. The mechanics at your neighborhood garage probably wear a special uniform. Today more and more people are getting into uniforms to go to work. According to psychologists, people who serve the public—especially those who are part of a group—often work best in uniform.[15] Wearing the same

Employees at Lowe's Companies, Inc. wear approved uniforms developed by a company that sells special-design career apparel.
Lowe's Companies, Inc.

A uniform worn by employees will often contribute to a spirit of teamwork. These uniforms are typical of those worn by chefs who are employed in fine restaurants.
Culinary Institute of America

uniform seems to create a sort of bond between coworkers. Thus, a uniform can make at least a small contribution to building esprit de corps at your local McDonald's restaurant or Holiday Inn motel.

Dress was the focus of a management decision at the GenCorp Automotive plant at Shelbyville, Indiana. The work force there is divided into twenty-five teams of twelve to fifteen production workers. To build company spirit, a decision was made to adopt the same "uniform" for all employees. Everyone, including managers, wears navy blue skirts or trousers and light blue shirts.[16]

The uniforms worn by UPS employees, airline reservation clerks, and the employees at your local restaurant might be classified as special-design career apparel. Some work uniforms are designed by top talents in the fashion industry. In addition to special-design uniforms, there is another type of career apparel, less formal and somewhat less predictable, worn by large numbers of people in our labor force. Here are some examples:

- A woman lawyer representing a prestigious firm would be appropriately dressed in a gray or blue skirted suit. A dress with a suit jacket would also be acceptable. She should avoid cute, frilly clothing that might reduce her credibility.

- A male bank loan officer would be appropriately dressed in a tailored gray or blue suit, white shirt, and tie. This same person dressed in a colorful blazer, sport shirt, and plaid slacks would be seen as too casual in a bank setting.

- A female receptionist at a prominent accounting firm would be appropriately dressed in a skirt and blouse. This same person would be inappropriately dressed if she showed up for work wearing designer jeans, a sweater, and sandals.

- A mechanic employed by an auto dealership that sells new cars would be appropriately dressed in matching gray, tan, or light blue shirt and pants. The mechanic would be inappropriately dressed in jeans and a sport shirt.

Selecting the correct clothing for a career can be difficult—for both men and women. The rules are usually unwritten and quite subtle. One psychologist who took an in-depth look at the subject made this observation:

> This whole business of dress and grooming is actually playing upon unconscious expectations and assumptions about the significance of clothing. For example, the man who's wearing a dark, three-piece suit projects to others that he's a conservative, predictable individual, while the man with frayed cuffs, or unshined shoes, is just naturally going to come off as careless and sloppy.[17]

The key idea presented here is **unconscious expectations.** Everyone has certain opinions about what is appropriate in terms of dress. Throughout life, we become acquainted with bank loan officers, nurses, police officers, and others employed in a wide range of occupations. We form mental images of the apparel common to each of these occupations. When we encounter someone whose appearance does not conform to our past experiences, we feel uncomfortable. Although today's public is more tolerant in matters related to dress, people still have certain expectations.

In general, three things will influence your choice of clothing for work: (1) the products or services offered by your employer, (2) the type of person served, and (3) the desired image projected by your organization.

Products and Services Offered Store A sells casual clothing such as blue jeans, corduroy slacks, multicolored shirts, and sweatshirts. Store B sells expensive suits, dress shirts, ties, and other accessories. You would not expect the employees working at Store A to wear a suit to work. Casual clothing, similar to that sold by the store, would be very acceptable. However, the employees working at Store B should dress up to meet the expectations of the clientele served. The customer who purchases an expensive suit will expect the salesperson to be dressed in a conservative manner. This person should wear clothing similar to that sold by the store.

Type of Person Served What are the expectations of your firm's customers and clients? This is always a key question when you are selecting career apparel. Consider the real estate firm that employs two sales teams: one team sells houses in urban areas and the other sells rural property, primarily farms. The urban home buyer expects to do business with someone who is conservatively dressed. The farmer, on the other hand, is apt to feel uncomfortable when dealing with someone who is dressed up (suit and tie, for example). A more casual outfit may represent appropriate apparel for these employees.

Desired Image Projected by the Organization Lowe's Companies, Inc. operates a chain of three hundred retail home-center stores. The company is attempting to project the image of an "upscale" discount retailer. The attractive stores are stocked with quality merchandise at competitive prices. Each employee wears neatly tailored apparel that was designed to complement the store image. The dress program was initiated to ensure that all employees present to customers a consistent professional look. (See photo on p. 206.)

Paul H. Pearson, president of Security Mutual Life Insurance Company, feels that people working for his company should project a well-groomed look. He also feels that top management should set the right example. Pearson states, "Personal grooming and clothing styles of top management should be consistent with the public image their corporation chooses to project."[18]

THINKING/LEARNING STARTER

Assume that you are planning to purchase: (1) a life insurance policy, (2) a Rolex wrist watch, and (3) eyeglasses. What types of career apparel would you expect persons selling these products to wear? What grooming standards would you recommend?

Wardrobe Engineering

The term **wardrobe engineering** was first used by John T. Molloy to describe how clothing and accessories can be used to create a certain image. This concept was later refined by William Thourlby, Jacqueline Thompson, Emily Cho, Susan Bixler, and other noted image consultants. In recent years, hundreds of books and articles on dress and grooming have been written. Although these authors are not in complete agreement on every aspect of dress, they do agree on a few basic points regarding your wardrobe.

1. *When meeting someone for the first time, you make an impression even before you open your mouth.* People judge your appearance before they know your talents! Keep in mind that nonverbal communication is the first and greatest source of impressions in direct, face-to-face interactions, and your choice of clothing is a major part of the nonverbal message you send to a new acquaintance.

2. *Establish personal dress and grooming standards appropriate for the organization where you wish to work.* Before you apply for a job, try to find out what the workers there are wearing. If in doubt, dress conservatively. If you find out the dress code is more relaxed, you can adjust to it later. When you actually begin work, identify the most successful people in the organization and emulate their manner of dress.

3. *Dress for the job you want, not the job you have.*[19] If you are currently a secretary and want to become the office manager, don't continue to dress like a secretary. Employees can communicate with their clothing

Reprinted by permission: Tribune Media Services.

that they are satisfied with their position. Emily Cho, author of *Looking Terrific*, says that the right wardrobe can transform a person from being part of the corporate scenery to being in the forefront. Some employers say they can walk into a business firm and see who is ready for a promotion.

4. *Avoid wearing the newest dress fad in a business or professional setting.* In most cases the world of work is more conservative than college, the arts, or the world of sports. If you are a fashion setter, you might be viewed as unstable or lacking in sincerity. To be taken seriously, avoid clothing that is too flashy.

   Women generally have more latitude than men in selecting appropriate attire, but they should still exercise some caution in choosing their wardrobe. In some cases, women are entering positions formerly dominated by men. They need to be taken seriously, and the wardrobe they select can contribute to this end.

5. *When you select a wardrobe, consider regional differences in dress and grooming standards.* Geography is a factor that determines how people should dress. What may be suitable apparel for a receptionist working in New York City may be inappropriate in Des Moines. Pay attention to local customs and traditions when establishing your personal dress and grooming standards.

6. *The quality of your wardrobe will influence the image you project.* Money spent on career apparel should be viewed as an investment, with each item carefully selected to look and fit well. A suit or dress purchased off the rack at a discount store may save dollars initially, but can cost you more if it doesn't help you get the promotion you want. Clothing purchased at bargain prices often wears out quickly. The less money you have, the more concerned you should be about buying quality clothing.

7. *Selection of a wardrobe should be an individual matter.* Diane Harris, a North Carolina-based image consultant who knows the rules about career dress for men and women, says, "Effective packaging is an individual matter based on the person's circumstances, age, weight, height, coloring, and objectives"[20] While you should consider the dress and grooming standards of others in your field, blind conformity or duplication are not advisable.

Getting a job, keeping a job, and getting a promotion depend to some degree on your wardrobe. Therefore, research your wardrobe as carefully as you would research a prospective employer. Although the practice of judging people solely by what they wear should not be encouraged, you need to recognize that people often are prejudiced regarding physical appearance. Make sure that your appearance helps you create a positive first impression.

Your Facial Expression

After your overall appearance, your face is the most visible part of you. Facial expressions are the cue most people rely on in initial interactions. They are the "teleprompter" by which others read your mood and personality.[21]

Studies conducted in nonverbal communication show that facial expressions strongly influence people's reactions to each other. The expression on your face can quickly trigger a positive or negative reaction from those you meet. How you rate in the "good-looks" department may not be nearly as important as your ability to communicate positive impressions with a pleasant smile.

If you want to identify the inner feelings of another person, watch the individual's facial expressions closely. A frown may tell you "something is wrong." A smile generally communicates "things are OK." Everyone has encountered a "look of surprise" and "a look that could kill." These facial expressions usually reflect inner emotions more accurately than words.

In many work settings, a cheerful smile is an important key to creating a positive first impression. On the other hand, a deadpan stare (or frown) can communicate a negative first impression to others. If you find it hard to smile, take time to consider the reasons. Are you constantly thinking negative thoughts and simply find nothing to smile about? Are you afraid others might misinterpret your intentions? Are you fearful that a pleasant smile will encourage communication with people with whom you would rather not spend time?

Your Entrance and Carriage

Susan Bixler, author of *The Professional Image,* says the way you enter someone's office or a business meeting can influence the image you project. She notes that "your entrance and the way you carry yourself will set the stage for everything that comes afterward."[22] A nervous or apologetic entrance may ruin your chances of getting a job, closing a sale, or getting the raise you have earned. If you feel apprehensive, try not to let it show in your body language. Hold your head up, avoid slumping forward, and try to project self-assurance. To get off to the right start and make a favorable impression, follow these words of advice from Bixler.

> The person who has confidence in himself or herself indicates this by a strong stride, a friendly smile, good posture, and a genuine sense of energy. This is a very effective way to set the stage for a productive meeting. When you ask for respect visually, you get it.[23]

Bixler says the key to making a successful entrance is simply believing—and projecting—that you have a reason to be there and have something important to present or discuss.

Your Voice

Several years ago a Cleveland-based company, North American Systems, Inc., developed and marketed Mr. Coffee, which makes a cup of coffee quickly and conveniently. Some credited the quick acceptance of this product to an effective advertising campaign featuring baseball Hall of Famer Joe Di Maggio. He came across to the consumer as an honest, sincere

Facial expressions can quickly communicate our inner thoughts to another person.
Deborah Kahn/Stock, Boston

person. When Joe Di Maggio said Mr. Coffee worked and made good coffee, people believed him.

The tone of your voice, the rate of speed at which you speak (tempo), and the volume of your speech contribute greatly to the meaning attached to your verbal messages. In the case of telephone calls, voice quality is critical, because the other person cannot see your facial expressions, hand gestures, and other body movements. You can't trade in your current voice for a new one. However, you can make your voice more pleasing to other people and project a positive tone.

Although there is no ideal voice for all business contacts, your voice should reflect at least these five qualities: confidence, enthusiasm, attention, optimism, and sincerity. Above all, try to avoid a speech pattern that is dull and colorless. Joanne Lamm, founder of Professional Speech Associates, says the worst kind of voice has no projection, no color, and no feeling.[24]

Assess your own speaking voice and determine if small changes will increase the effectiveness of your verbal communication with others. Try recording your voice to find out how you sound to others. To evaluate the quality of your voice, tape your conversation with another person. Play back the tape and rate yourself according to the five qualities listed in the previous paragraph.

Your Handshake

When two people first meet, a handshake is usually the only physical contact between them. The handshake can communicate warmth, genuine concern for the other person, and strength. It can also communicate aloofness, indifference, and weakness. The message you send the other party via your handshake will depend on a combination of the following factors.

1. *Degree of firmness.* Generally speaking, a firm handshake will communicate a caring attitude, whereas a weak grip communicates indifference.

2. *Degree of dryness of hands.* A moist palm is not only unpleasant to feel, but it can communicate the impression that you are nervous. A clammy hand is likely to repel most people.

3. *Duration of grip.* There are no specific guidelines about the ideal duration of a grip. However, by extending the handshake, you can often communicate a greater degree of interest in and concern for the other person.

4. *Depth of interlock.* A full, deep grip is more apt to convey friendship and strength to the other person.

5. *Eye contact during handshake.* Visual communication can increase the positive impact of your handshake. Maintaining eye contact throughout the handshaking process is important when two people greet each other.[25]

The message we communicate via our handshake can be quite powerful. It can communicate warmth, concern for the other person, and strength.
Hazel Hankin/Stock, Boston

Most individuals have shaken hands with hundreds of people but have little idea whether they are creating positive or negative impressions. It is a good idea to obtain this information from those coworkers or friends who will express candid opinions. Like all other human relations skills, the handshake can be improved with practice.

Your Manners

More than a decade ago Judith Martin started writing a column called "Miss Manners." To her surprise, the column has become extremely popular throughout the United States. Today, more than 250 newspapers carry the column. A growing number of people are seeking expert advice on such topics as how to deal with a coworker who cracks his or her knuckles or how to respond to a customer service representative who tells customers offensive stories. Renewed interest in manners has also been stimulated by the writings of Letitia Baldrige, author of *Letitia Baldrige's Complete Guide to Executive Manners*. It is her view that good manners are cost effective.

A study of manners (sometimes called etiquette) reveals a number of ways to improve first impressions. Jonathan Swift recognized the impor-

---

TOTAL PERSON INSIGHT

❝ In a society as ridden as ours with expensive status symbols, where every purchase is considered a social statement, there is no easier or cheaper way to distinguish oneself than by the practice of gentle manners. ❞

Judith Martin

---

tance of good manners when he said, "Good manners is the art of making people comfortable. Whoever makes the fewest people uncomfortable has the best manners." Making people feel comfortable is at the heart of good human relations. Good manners is a universal passport to positive relationships and respect.

One of the best ways to develop rapport with another person is to avoid behavior that might be offensive to that individual. Although it is not possible to do a complete review of this topic, some of the rules of etiquette that are particularly important in an organizational setting are covered here.

1. *When establishing new relationships, avoid calling people by their first names too soon.* Jacqueline Thompson says that assuming that all work-related associates prefer to be addressed informally by their first names is a serious breach of etiquette.[26] Use titles of respect—Miss, Mrs., Ms., Mr., or Dr.—until the relationship is well established. Too much familiarity can breed irritation. When the other party says "Call me Susan" or "Call me Roy," it's all right to begin using the person's first name. Informality should develop by invitation, not by presumption.

2. *Avoid obscenities and offensive comments or stories.* In recent years, standards for acceptable and unacceptable language have changed considerably. Obscenity is more permissible in everyday conversation than it was in the past. However, it is still considered inappropriate to use foul language in front of a customer, a client, or, in many cases, a fellow worker. According to Bob Greene, syndicated columnist, an obscenity communicates a negative message to most people.

   > What it probably all comes down to is an implied lack of respect for the people who hear you talk. If you use profanity among friends, that is a choice you make. But if you broadcast it to people in general, you're telling them that you don't care what their feelings might be.[27]

   Never assume that another person's value system is the same as your own. Foul language and off-color stories can do irreparable damage to interpersonal relations.

3. *Never smoke in the presence of a fellow employee, customer, or client unless you are sure he or she will not be offended.* The practice of smoking is

viewed with disapproval by a growing number of people. Many organizations are restricting smoking to designated areas only. Some people are allergic to smoke and others simply dislike the odor. People who do not smoke will appreciate your consideration of their comfort and health.

4. *Avoid making business or professional visits unless you have an appointment.* Walking into someone's office without an appointment is generally considered rude. A good rule of thumb is always to make an appointment in advance and arrive promptly. If you are late, quickly voice a sincere apology.

5. *Express appreciation at appropriate times.* A simple thank you can mean a lot. Failure to express appreciation can be a serious human relations blunder. The secretary who works hard to complete a rush job for his or her boss is likely to feel frustrated and angry if this extra effort is ignored. The customer who makes a purchase deserves to receive a sincere thank you. You want your customers to know that their business is appreciated.

6. *Be aware of personal habits that may be offensive to others.* Sometimes an annoying habit can be a barrier to establishing a positive relationship with someone else. Chewing gum is a habit that bothers many people, particularly if you chew gum vigorously or "crack" it. Biting fingernails, cracking knuckles, scratching your head, and combing your hair in public are additional habits to be avoided.

Letitia Baldrige says that in the field of manners, "Rules are based on kindness and efficiency." She also believes that good manners are those personal qualities that make life at work more livable.[28] A knowledge of good manners permits us to perform our daily work with poise and confidence.

SUMMARY

People tend to form impressions of others quickly at the time they first meet them, and these first impressions tend to be preserved. Leonard and Natalie Zunin describe the four-minute barrier as the average time people spend together before a relationship is either established or denied. In an organizational setting, the time interval is often reduced to seconds. Positive first impressions are important because they contribute to repeat business and greater customer loyalty.

The impression you form of another person during the initial contact is made up of assumptions and facts. When meeting someone for the first time, people tend to rely heavily on assumptions. Many of your assumptions can be traced to early cultural conditioning. Assumptions are also based on our perceptions of surface language. The Zunins describe surface language as a pattern of immediate impressions conveyed by appearance. The clothing and jewelry you wear, your hair style, and the fragrances you use all combine to make a statement about yourself to others

Egon Von Furstenberg, author of *The Power Look*, contends that discrimination on the basis of appearance is still a fact of life. The clothing you wear is an important part of the image you communicate to others. Three things tend to influence your choice of clothing for work: (1) the products or services offered by the employer, (2) the type of person served, and (3) the desired image projected by the organization.

In addition to clothing, research indicates that facial expressions strongly influence people's reactions to each other. The expression on your face can quickly trigger a positive or negative reaction. Similarly, your entrance and carriage, voice, handshake, and manners also contribute to the image you project when meeting others.

KEY TERMS

primacy effect
assumptions
cultural conditioning
image
surface language

career apparel
unconscious expectations
wardrobe engineering
four-minute barrier

REVIEW QUESTIONS

1. Image has been described as "more than exterior qualities such as dress and grooming." What other factors shape the image we project?

2. Define the term *primacy effect*. How would knowledge of the primacy effect help someone in sales or customer service?

3. Why do people tend to rely more heavily on assumptions than facts during the initial meeting?

4. Why should career-minded people be concerned about the image they project? What factors contribute to the formation of one's image?

5. What are some of the major decisions people make about others based on career apparel?

6. What are the three things that will influence your choice of clothing for work?

7. What is meant by the term *unconscious expectations?*

8. Describe the type of speaking voice that will increase one's effectiveness in dealing with people.

9. Jonathan Swift, Letitia Baldrige, and Judith Martin have voiced strong support for the study of manners. What reasons do they give for developing an understanding of good manners?

10. The Total Person Insight on page 202 suggests that we have only two to four minutes to create a positive first impression. Do you agree with the views of Janet G. Elsea?

CASE 8.1

What You See Isn't Necessarily What You Get

The clothing men and women wear at work shapes our expectations of them. Feelings about people's competence, intelligence, attitudes, trustworthiness, and many other aspects of their personalities are conveyed by the colors, styles, and fit of their attire. Writers for *Communication Briefings* (June 1987), for example, suggest that women's clothing should fall somewhere between the very feminine soft and frilly look and the more masculine, dark three-piece suit look to be appropriate in many work settings. And Kathleen A. Hughes, writing for *The Wall Street Journal* (September 1, 1987), suggests that women executives need to avoid clothes that are too tight and hemlines that are too short if they want to be taken seriously as professionals. Some companies, such as the Signet Bank in Virginia and the Century 21 chain of real estate firms, have begun to require their employees to wear specially designed uniforms, called "career wear," to ensure that the employees will convey the "right" message and instill confidence in their customers.

Just how important is the "right look," and how does what people wear influence our expectations of them? Imagine that you have just checked into a hospital to be operated on the next day. When you get to your room, you are told that the following people will be coming to speak with you within the next several hours:

1. the surgeon who will do the operation
2. a nurse
3. the secretary for the department of surgery
4. a representative of the company that supplies televisions to the hospital rooms
5. a technician who does laboratory tests
6. a hospital business manager
7. the dietitian

You have never met any of these people before and don't know what to expect. The only thing you do know is that they are all women.

About half an hour after your arrival, a woman appears at your door dressed in a straight, red wool skirt, a pink and white striped polyester blouse with a bow at the neck, and red medium-high-heel shoes that match the skirt. She is wearing round gold earrings, a gold chain necklace, a gold wedding band, and a white hospital laboratory coat. She is carrying a clipboard.

Sources: "How Should Women Dress?" *Communication Briefings*, June 1987, p. 4; "Dressing for Success," *INC.*, April 1988, p. 129; Kathleen A. Hughes, "Businesswomen's Broader Latitude in Dress Codes Goes Just So Far," *The Wall Street Journal*, September 1, 1987, p. 33; Melinda J. Payne, "Corporate Clothes," *Roanoke Times & World-News*, May 9, 1988, pp. 1, 3.

Questions

1. Of the seven people listed, which of them do you think is standing at your door? Why?
2. If the woman had not been wearing a white hospital laboratory coat, how might your perceptions of her differ? Why?
3. If you find out that she is the surgeon who will be operating on you in the morning, and thought she was someone different initially, how confident do you now feel in her ability as a surgeon? Why?

CASE 8.2

Do We Need an Employee Handbook?

Connie Bayer and Rose Lamas met for the first time at a Sales and Marketing Executives (SME) dinner meeting. A strong friendship developed quickly because they had a great deal in common. Connie was a successful real estate broker working for Hilldale Real Estate, a well-established firm serving the St. Louis metropolitan area. Rose was a part-time community college instructor who taught real estate broker courses. Prior to becoming an instructor, she had sold real estate for five years.

After the initial meeting, Connie and Rose met several times at SME-sponsored dinner meetings and occasionally for lunch. At one of these meetings, Connie discussed her plan to start her own real estate business. She explained in detail the type of business she hoped to establish and then said, "Rose, I have been thinking about a partnership. Would you be willing to join me as a full partner?" At first Rose was tempted to say yes. She had also dreamed of owning her own business someday. But she knew that business partnerships often failed. She also knew that a major factor contributing to failure was dissension. She said, "Before I make this decision, I feel we should discuss our basic beliefs regarding business policies and practices."

A few days later, Connie and Rose met to discuss their views on business operations. Here is a portion of that conversation.

Connie: I believe that customer relations is a very important key to business success. I feel we should develop a detailed employee handbook that outlines policies and practices in such areas as stress and grooming, use of the telephone, methods of greeting the customer, service after the sale, and so on.

Rose: I believe that everyone associated with the firm should project a professional image and that good service is the key to business success. However, I wonder if a detailed employee handbook is necessary. I feel a handbook is simply a crutch used by managers who do not want to spend time on employee development.

Connie: I don't think I understand what you mean.

Rose: When I worked for Hilldale Real Estate, the manager never discussed his expectations in the area of customer service. New employees were given a list of policies and told to read them. I feel customer service requires constant attention. I would want to schedule weekly meetings to improve this area of the business. I would involve the entire staff in making these decisions.

Questions

1. Would you agree or disagree with Rose? Explain your answer.

2. What customer service policies and practices related to the area of first impressions should be given attention before the new business is opened?

SUGGESTED READINGS

Baldrige, Letitia. *Letitia Baldrige's Complete Guide to Executive Manners.* New York: Rawson Associates, 1985.

Bixler, Susan. *The Professional Image.* New York: Perigee Books, 1984.

Carnegie, Dale. *How to Win Friends and Influence People.* New York: Pocket Books, 1964.

Collins, Julia M. "Off to Work," *Harvard Business Review,* September/October 1989, pp. 105–109.

Elsea, Janet G. *The Four-Minute Sell.* New York: Simon & Schuster, 1984.

Fenton, Lois (with Edward Olcott). *Dress for Excellence.* New York: Rawson Associates, 1986.

Gray, James. *The Winning Image.* New York: American Management Associations, 1982.

Jackson, Carole (with Kalia Lulow). *Color for Men.* New York: Ballantine Books, 1987.

King, Norman. *The First Five Minutes.* New York: Prentice-Hall, 1987.

Martin, Judith. *Common Courtesy: In Which Miss Manners Solves the Problem That Baffled Mr. Jefferson.* New York: Atheneum, 1986.

Molloy, John T. *Live for Success.* New York: Morrow, 1981.

Molloy, John T. *New Dress for Success.* New York: Warner Books, 1988.

Molloy, John T. *The Woman's Dress for Success Book.* New York: Warner Books, 1977.

Thompson, Jacqueline. *Image Impact.* New York: Ace Books, 1981.

Thourlby, William. *You Are What You Wear—The Key to Business Success.* Kansas City, Mo.: Sheed Andrews and McMeel, 1978.

Zeldis, Yona. *Coping with Social Situations: A Handbook of Correct Behavior.* New York: Rosen Publishing Group, 1987.

Zunin, Leonard, and Natalie Zunin. *Contact—The First Four Minutes.* New York: Ballantine Books, 1972.

NOTES

1. James Gray, Jr., *The Winning Image* (New York: American Management Associations, 1982), p. 3.
2. "Image Consulting Looks Better All the Time," *Training and Development Journal,* September 1984, p. 10.
3. Joel Kotkin, "City of the Future," *INC.,* April 1987, p. 60.
4. Julia H. Martin and Donna J. Tolson, "Changing Job Skills in Virginia: The Employer's View," *Newsletter,* University of Virginia, January 1986, p. 2.
5. Zick Rubin, "The Rise and Fall of First Impressions—How People Are Perceived," in *Interpersonal Communication in Action,* ed. Bobby R. Patton and Kim Fiffen II (New York: Harper & Row, 1977), p. 150.
6. Leonard Zunin and Natalie Zunin, *Contact—The First Four Minutes* (New York: Ballantine Books, 1972), p. 5.
7. Jacqueline Thompson, *Image Impact* (New York: Ace Books, 1981), p. 8.
8. "Postal Polish: Improved Image Is Aim of Efforts at Postal Service," *Roanoke Times & World-News,* January 1, 1989, p. D–1.
9. Zunin and Zunin, p. 17.
10. Gray, pp. 3–5.
11. Ibid., p. 6.
12. John T. Molloy, *Dress for Success* (New York: Peter H. Wyden, 1975); and John T. Molloy, *The Woman's Dress for Success Book* (New York: Warner Books, 1977).
13. Egon Von Furstenberg, *The Power Look* (New York: Holt, Rinehart & Winston, 1978), p. 5.
14. William Thourlby, *You Are What You Wear—The Key to Business Success* (Kansas City, Mo.: Sheed Andrews and McMeel, 1978), p. 1.
15. Anita Porter, "What a Difference a Uniform Makes," *TWA Ambassador,* June 1978, p. 18.
16. "Workers Voice Needs," *Roanoke Times & World-News,* January 1, 1989, p. D–1.
17. Gerald Egan, "Dressing for Success in Richmond," *New Dominion Lifestyle,* September 1977, p. 24.
18. Lois Fenton (with Edward Olcott), *Dress for Excellence* (New York: Rawson Associates, 1986), p. 14.
19. "Does What You Wear Tell Where You're Headed?" *U.S. News and World Report,* September 25, 1978, p. 59.

20. Dave Knesel, "Image Consulting—A Well-Dressed Step Up the Corporate Ladder," *Pace*, July/August, 1981, p. 74.
21. Janet G. Elsea, *The Four-Minute Sell* (New York: Simon & Schuster, 1984), p. 34.
22. Susan Bixler, *The Professional Image* (New York: Perigee Books, 1984), p. 217.
23. Ibid., p. 219.
24. Martha Sherrill Dailey, "The Way We Sound," *Roanoke Times & World-News*, May 8, 1988, p. 1.
25. Adapted from Zunin and Zunin, pp. 102–108.
26. Thompson, p. 131.
27. Bob Greene, "Why Must We Say Things Like . . . and . . . ?" *Roanoke Times & World-News*, April 27, 1980, p. 7.
28. Letitia Baldrige, *Letitia Baldrige's Complete Guide to Executive Manners* (New York: Rawson Associates, 1985), p. 13.

Chapter 9

Coping with Personal and Professional Life Changes

CHAPTER PREVIEW

After studying this chapter, you will be able to

1. Describe conditions that create the need for change in organizations.

2. Better anticipate and manage your life's transitions.

3. Understand why individuals resist change.

4. Summarize ways of actively adapting to change.

5. Explain how individuals can counteract stress.

6. Describe how organizations can help their employees manage stress.

he headline in *Business Week* announced "Big Changes at Big Blue." This story attracted the attention of many people interested in the fortunes of International Business Machines Corp. (IBM), the nation's largest maker of information processing equipment. Faced in the mid-1980s with declining market share and profits, the company found it necessary to cut costs and reduce the size of its work force. One of the most cherished traditions at IBM is a no-layoff practice, so the company had to find different ways to develop a leaner work force. One solution was to retrain 9,400 employees for new jobs in the areas of sales, computer programming, and customer service. Sales representatives were needed in the field to sell in a more competitive atmosphere. Approximately 21,000 workers were voluntarily or involuntarily moved to fill job openings

At IBM's Raleigh, N.C. plant Michael Bessard has begun a new career in robotics maintenance as part of IBM's retraining programs.
Courtesy of International Business Machines Corporation

in other parts of the nation. Regardless of this upheaval, IBM's no-layoff tradition remained intact.

D. Quinn Mills, a Harvard Business School professor, did 100 personal interviews with IBM employees, plus an additional 250 through written questionnaires. He estimates that of the IBM employees who took new jobs, only one-quarter thought they had made a sacrifice to the company. The rest saw their new jobs as promotions. It appears IBM took what could have been perceived as a devastating blow and helped its employees view it as an opportunity.[1]

CHANGE AND THE ORGANIZATION

In the preface to his book *Thriving on Chaos*, Tom Peters discusses the semantic decision he made in determining the name of the book. Was it to be "Thriving *Amidst* Chaos" or "Thriving *on* Chaos?" To thrive "amidst" chaos means to cope or to come to grips with it, to succeed in spite of it. After careful consideration he decided that this represented a reactive approach to change. To merely cope misses the point. "The winners of tomorrow will deal proactively with chaos. The true objective is to take the chaos as given and learn to thrive *on* it."[2] Violent and accelerating changes, now commonplace, will become the opportunities of the future. Losers will view such confusion as "a problem to be dealt with."

Seldom does a week pass by without a major joint venture, or stock take-over, involving various companies. Many such ventures involve international deals. In the last six years, General Electric Co. has acquired over 325 businesses, then turned around and sold over 225 of them. Economists estimate that as many as 30 million people have been dislocated by the "restructuring" in manufacturing during the last decade. Since 1980, Fortune 500 companies have shed a staggering 2.8 million jobs! No organization can guarantee against change. IBM was declared dead in 1979, the best of the best in 1982, and dead again in 1986. People Express Airlines, Inc. was the model "new look" organization, then flopped two years later.[3] We used to be able to divide our organizations into neat little boxes and say this is a bank, this is a retail store, this is a hospital, this is a school. But now we are erasing the lines that draw the boxes. You can walk into a K mart and open a money market account. You can walk into a freestanding emergency medical center that is run like a business, and often receive better and less expensive service than you would at a nonprofit hospital.[4]

In the past two centuries, much of the world has experienced an acceleration in the rate of change. Events happen more rapidly than people can absorb and adjust to them. Author Alvin Toffler called this phenomenon **future shock**. Each generation in the twentieth century has grown up with products, technological advances, and discoveries unknown to the previous generation. Change shows no sign of slowing down in the future.

In most organizations, change is necessary for survival. The turmoil of the 1970s and 1980s, brought about by the stiff competition of a global marketplace and the move from an industrial base toward an information and service base, represents the necessity of adjusting to economic realities. Such changes are not a matter of simply reshuffling top management or altering a product line. Rather, they entail reshaping the culture of an organization to make it more competitive, more efficient, and better able to adapt to an environment in constant flux. An organization must consider making changes when one or more of the following conditions arise.[5]

1. *The organization is in a highly competitive industry and a quickly changing environment.* Organizations that pay close attention to customer needs and believe in the value of quickly adapting to those needs can maintain a competitive edge. They have created a corporate culture open to the evolutionary process of change and have institutionalized the ability to adapt quickly.

   Dave Boyer, president of Teleflex Incorporated, a profitable maker of high-tech control systems, describes his automotive division's rapid growth from $10 million to $60 million. He attributes the growth to new product introduction which resulted in 50 percent of sales coming from products launched in the last year. The key to that success rate is what Boyer calls "failing forward": that is, failing fast—and learning from it so as to make the next and smarter step quickly.[6]

   Soichiro Honda, founder of Honda Motor Co., Ltd., says: "Many people dream of success. To me success can only be achieved through repeated failure and introspection. In fact, success represents the 1 percent of your work which results only from the 99 percent that is called failure." To support failure is to demand that something be learned from each failure, and that it be quickly followed with a new modification.[7]

   In contrast, John Young, Hewlett-Packard CEO, says, "Doing it fast forces you to do it right the first time."[8] He insists that HP develop, manufacture, and deliver products faster than ever before and faster than the competition. "Our competitors abroad have turned new technologies into new products and processes more rapidly. And they've reaped the commercial rewards of the time-to-market race."[9] HP has now created a company-wide program called BET (breakeven time). Employees are challenged to cut by half the time it takes to move from a new product's conception to its profitability.

   Although these companies have chosen different means of adapting, all are responding to the intense competition and the rapid-paced market in which they operate. Table 9.1 lists some examples of companies that have managed to reduce their development and production schedules to remain competitive.

TABLE 9.1   Success Through Speed

Superfast Innovators			
Company	Product	Development Time	
		Old	New
Honda	cars	5 years	3 years
AT&T	phones	2 years	1 year
Navistar	trucks	5 years	2.5 years
Hewlett-Packard	computer printers	4.5 years	22 months

Superfast Producers			
Company	Product	Order-to-finished-goods Time	
		Old	New
GE	circuit breaker boxes	3 weeks	3 days
Brunswick	fishing reels	3 weeks	1 week
Hewlett-Packard	electronic testing equipment	4 weeks	5 days
Motorola	pagers	3 weeks	2 hours

Source: "How Managers Can Succeed Through Speed," *Fortune*, February 13, 1989, p. 56.
© 1989 The Time Inc. Magazine Company. All rights reserved.

2. *The organization is in financial trouble.* A company that is losing money will need to make radical changes to survive. Lee Iacocca turned Chrysler Corporation around by emphasizing quality construction, customer service, and attention to consumer tastes.

   The world's largest merchant, Sears, Roebuck, has experienced tremendous pressure from much more efficient retailers and appears to lack the corporate flexibility necessary to quickly make the required changes. In 1987 Sears had revenues of more than $48 billion and net earnings of $1.65 billion. Nine months later Sears earnings tumbled 18 percent. In the previous ten years Sears had given up $8.5 billion in sales to K Mart Corporation, Wal-Mart Stores, Inc., and J. C. Penney Co., Inc. In the article "Why Bigger Is Badder at Sears," author Patricia Sellers says, "Compared with these fleet-footed competitors, Sears is a 2,000 pound centipede."[10]

3. *The organization is on the verge of becoming very large.* When a company is growing rapidly toward stability and success, it may also begin to acquire the trappings of a bureaucracy in terms of formal policies and systems. As a result, the original values that maintained the company

during its earlier, entrepreneurial years may be threatened. Hewlett-Packard has experienced the process of such a transition. The decentralized management that HP forged over the years—although responsible for the company's early success—also resulted eventually in overlapping products, lagging development, and a piecemeal approach to key markets as the company grew. It was a difficult task to keep the spirit of entrepreneurship alive while at the same time orchestrating the company's new direction into the computer field.[11] Hewlett-Packard knew, however, that this was a transition it had to make.

4. *The environment undergoes a fundamental change, and the organization is driven by traditional values. "Traditional values"* in this sense means that management believes that what worked in the past is bound to work in the future, regardless of change. Some airlines that competed well in a regulated environment suddenly found themselves in a deregulated situation. The American auto industry assumed that consumers would always value the large car, symbol of affluence and high standard of living, and needed to change this assumption when consumer taste changed. Many small and medium-sized oil companies geared their corporate culture to the world's continuing demand for energy, never suspecting that within a short time there would be an oil glut on the market. In a rapidly changing environment, adherence to traditional values can quickly bring an organization to the brink of disaster. Traditional values may need to be adjusted to allow the organization to respond to market and competitive pressures.

THINKING/LEARNING STARTERS

1. What change in the business environment have you witnessed recently that has caused a company to alter the way it conducts its business? Were the results of the alteration successful or unsuccessful?
2. Is there a traditional "family" business in your area that has not changed with the needs of its customers? How does this company inflexibility affect its employees personally and professionally?

CHANGE AND THE INDIVIDUAL

In a world moving as fast as ours, change will be a fact of life, and individuals will need to accept its inevitability. With that firmly in mind, we can learn to manage the transitions.

Transitions

A **transition** can be defined as the experience of being forced to give up something and face a change. People are affected by transition much more than we previously thought. In recent years we have learned that life transitions are like little deaths, and most organizations are full of people coping with them. If present trends continue, workers can expect to experience a series of work-related transitions. There are at least three different kinds of transitions related to a person's life as a worker.[12]

1. *Trying to change jobs or careers because of personal dissatisfaction with one's present job.* In this category are some 20 to 25 million people in America. Put another way, about one out of every four workers is (secretly or openly) contemplating a career or job change. The fact that about 30 percent of all workers wind up in a different occupation every five years indicates that many people do indeed move to different jobs.

2. *Trying to hold on to a job that is rapidly changing.* The United States is making the transition from the industrial age into the information and service age.[13] The next decade or two may result in as much change in the way Americans work as the Industrial Revolution fostered only a century ago. More companies are investing in robotics and automated equipment. Word processing centers have replaced the traditional typing pool. Optical scanners have changed the skills necessary to work in a retail center. Many Americans see automation as a tool to reduce the need for workers. Others see it as a tool to aid workers by adding value to the product they sell. To some observers, computer technology is the harbinger of a brighter and more secure future. Others see serious consequences of spending long hours with machines. Craig Brod, author of *Technostress*, notes that "the computer in many situations is generating very little interesting work, except for executives or research and development workers."[14] He also points out that the computer provides neither variety nor balance.

   In addition to technological changes, we are observing several other factors contributing to changes in the workplace. These include changes

---

TOTAL PERSON INSIGHT

66 The world is a highly unreliable place. No living creature is exempt from uncertainty. This is particularly true of the creature generically known as man, who is subject not only to the whims of nature, but to the multiple uncertainties he has created for himself. 99

The Royal Bank Letter

Between 15 and 20 million adults per year are undergoing transitions in their work lives. Many unemployed people need to be retrained before they are employable in today's organizations.
Jeffrey Dunn/The Picture Cube

attributable to mergers and the subsequent "cuts" that often result, changes in job descriptions, and shifts in organization from supervisor-employee relationships to self-management teams.

3. *Unemployed but trying to obtain a job.* Between 15 and 20 million adults are estimated to be in this transition category in an average year. These people are either going to work for the first time or are trying to reenter the work force after being fired, quitting, or taking time out for whatever reason. It is estimated that about 10 million Americans leave their jobs involuntarily every year.[15] The uncertainties of the labor market can create a great deal of anxiety in the minds of both employed and unemployed people.

The movement from being an unemployed worker to an employed worker is often a long and difficult journey. Many of the people who lost jobs in auto, steel, and other "smokestack" industries must first be retrained before they can search for a new job. If the new job is in the service sector, the worker will likely take a cut in pay. Coping with the demands of a new job and learning to live on less income are major challenges to most people.

Why We Resist Change

Few of us are comfortable when our lives are disturbed in any fundamental way. Usually, the greater the degree of change, the stronger the resistance from those affected by it or those who must implement it. Understanding the factors that make change stressful and so often unwelcome can help us better cope with life's transitions. In this section we present several reasons why people resist change.

Feelings of Inadequacy   When people must learn new skills, accept more responsibility, or take on challenges that stretch their abilities, they are apt to feel inadequate to the task. Usually resistance is based more on lack of self-confidence than on lack of ability. Carl Wolf of Chase Econometrics/Interactive Data Corp. introduced personal computers into his company by letting his employees take them home. After they got accustomed to using the new equipment, the workers lost their fear of computers and began using them at work.[16] A good manager can help workers overcome their lack of self-confidence and encourage them to try new projects and learn new skills.

Threat to Personal Security   Personal security—physical or psychological—is one of everyone's basic needs. Substantial changes in the nature of your work may make you wonder if you will be laid off or asked to do more work for the same pay. If you perceive a change as a demotion or loss of status, you may feel your worth as a person is being diminished. When executive secretaries in an insurance firm were moved into a word processing center, they lost their status as private secretaries and now worked for several bosses instead of only one. They were afraid that some of them would be let go as the office became more automated. Changes that threaten security inevitably cause problems in employee motivation, productivity, and morale.

Fear of the Unknown   Fear of the unknown is a common reaction to a new situation. When changing economic conditions threaten the stability of an organization, the grapevine begins to spread rumors. At John Deere Company, a major farm implement manufacturer, the farm crisis of the mid- and late 1980s exerted tremendous pressure on employees' lives. Daily conversations reflected employees' concerns. Will there be a layoff? How many will go this time? Will I be on the list, or will I survive another cut? If I do survive, will my job responsibilities be the same? Family and professional lives remain in limbo until the answers are known, and tension is high as employees consider the possibilities and options. Management can help alleviate this fear by maintaining good communication with employees and explaining in detail what any change means and how it will affect each employee.

Lack of Trust   Sometimes resistance to change is not directed at the change itself but at those who introduce it. The degree of openness and trust between management and employees often determines how readily change is accepted or opposed. Management may feel that employees should not be involved in the planning stages for a transition or in decisions about how and when it should take place. Employees may not believe what management tells them. As a result, an organization can quickly become a rumor mill. This lack of trust may mean that if change is forced on employees, it may leave in its wake reduced productivity, resentment, and even greater distrust of management.

Inability to See the Big Picture   If employees are not included in the process of change from the beginning, they often cannot see beyond their own attitudes and opinions or understand the change in terms of the goals of the organization. For example, a new method for shipping deliveries may inconvenience an individual but help the company control costs and reduce operating expenses. If employees are helped to understand that change will improve the overall organization, they probably will support it.

Changes often happen more rapidly than expected, and there may not always be time for someone to explain them to you and help you cope with the new situation. It is best to be ready to accept change and notice the positives of the situation as soon as possible. Perhaps there will be times when you hear of a new technique from a colleague in another organization or read in a trade journal about a more effective way to complete a task. When you see this trend toward a change, mentally prepare yourself for it.

Adapting to Change

Adapting to change is basically a matter of attitude and adjusting established values to new situations. Most changes involve some type of loss, but they can also offer new opportunities.

The Values Test   Many people, when confronted with sudden changes, lose sight of their basic values and make decisions on impulse. Yet values can act as guidelines for dealing with change. A young manager who has always valued close family and community relations may receive an offer to work overseas or relocate in another region of the country. An engineer who values a small-company working environment may be tempted by offers of a sizable salary increase to join a multinational firm. Such changes can create value conflicts. Throughout your career, you will need to clarify your value priorities to determine whether changes will lead you to achieve your personal or professional goals.

Active Adaptability   When faced with an unexpected or possibly threatening situation, human beings—like animals—react with the **fight or flight syndrome.** This term was coined in the 1920s by Dr. Walter B. Cannon of the Harvard Medical School. When a person is experiencing the fight or flight syndrome, adrenalin pours into the blood stream, heart rate and blood pressure increase, breathing accelerates, and muscles tighten. The body is poised to fight or run. Unlike animals, however, human beings have a third choice: the ability to adapt consciously to change. Not only are people capable of choosing their responses to a situation, but they can also think about the consequences of their choice. The ability to analyze possible choices and consequences *before* acting is called **active adaptability.**

The key to active adaptability is the realization that change can be constructive, even if the initial event appears to be a negative one. A machinist laid off from work at first believed he would never find another job. His skills were no longer needed, and his future seemed lost in the shuffle of factory closings. After a few weeks, however, he decided to take a chance and enroll in a federally funded training program. Eventually, he became a writer and consultant on skilled craft work, a job he found more satisfying than his old one. He turned a potential crisis into a new opportunity. An ancient Chinese proverb refers to crisis as an opportunity riding on a dangerous wind.

The need to adapt to change is also creating new demands for adult education, much of it related to job and career. Each year more than 20 million adult learners complete some type of training and development course, seminar, or workshop. Over half of these people complete instruction that is job related.

As mentioned earlier, IBM had to cut thousands of employees in the late 1980s. Through early retirements and normal attrition and elimination of overtime and temporary employees, 12,500 full-time jobs were eliminated. As another step, IBM fell back on its famous retraining program. Over 9,400 employees volunteered for retraining courses lasting up to eighteen months. Some 3,700 were trained as programmers, and 4,600 learned to be salespeople or customer consultants. Although there were no outright layoffs, more than 21,000 employees had to change locations, including 4,600 who went from the head office to the field.[17] These IBM employees had the opportunity to implement their "active adaptability" skills by viewing their new training in a positive light rather than negatively.

Active adaptability not only helps individuals adjust to change but can also strengthen their human relations. As employees face change head-on, they find positive ways of adapting and adjusting. This feeling of being in control, rather than being controlled by the change, builds the individuals' self-esteem. Positive self-esteem helps promote teamwork among coworkers as they face change together.

THINKING/LEARNING STARTERS

1. What changes have you had to cope with in your personal and work life? What is your basic attitude toward change?
2. Have you been able to call upon your value priorities as guidelines when confronted with major changes in your life? How did you adapt to these changes?
3. What changes do you anticipate facing in the next three to five years? How can you prepare for these changes?

CHANGE CAUSES STRESS

Most of the changes in our life, regardless of how beneficial, can cause tension or stress. **Stress** is typically defined as any action or set of circumstances under which an individual cannot respond adequately or can only respond at the cost of excessive wear and tear on the body.[18] Under stress, we are in a state of imbalance. Stress is the tension we feel when we try to adapt—whether changing jobs, learning to operate a computer, moving into a new home, or getting married—all the while struggling to regain our old equilibrium.

Although most of what is written about stress today focuses on its negative consequences, it is important to realize that some stress is beneficial. John Lawrie, president of Applied Psychology, Inc., states that too much stress can sap your energy, undermine your personal life, and ruin your effectiveness on the job. But too little can stall your personal growth and lead to stagnation.[19] Lawrie says that the goal is not to eliminate stress but to determine when you've passed your limits and then to do something about it. Table 9.2 lists some of the most common life stressors, with point values assigned to each indicating the degree of stress potential it represents. An accumulation of these events could easily lead to an unproductive level of stress.

Technostress: A New Threat in the Workplace

The computer revolution has created a new form of stress that is causing mental and physical health problems among many workers. Craig Brod, a consultant specializing in stress reduction, uses the term *technostress* to describe a modern disease caused by an inability to cope with new computer technologies in a healthy manner.[20] Brod notes that technostress manifests itself in two distinct but related ways. First, stress is apt to surface as we

TABLE 9.2   Life Events Scale for Measuring Stress

Besides on-the-job stress, there are other sources of stress. Thomas Holmes and Richard Rahe, two psychiatrists at the University of Washington Medical School, have developed a life events scale that measures the potential for stress-related illness.

To figure your stress potential, add up the points for each item that has occurred in your life in the past year.

Rank	Crisis	Points	Rank	Crisis	Points
1.	Death of a spouse	100	23.	Departure of son or daughter from home	29
2.	Divorce	73			
3.	Marital separation	65	24.	Trouble with in-laws	29
4.	Jail term	63	25.	Outstanding personal achievement	28
5.	Death of a close family member	63			
6.	Personal injury or illness	53	26.	Spouse's beginning or stopping work	26
7.	Marriage	50	27.	Beginning or end of school	26
8.	Job firing	47	28.	Change in living conditions	25
9.	Marital reconciliation	45	29.	Change of personal habits	24
10.	Retirement	45	30.	Trouble with boss	23
11.	Change in health of family member	44	31.	Change in work hours or conditions	20
12.	Pregnancy	44	32.	Change in residence	20
13.	Sexual difficulties	39	33.	Change in schools	20
14.	Gain of new family member	39	34.	Change in recreation	19
15.	Business readjustment	39	35.	Change in church activities	19
16.	Change in financial state	38	36.	Change in social activities	18
17.	Death of a close friend	38	37.	Mortgage or loan less than $10,000	17
18.	Change to different line of work	36	38.	Change in sleeping habits	16
19.	Change in number of arguments with spouse	35	39.	Change in number of family gatherings	15
20.	Mortgage more than $10,000	31	40.	Change in eating habits	15
21.	Foreclosure of mortgage or loan	30	41.	Vacation	13
			42.	Christmas	12
22.	Change in work responsibilities	29	43.	Minor violation of law	11

LOW	*MEDIUM*	*HIGH*
(150–200) 37% chance of getting seriously ill in the next two years.	(225–300) 51% chance of getting seriously ill.	(325–375) 80% chance of getting seriously ill in the next two years.

Source: Reprinted with permission from *Journal of Psychosomatic Research,* Vol. 11, Thomas Holmes and Richard Rahe, "The Social Readjustment Rating Scale," Copyright 1967, Pergamon Press, plc.

TOTAL PERSON INSIGHT

❝ We have come to expect from people the perfection, accuracy, and speed to which computers have made us accustomed. Busy following standardized procedures and ultralogical reasoning in order to interact with computers, we have begun to think of conversation as data transfer and memory as a search procedure. We already are beginning to speak like machines: "I need more data" or "I can't access that." The directory-assistance operator, the bank teller, the ticket agent, the librarian have all become computer operators with whom we "interface." As we grow more and more impatient with human imperfection and variation, we move further and further away from the very essence of our own humanity. ❞

Craig Brod

---

struggle to learn how to adapt to computers in the workplace. Adaptation to the new computer technology often provokes anxiety.

> As the rhythm of the workplace speeds up to match that of the computer, the resulting increase in both load and rate of work, aggravated by the reliance on symbols and abstractions that the computer demands, creates new physical and psychological pressures. Our reaction to these pressures is expressed in the symptoms of technostress.[21]

Overidentification with computer technology is the second way that technostress manifests itself. Some workers have adopted a machinelike

Technostress results from the increased speed and workload brought on by the prevalence of computers in the workplace. Philip Jon Bailey/The Picture Cube

mindset that reflects the characteristics of the computer itself. Brod notes that some people have too successfully identified with computer technology and have lost the capacity to feel or relate to others.

> Technocentered people tend to be highly motivated and eager to adapt to the new technology. Unwittingly, however, they begin to adopt a mindset that mirrors the computer itself. Signs of the technocentered state include a high degree of factual thinking, poor access to feelings, an insistence on efficiency and speed, a lack of empathy for others, and a low tolerance for the ambiguities of human behavior and communication.[22]

In some cases, spouses have reported that their technostressed partners view them almost as machines. The wife of a director of computer services for a large bank recalls that when she first met her spouse he was a warm, sensitive person. Today she says he has no close friends, and his only recreational activity is watching television. He has no patience for the easy exchange of informal conversation. He displays many of the symptoms of technostress.[23]

These two manifestations of technostress have been termed **cyberphobia** (excessive fear of new computer technology), and **cyberphrenia** (addiction to new computer technology to the extent that it totally dominates one's life).

Eliminating technostress is always a cooperative venture. Organizational leaders must implement a humane policy regarding the introduction and use of computer technology. They must recognize and plan for the process of adaptation that people will need to go through. A research study conducted by the Administrative Management Society Foundation identified four critical problems involving human resources and office automation. Organizational leaders would do well to address these problems in forming a policy to reduce technostress.

- maintaining a human perspective in automated office settings so that individuals continue to obtain deserved recognition for their accomplishments and are not made to feel controlled by technology
- designing meaningful and satisfying jobs in which employees can succeed in an automated office environment
- ensuring that automated office systems are user and not equipment oriented
- helping employees who work primarily at terminals to maintain job satisfaction[24]

On the individual level, we must engage in some honest self-appraisal to avoid becoming a technocentered person. Do those of us who work with computers find it more difficult to deal with humans? Are we losing our sensitivity to the needs and feelings of others? Are we less patient with those around us? It is important to be alert to the warning signs.

Warning Signs of Too Much Stress

Because of our ability to adapt to increasing levels of stress, we may not always be aware of the amount of pressure we are under. Over short periods of time, stress is seldom damaging. However, over extended periods and in very intense circumstances, it can be harmful, creating numerous medical problems, including lower back pains, headaches, coronary problems, and cancer (see Table 9.3). Among the psychological problems that can result from too much stress are anxiety, depression, irritability, loss of appetite, reduced interest in personal relationships, and paranoia.

Stress affects people at all levels of the organization. Although executives may be exposed to more stress-producing situations than others, they generally have the authority to do something about the problems. Employees who are subject to heavy demands but who have the authority to correct problems are often less stressed than those with fewer responsibilities but no authority to implement solutions.

Supervisors need to be aware of the warning signs of too much stress in themselves and their employees. Some of these signs are the following:

- an increase in working long hours or an increase in tardiness and absenteeism
- difficulty in making decisions
- an increasing number of careless mistakes
- problems interacting and getting along with others
- focusing on mistakes and personal failures[25]

TABLE 9.3   Physical Warning Signals of Too Much Stress

Pounding of the heart	Chronic pain in the neck or lower back
Dryness of the throat and mouth	Vomiting or nausea, with no apparent physical cause
Chronic fatigue, with no apparent physical cause	Stomach pain
Trembling and nervous tics	Decreased or increased appetite
High-pitched nervous laughter	Nightmares
Stuttering and other speech problems not usually apparent	Overpowering urge to cry or run and hide
Inability to concentrate	Difficulty breathing
Insomnia	Constipation
Frequent urination	Chest pains, with no apparent physical cause
Diarrhea and cramping	
Irregular or missed menstrual periods	

*"I'll have to take a rain-check.
Things are piling up here."*
© by Vietor. Used by
permission.

A long-term pattern of such occurrences suggests a person is overly stressed. The psychological and physical disorders that may result can cause low productivity and lost workdays.

Counteracting the Effects of Stress

When we are faced with stressful situations, our adrenal glands release adrenalin to prepare us for instant action. Heart rate and blood pressure shoot up, and blood rushes to the muscles, where it will be needed for a physical fight. In today's world, fighting is rarely an option; the body is prepared for a physical response when such a response is not possible. It takes time for the body to return to normal. For instance, it takes four to six hours to burn off the adrenalin created in the two to four seconds following a startling noise. The longer the adrenalin remains in the blood stream, the more damage can be done to the heart, blood vessels, and vital organs. Even though stress causes a physical response, you can take steps to alleviate your body's reaction to it.

Gaining Control   Stress often occurs when people feel they do not have control over their lives. In many cases, planning ahead is all that is needed to avoid a stressful situation. If a deadline is coming up, map a plan of action that will prevent a crisis situation. Structure your long-term goals just out of reach but not so far out of sight that they add stress instead of leading you in the direction you want to go. Too much stress is often the result of a mismatch between your expectations and your current environment. You can regain control by changing either one. Or sometimes you simply have to learn to accept a situation instead of resist. You can recognize your own limitations, learn when to pull back, and rearrange your schedule when necessary to allow for quiet time and activities outside the job. Taking control of your life is desirable, but using artificial controls such as smoking, drugs, and alcohol to do so is not. These artificial controls deal with the symptoms and not the causes of stress, and are not effective in combatting it.

Nutrition   The food you eat can play a critical role in helping you manage stress. Health experts agree that the typical American diet—high in saturated fats, refined sugar, additives, caffeine, and even too much protein— is actually the wrong menu for coping with stress. The U.S. Senate Select Committee on Nutrition and Human Needs has advised cutting down on fatty meats, dairy products, eggs, sweets, and salt. Fatty deposits can build up in the arteries, forming plaque. When stress increases the blood pressure, this plaque can tear away, damaging the arteries. Too much salt or caffeine overstimulates the heart. Refined sugar acts first as a stimulant and then a depressant to the central nervous system. The committee encourages greater consumption of fresh fruits, vegetables, whole grains, poultry, and fish. Eating the right foods in the proper balance can replenish the vitamins and minerals the body loses when under stress and can also have a calming effect on your nervous system.

Exercise   An effective exercise program can "burn off" the adrenalin and other harmful chemicals that build up in your blood stream as a result of a prolonged reaction to stress. Most people have a favorite form of exercise: jogging, tennis, golf, racquetball, or walking. Table 9.4 lists some of the most common forms of exercise and the number of calories they burn per hour. However, the effect of exercise on stress is minimal unless the regimen is fairly extensive and regular. No matter how strenuous the program, it must be done at least three times a week for at least thirty minutes each time to be effective. It is also important that the exercise program you choose be enjoyable. Otherwise, you will probably abandon it after a few weeks. John Lawrie recommends a "stress recess" at least once a week. This "recess" may or may not include strenuous exercise (he chooses fishing). The object is to remove yourself from the stressors of everyday life. Once you have determined which activity to pursue during your stress recess, decide which day (or days) of the week it would do you the most good.

Mental Relaxation   According to many physicians and researchers in human behavior, the stress response to events is one we *learn*. Individuals can unlearn this response by acquiring techniques of **mental relaxation.** Dr. Mary Asterita of the Indiana University School of Medicine says, "In the same way you have learned to speed up your biochemical processes when

TABLE 9.4   **Cardiovascular Fitness**

Aerobic Activities	Calories Burned/Hour	Anaerobic Activities	Calories Burned/Hour
Basketball	360–660	Calisthenics	360
Bicycling	240–420	Golf (power cart)	240
Bicycling (uphill)	500	Golf (pulling bag cart)	300
Cross-country skiing	600		
Dancing	240–420		
Rowing	250–420		
Running (11 min. mile)	540		
Skating	350–400		
Squash/Handball	600		
Swimming	540–660		
Tennis (singles)	420		
Walking (3 mph)	210		

Source: American Health Foundation, *Health Passport*, 1987. p. 11. Reprinted by permission.

aroused or alerted, you can learn to slow down the processes and return your body to a normal, balanced state."[26]

Relaxation techniques that Dr. Asterita and others recommend to employees include deep, rhythmical breathing, visualization exercises (such as imagining yourself in pleasant situations), and guided meditations. They have found that the nervous system cannot tell the difference between a real and a vividly imagined experience. If an individual visualizes a relaxing scene strongly enough, the nervous system will believe that the experience is actually occurring. Blood pressure drops, breathing slows down, and the fight or flight reaction recedes.

Converse Inc. in Wilmington, Massachusetts, is one of many organizations that provide in-house seminars to teach personnel how to use mental relaxation techniques.[27] Some organizations have special soundproof rooms with slides of quiet scenery projected on a movie screen. Other organizations encourage employees to take classes in yoga or meditation. These programs teach people how to take advantage of the mind's natural tranquilizers.

Emotional Expression   Stress can trigger two of your strongest emotions, anger and fear. These emotions must be given a healthy outlet, especially during times of change. Often you will feel better just by having someone listen to your concerns; everyone needs emotional support and a chance to vent their feelings. There are many excellent support groups that have been created for individuals who want to self-disclose. Emotions Anonymous (EA) offers weekly meetings in most cities. EA provides a fellowship of persons who share their experiences, strengths, weaknesses, feelings, and their hopes with one another to solve their emotional problems and to learn to live at peace with unsolved problems.

The best listeners are usually those who have an understanding of the nature of your work but who are not directly associated with it. In some cases you may want to consult a psychotherapist. Psychotherapy is no longer considered shameful, and it need not be time consuming or expensive. In addition, constructive disclosure of your feelings often reduces stress when you discuss situations as they happen and attempt to describe your emotions accurately. When you select the right time, place, and listener, expressing your emotions can offset the detrimental physical effects of stress.

Regardless of your physical condition, stress can harm—and even kill—you when you neglect to take control of your life and your body. Stress can have a great effect on your physical and psychological well-being, and you cannot assume that you will be aware of dangerous stress levels as they build. The long-term effects of stress are much like many cancers that do not make themselves evident until extensive damage has already occurred. Some people hold up well under stress for extended periods; others do not. But everyone should make the effort to put stressful situations into their proper perspective, and take steps to reduce their effects.

THINKING/LEARNING STARTERS

1. To what extent are you aware of your nutrition and feed your body healthy foods? Give examples.
2. What forms of exercise do you do? Would you like to add some form of exercise to your schedule? Which one? When will you start?
3. Total your stress potential points on the Life Events Scale for Measuring Stress (Table 9.2). Do you have any of the physical warning signs of stress listed in Table 9.3 ? List them and explain how you are attempting to counter these symptoms.

EAPs: AN ORGANIZATIONAL APPROACH

Personal and professional life transitions annually affect 16 percent of all full-time workers. Employees experiencing life transitions typically enter into a four- to six-month period of adjustment during which they produce less than half of their usual output. Corporate America is now beginning to pay closer attention to the dynamics of these transitions and the resulting $80 to $90 billion annual losses.[28] The most direct, effective, legally acceptable, and humane means of reducing the costs resulting from employee transitions have proven to be **employee assistance programs (EAPs).** These programs usually include **wellness programs** and various counseling opportunities. What might once have been considered an intrusion into an employee's personal life has come to be considered a benefit in the business environment of an information and service society, where people are a company's strategic resource.

Wellness Programs

One expression of the importance of human capital is the new corporate emphasis on health and fitness. Corporations are encouraging their people to stop smoking, lose weight, exercise, and learn to manage stress. They have discovered that stressed-out employees can be bad for business. They are, more apt to get sick, tend to miss deadlines, and often lack creativity.[29] Today, more than one-fourth of the employers with fifty or more employees have some type of stress management program. Here are some examples.

> **Item:** At Guild Investment Management, Inc., of Malibu, California, executives gather in a conference room for transcendental meditation. One vice president with the company said that after twenty minutes "you feel like you've had a five or six hour nap."[30]

> **Item:** The U.S. Air Force has sponsored one-day workshops on "The Humor Option." C. W. Metcalf, the workshop instructor, helps participants learn how to use humor to reduce stress.[31]

> **Item:** At Corning Glass Works, employees under a great deal of stress have learned to juggle tennis balls. This prescription for stress reduction was introduced by Dr. Steve Allen, Jr., a medical doctor and son of entertainer Steve Allen. How does juggling help? Allen says, "Juggling helps you laugh at yourself."[32]

As might be expected, there are financial reasons organizations are placing more emphasis on wellness programs for their employees. American business pays $80 million each year in health insurance premiums.[33] Health care costs are steadily rising. Medical costs of companies offering wellness programs, however, are 25 percent lower than those of companies that do not provide such programs. Wellness clinics also increase employee productivity and reduce absenteeism by as much as 17 percent.[34] The Lockheed Missiles & Space Company, Inc., estimates that in five years it saved $1 million in life insurance costs through its wellness programs.[35] But wellness programs are not advantageous just for giant corporations. The fewer employees a company has, the greater the relative impact of a disabling illness of a single key worker.

Physical Fitness Programs   In many work environments, employees typically use their heads all day and not their bodies. It is therefore appropriate that organizations are becoming involved in health and fitness. Judging from jogging trails in small towns to multimillion dollar gymnasiums at major corporate centers, the new emphasis on health and fitness programs in business is not likely to fade. A study by the Canadian Fitness and Lifestyle Project showed that company fitness programs saved $233 per employee each year. In Dallas, Texas, teachers who enrolled in a fitness program took an average of three fewer sick days per year, at a savings of $452,000 in substitute pay alone.[36] More and more companies are instituting physical fitness programs for their employees, not only because employees enjoy them but also because they are cost effective.

Item: Xerox Corporation has thirteen physical fitness facilities throughout the United States. One is in Stamford, Conn., where 50 percent of the employees use the facility regularly.[37]

Item: Sky Brothers Inc., a food distributor in Altoona, Penn., rewards those of its employees who participate in its fitness program by paying a part of the membership fee to a health club.[38]

Item: Plaskolite, Inc., a plastics manufacturer in Columbus, Ohio, has an on-site fitness program that includes the use of twelve weight-lifting machines.[39]

Organizations too small to invest in private physical fitness facilities make arrangements with nearby health clubs, where employees can work out—often at company expense and sometimes on company time.

The Fitness Center at Mannington Mills, Inc. (Salem, N.J.) contains a fully equipped exercise room with individually tailored programs provided by professionally trained staff.
Mannington Mills, Inc.

While companies benefit financially from these programs, employees benefit from improved muscle tone, loss of body fat, a more optimistic outlook, improved sleep, increased energy, decreased stress, and a reduced risk of heart disease. For some employees, enrollment in an exercise program becomes the stimulus for other life changes. They may stop smoking, reduce their alcohol consumption, or start eating healthier foods.

Nutritional Programs   Unless an organization has a full-time food service for all employees, it is almost impossible to monitor the diets of individual employees. Even when the company cafeteria offers well-balanced meals, employees generally eat breakfast and the evening meal at home. Although most organizations understand the value of a balanced diet, their opportunities for improving employees' dietary habits are limited.

The most effective way to get employees interested in improving their diets is to provide in-house workshops taught by nutritionists. Individual daily eating logs can show employees how much sugar, salt, and fat they are consuming. Speakers from Weight Watchers International Inc., Nutri/System, Inc., and other established weight- reduction programs can also be of help.

Organizations can also remove vending machines that sell candy and other unhealthy snacks and replace them with machines that offer fruit, whole-grain crackers, and other nutritious foods. Coffee pots and coffee machines can dispense only decaffeinated coffee, and fruit juices can replace soft drinks, which are often high in sugar and caffeine. When someone joins the organization, coworkers and managers can make clear that birthday celebrations, holidays, and special occasions do not need to include doughnuts and cakes laden with refined sugar. Researchers estimate that as many as 10 million American suffer from such reactions to sugar as fatigue, inability to concentrate, irritability, and anxiety.[40]

Health-conscious organizations can help ensure that human relations problems are not exacerbated by poor nutrition and exhausted employees. Fitness planners believe that the camaraderie and enthusiasm generated by wellness programs promote management-employee relations better than any number of memos or conferences ever could.

Counseling Programs

If an employee is in fit shape, this does not necessarily mean that his or her mind is clear and operating productively. Personal and professional life changes may manifest themselves in behavioral changes that only direct counseling can address. Many organizations, therefore, offer various types of counseling aimed at alcohol and drug abuse; emotional and stress reduction; and preretirement, marital, termination, career, financial, legal, and elder care matters (see Table 9.5).

TABLE 9.5   **Keeping Counsel**

Type of Counseling	Percentage of Companies Offering Such Counseling Under an Employee Assistance Program
Alcohol/drug abuse	50%
Emotional/stress	44
Preretirement	38
Marital	31
Termination	34
Career	27
Financial	25
Legal	20
Elder Care	13

Source: Published with the permission of the Administrative Management Society Foundation, Trevose, Pennsylvania.

One behavioral problem affecting employees today is drug and alcohol abuse. Not long ago, people caught drinking or using drugs on the job were fired automatically. Today, organizations are realizing that pressure on the job can encourage alcohol and drug abuse as workers seek to cope with stress. Norfolk and Western Railway Co. established a preventive program after discovering that alcohol-related problems—absenteeism, accidents, and mistakes—were costing the company nearly $8 million annually. Other organizations employ trained counselors who facilitate alcohol and drug abuse control programs. These sessions concentrate on early detection of stress-related problems and on helping individuals find healthy ways to cope with stress.

According to the National Institute of Alcohol Abuse and Alcoholism (NIAAA), occupational alcoholism programs are among the most successful of all alcoholism programs. The rehabilitation rate of alcoholic workers has been between 50 to 60 percent of cases treated, and many programs report success rates as high as 70 to 80 percent.[41] The National Council on Alcoholism (NCA) has for many years been a leader in employee assistance programs. Approximately three-fifths of the employees referred to an EAP have alcohol or other drug dependency problems. The remainder are people experiencing unresolved grief, financial or family difficulties, emotional problems, or stress of impending retirement—problems that may lead to alcohol or drug abuse. Currently, over five thousand organizations have implemented the NCA employee assistance program.

A pattern of changed behavior may indicate that a worker is using drugs or alcohol. For instance, a normally calm individual may become angry very quickly. Compared with past performance, the work of alcohol- or drug-dependent employees may become sloppy or erratic. Executives may be reluctant to take on more responsibility. Drug-dependent employees are often late to work or absent on Mondays and Fridays. Since drugs are expensive, employees may experience persistent financial problems. An unusually high use of health insurance benefits may also indicate a drug or alcohol problem. Once an employee is identified as having a drug- or alcohol-related problem, the EAP is usually initiated with two steps. First, the employee is referred to the appropriate psychologist or counseling staff person. Second, the employee is given one or more warning interviews in which he or she is given the choice of continuing in the EAP (which may consist of individual or peer-group counseling or many other forms of treatment), referral to an outside agency, or accepting the consequences of unacceptable job performance.[42] No matter what the process, however, the employee's confidentiality is always ensured.

Even in a supportive work environment that attends to the need for physical and mental health, many people find they occasionally slip out of balance when their job becomes overly predominant in their lives. A woman who is treasurer of a high-technology company confessed during a counseling session, "After getting up early each day, arriving at my job before most of my peers, looking well groomed and attractive, and working hard for ten-plus hours, there was simply nothing left of me when I arrived home. The last thing I was ready for was cooking dinner and being pleasant for my family. I was no longer willing nor able to make the effort to play the 'Ms. Competency' role twenty-four hours a day. I am now divorced."[43] This book is focused on developing human relations skills for the *total person*. With all the personal and professional stresses of daily living, maintaining balance in one's life is critical for the individual, and in turn for the organization.

SUMMARY

Change is a necessary and exciting part of individual and organizational growth and development. Without it, there would be no growth. Learning to make the most of the changes with which you are confronted will enhance your life and your relationships.

Organizations may be forced to change in order to remain competitive in a quickly changing environment. If the organization is in financial trouble or in the process of unusual growth, changes will be inevitable. Also, organizations driven by traditional values will need to make the necessary adjustments as the environment undergoes fundamental changes.

People tend to resist change because they feel inadequate to meet the challenge, feel their security is threatened, fear the unknown, mistrust those initiating the change, or lack the ability to see the big picture. Individuals can actively adapt to change by using their values as a guideline for making decisions and achieving goals.

Any change produces tension or stress. Although many people thrive on stress, too much can cause physical or psychological harm. Technostress, the inability to cope with new computer technology in a healthy manner, is a significant contemporary threat to individuals and organizations. Individuals can counteract the effects of stress by controlling their goals, expectations, or working environment; eating a balanced diet; exercising regularly; taking time for mental relaxation; and effectively expressing their emotions. Organizations can help employees cope with stress by providing employee assistance programs, including physical fitness programs, nutrition training, and counseling programs to address such problems as alcohol and drug abuse.

KEY TERMS

future shock
transition
fight or flight syndrome
active adaptability
stress
technostress

cyberphobia
cyberphrenia
mental relaxation
employee assistance program
    (EAP)
wellness program

REVIEW QUESTIONS

1. Under what circumstances do many organizations find it necessary to change?
2. What are three work-related transitions most people face?
3. Explain the relationship between technostress and future shock.
4. Explain how people can actively adapt to change.
5. List five of the reasons people resist change.
6. List some of the warning signs of too much stress.
7. How can physical exercise and mental relaxation counteract the effects of stress?
8. Describe the most effective way or ways organizations can counteract stress in their employees.
9. Why should organizations try to eliminate worker stress?
10. Refer to the Total Person Insight on page 229. Describe the changes you may personally encounter in the next ten years.

■ CASE 9.1

Bye-Bye Bell System

The biggest organizational change in history took place on January 1, 1984, when the Bell System—also known as AT&T—divested itself of seven regional telephone companies. The regional companies are now separate and independent firms that provide local telephone service. The new streamlined AT&T sells long-distance service and telephone equipment.

AT&T's employees were aware that the breakup was to occur, but few were able to foresee its full effects. Even on the surface, the change was drastic: On January 1, some six hundred thousand former AT&T employees began working for the new regional companies. Many returned to their workplaces to find that blue or yellow tape had been placed across the floor; those on one side of the tape worked for AT&T, while those on the other side were employed by a regional company. The two groups now had to wear different identification badges and could not share facilities in the same building; people who had formerly worked together and exchanged work information could no longer do so, by order of the Federal Communications Commission.

At another level, it seemed to many employees that the entire working atmosphere had changed. AT&T had been a stable and profitable firm whose employees were generally well paid and secure in their jobs. But with divestiture came a concern for competitive effectiveness and the bottom line. To reduce operating costs, executive salaries were frozen and AT&T sought wage concessions from its unions. Thousands of positions were eliminated through early retirement, normal attrition, and some firing. Reorganizations resulted in increased responsibilities for many managers, entirely new responsibilities for others, relocation for some, and a general uneasiness about what the future would bring for all. According to one regional executive, the changes and regroupings came so fast that he didn't know who his boss was from one day to the next.

Not only jobs were in jeopardy, but decision making as well. Before the breakup, regional company executives based their decisions on AT&T policies and guidelines. After the breakup, they were left without any outside guidance at all. Moreover, they were now forced to deal with competition from a variety of new telecommunications firms. Costs, prices, development and production lags, and the market for their products became important considerations—in many cases for the first time. Some managers found that their previous experience was close to worthless, and that they had to work by an almost completely new set of rules.

Although many researchers focus on the negative effect of the changes, there have been many positive results as well. The new competition has forced rapid technological change and increased communications research. William McGowan, president of MCI, says: "Divestiture was essential. If we had not done this, the United States would now be at a competitive disadvantage with the world."[1]

Although AT&T revenues have shrunk about 50 percent since the breakup, the company has increased its research and development budget from $2 billion to $2.7 billion. Bell Telephone Laboratories Inc. has received over twenty-five thousand patents since it was founded in 1925, and still wins a new one each day.

Sources: Kenneth Labich, "Was Breaking up AT&T a Good Idea?" *Fortune,* January 2, 1989, pp. 82–87; Maya Pines, "Ma Bell and Hardy Boys," *Across the Board,* July/August 1984, pp. 37–42; Michael E. Pollock and Aaron Bernstein, "After the Bell Breakup: 'A Different Ballgame' for Unions," *Business Week,* May 13, 1985, pp. 50, 52.

Questions

1. Which basic consequences of the AT&T breakup probably gave rise to the most stress for employees? Why?
2. How could AT&T and the regional "baby bell" companies have helped their employees cope with the changes?
3. What steps could individual AT&T employees have taken to better cope with the changes?

CASE 9.2

Wellness Programs Start Small

Three years ago, Plaskolite, Inc., a medium-sized producer of plastics, began an employee wellness program. At first, the program was mainly a cash bonus plan: bonuses were given to employees who participated actively in sports and to those who didn't smoke. Now the program includes an in-plant weight room and periodic fitness tests, as well as smoking cessation, weight loss, and stress management clinics.

The goal of the program is to reduce the company's medical costs over the long term by increasing employee fitness. Monetary benefits were not expected for perhaps ten years, when the effects of the program would show up in lower incidences of such "life-style diseases" as diabetes and heart attacks. Yet Plaskolite's insurance has already decreased, and the fitness tests show continual improvement. In addition, the firm has found that its wellness program is of help in both recruiting and employee relations.

Cullinet Software, in Westwood, Massachusetts, has progressed from an initial small effort to a full commitment to wellness. They employ many people who spend all day at computer terminals. When their building was

---

[1] Kenneth Labich, "Was Breaking up AT&T a Good Idea?" *Fortune,* January 2, 1989, p. 82.

designed, a fitness component was included to counteract the sedentary work style. Employees may now take a fitness break anytime during the day and then work until 7:00 P.M. When Maggie Weinstock, director of health and fitness for the company, talks about the program, she says, "It is a stress release and provides a social atmosphere at work. As a result, we see a definite positive impact on productivity and a lowering of absenteeism."[1]

Most wellness programs involve three stages:

1. an *informational* stage, in which the benefits of fitness are carefully explained to employees
2. a *motivational* stage, in which employees are encouraged to participate in the program
3. a *behavioral* stage, in which employees do participate and find that, as a result, they feel healthier and actually are in better physical shape

The cost of the program, and of each stage, depends on how extensive it is—and that obviously varies from organization to organization. But even the smallest firm can take steps toward employee wellness by spotlighting informational notices regarding wellness, offering small cash bonuses for participation (as Plaskolite did at first), and following through to ensure that employees' fitness goals are met.

Sources: Judith A. Webster and Vicki A. Moss, "To Your Health," *Nation's Business*, March 1986, p. 65; Donna Fenn, "Keeping Fit," *INC.*, February 1986, pp. 101–102; Leonard Abramson, "Boost to the Bottom Line," *Personnel Administrator*, July 1988, pp. 36–39.

Questions

1. Suppose you were asked to devise an inexpensive wellness program for a real estate agency with about twenty-five employees. How would you determine which areas of fitness to work on first?
2. How would you implement the three stages of the program in the areas of (a) physical fitness and (b) smoking cessation?
3. How would you justify the cost of the program to the owner of the agency?

SUGGESTED READINGS

Allen, George. *Game Plan for the Healthy Life*. Battle Creek, Mich.: Kellogg Company, 1988.

Benson, Herbert. *The Relaxation Response*. New York: Morrow, 1975.

Blanchard, Kenneth, D. W. Edington, and Marjorie Blanchard. *The One Minute Manager Gets Fit*. New York: Morrow, 1986.

---

[1] Leonard Abramson, "Boost to the Bottom Line," *Personnel Administrator*, July 1988, p. 38.

Brod, Craig. *Technostress: The Human Cost of the Computer Revolution.* Reading, Mass.: Addison-Wesley, 1984.

Dietary Guidelines for Americans, Second Edition. U.S. Department of Health and Human Services, 1985.

Gawain, Shakti. *Creative Visualization.* San Rafael, Cal.: Whatever Publishing, 1978.

Kanter, Rosabeth Moss. *The Change Masters.* New York: Simon & Schuster, 1983.

Peters, Tom. *Thriving on Chaos: Handbook for a Management Revolution.* New York: Alfred A. Knopf, 1988.

Schafer, Walt. *Managing Stress.* New York: International Dialogue Press, 1982.

NOTES

1. "Big Changes at Big Blue," *Business Week,* February 15, 1988, pp. 92–98; Carol J. Loomis, "IBM's Big Blues: A Legend Tries To Remake Itself," *Fortune,* January 19, 1987, pp. 34–53.

2. Tom Peters, *Thriving on Chaos: Handbook for a Management Revolution* (New York: Alfred A. Knopf, 1987), p. xi, xii.

3. Ibid., pp. 1–9.

4. John Naisbitt and Patricia Aburdene, *Re-Inventing the Corporation* (New York: Warner Books, 1985), p. 298.

5. Terrence E. Deal and Alan A. Kennedy, *Corporate Culture: The Rites and Rituals of Corporate Life* (Reading, Mass.: Addison-Wesley, 1982), pp. 159–161.

6. Peters, p. 261.

7. Ibid., p. 259.

8. Brian Dumaine, "How Managers Can Succeed Through Speed," *Fortune,* February 13, 1989, p. 54.

9. Ibid., p. 58.

10. Patricia Sellers, "Why Bigger Is Badder at Sears," *Fortune,* December 5, 1988, p. 79.

11. "Can John Young Redesign Hewlett-Packard?" *Business Week,* December 6, 1982, pp. 72–78.

12. Richard Bolles, "The 'Warp' in the Way We Perceive Our Life in the World of Work," *Training and Development Journal,* November 1981, p. 22.

13. Jerry Main, "Work Won't Be the Same Again," *Fortune,* June 28, 1982, pp. 58–59.

14. Craig Brod, *Technostress: The Human Cost of the Computer Revolution* (Reading, Mass.: Addison-Wesley, 1984), p. 5.

15. Richard Kirkland, Jr., "Why America Creates the Most Jobs," *Fortune,* December 21, 1987, p. 178.

16. Theresa Engstrom, "How Do You Change Employees? Let Them Experiment," *Personal Computing,* December 1982, pp. 128–129.

17. "How IBM Cut 16,200 Employees—Without An Ax," *Business Week,* February 15, 1988, p. 98.

18. Vandra L. Huber, "Managing Stress for Increased Productivity," *Supervisory Management,* December 1981, pp. 2, 3.

19. John Lawrie, "Three Steps to Reducing Stress," *Supervisory Management,* October 1985, pp. 8, 9.

20. Brod, p. 16.

21. Ibid., p. 30.

22. Ibid., p. 17.

23. Craig Brod, "Technostress," *Review,* September 1984, p. 28.
24. Harold T. Smith, C.A.M., *The Office Revolution: Strategies for Managing Tomorrow's Workforce,* Administrative Management Society Foundation, 1983, pp. 66–68.
25. Shane Premeaux, Wayne Mondy, and Arthur Sharplin, "Stress and the First-Line Supervisor," *Supervisory Management,* July 1985, p. 37.
26. "Mind Games That Melt Away Stress," *Executive Fitness Newsletter,* November 27, 1982.
27. Linda Standke, "Advantage of Training People to Handle Stress," *Training/HRD,* February 1979, p. 25.
28. Richard Sprague, "The High Cost of Personal Transitions," *Training and Development Journal,* October 1984, pp. 61–62.
29. Laurie Hays, "But Some Firms Try to Help," *The Wall Street Journal,* April 24, 1987, p. 16D.
30. Meg Sullivan, "Pressure, Pressure Everywhere . . . ," *The Wall Street Journal,* April 24, 1987, p. 16D.
31. "A Cure For Stress?" *Newsweek,* October 12, 1987, p. 64.
32. Ibid., pp. 64, 65.
33. Richard H. Lambert, "Good Health Means Good Business," *DIY Retailing,* February 1985, p. 9.
34. Kim Wright Wiley, "Corporate Fitness Programs, Encouraging Employee Health," *Piedmont Airlines,* September 1985, p. 81.
35. Jane Brody, "Companies Promote Better Health Among Employees," *Roanoke Times & World-News,* December 2, 1985, p. C–1.
36. Ibid.
37. John Perham, "Fitness Programs Down the Line," *Dun's Business Month,* October 1984, p. 106.
38. Donna Fenn, "Keeping Fit," *INC.,* February 1986, p. 101.
39. Ibid.
40. Stuart Berger, "Food Can Change Your Mood," *Parade Magazine,* December 23, 1984, p. 13.
41. Lin Grensing, "Driving Them Away from Drink," *Training,* December 1984, pp. 123–125.
42. Ibid.
43. Nancy Collins, Susan Gilbert, and Susan Nycum, *Women Leading* (Lexington, Mass.: Stephen Greene Press, 1988), pp. 11–12.

Name Index

Subject Index